A Diplomacy of the Oppressed

New Directions in International Feminism

Edited by
Georgina Ashworth

Zed Books Ltd
LONDON AND NEW JERSEY

A Diplomacy of the Oppressed was first published by
Zed Books Ltd, 7 Cynthia Street,
London NI 9JF, UK, and
165 First Avenue, Atlantic Highlands,
New Jersey 07716, USA,
in 1995.

Cover designed by Andrew Corbett.
Typeset in Monotype Baskerville by Philip Armstrong
Printed and bound in the United Kingdom
by Biddles Ltd, Guildford and King's Lynn.

A catalogue record for this book is
available from the British Library.

US CIP data is available from
the Library of Congress.

ISBN 1 85649 143 9 Cased
ISBN 1 85649 144 7 Limp

Contents

meetings and correspondence with the authors. There was no funding for its creation. So my thanks are entirely due to my patient colleagues in CHANGE, Mia Hyun, Elizabeth Ighodaro, Sreelatha Sashikaran, Amanda Waite, with Rachel Coulson and Sarah Robinson in particular, and to my immediate family, Roy, Jessica and Simon Ashworth.

The Contributors

Anita Anand is a director of the Women's Feature Service in New Delhi.

Georgina Ashworth is a writer on women's human rights, democracy and governance, and is engaged in lobby and advocacy training.

Eva Cox is founder of the consultancy group, Distaff. Her work in feminist economics has focused on methods of recognising women's domestic and volunteer management skills.

Leith Dunn, former Caribbean Desk Officer at Christian Aid, now works in Jamaica as a consultant on economic and political developments.

Gwyn Kirk started her peace and environmental activism in Wales, and is now teaching women's studies – and mobilisation – at various universities in the US.

Olayinka Koso-Thomas is a medical doctor and campaigner in Sierra Leone, Nigeria, and other West African countries.

Judith Large is a tutor with Responding to Conflict, Birmingham, UK, and works in an advisory capacity with NGO and voluntary organisations in Eastern Europe.

Yayori Matsui, formerly of *Asahi Shimbun*, is a writer and campaigner. She is author of *Women's Asia* (Zed Books, 1989).

Andrée Michel has been a writer and activist since her retirement from the Centre for National Scientific Research.

Ginny NiCarthy, former editor of the newsletter of the International Network Against Violence Against Women, is a writer and campaigner on women's rights.

Ursula Paredes is currently Communications Director of INSTRAW, after having worked with IOCU in Montevideo.

Jacqueline Pitanguy is a former President of the National Council of Women's Rights, and a Visiting Professor at Rutgers University.

Paula Rose worked for a long period in Brussels with Nato Alerts and other action groups, and now divides her time between Belgium and southern France.

Rose Waruhiu left her parliamentary seat in Kenya and was the first African to receive a scholarship to the J.F. Kennedy School of Government in New York. She is now with the Democratic Foundation of Kenya.

Judith Zinsser, author of *A History of Their Own*, teaches at Miami University, Ohio, where she continues to be engaged in feminist approaches to curriculum development.

1

Introduction

Georgina Ashworth

Feminism is a proposal for social transformation as well as a movement that strives to end the oppression of women. In this double aspect, feminism has always existed as part of the historical societies in which it has developed: it has been influenced by the specific social, economic and political traits of its society. As a movement, feminism has a long history of rebellion, more or less organised but always expressing opposition to the social institutions that made possible the inferiority of women. This opposition has not been isolated from other forms of social struggle and this relationship has influenced both the ideology and the organisation of the movement.

Judith Astellara[1]

Feminism developed from the conflict and experience of women who are oppressed. What Third World women have given to feminism is a widening of the view of feminism to cover many forms of oppression ... feminism looks at the whole of society ... feminism also means activism. Feminism abhors violence; feminism reasserts the importance of community; feminism is a belief in sisterhood and that actions with lasting effects are taken collectively; feminism stands for equality of all people in society. Feminism stands for social justice.

Amelia Rokotuivna, Fiji[2]

Feminism is a way of life which is characterised by understanding, friendship, love, communication and solidarity amongst women. We understand that communities usually use all these values in order to persuade women to stay *inactive,* but they are all essential when used as a means to develop an atmosphere of co-operation to help women to face all the difficulties in their relations in the family and in society.

a Greek participant in an international seminar 1986[3]

Feminism is an awareness of women's oppression and exploitation in society, at work and within the family, and conscious action by women and men to change this situation ... a struggle for the achievement of women's equality, dignity and freedom of choice to control our lives and bodies within and outside the home ... for a just and equitable society for women and men both.

Kamla Bhasin and Nighat Said Khan[4]

Feminists, despite and because of their diversity and pluralism, have become a new force in international politics. It is a force of ideas, invention and commitment rather than economic resources, of courage, morality and justice instead of technology and tanks. This force is the diplomacy of the disempowered, addressing, modifying and seeking to transform every issue on the international agenda with the realities, knowledge, pain and demands of the dominated; it is part of our own transformation from victimhood to survival, and from survival – whether of personal or structural violence – to power. If governments can send embassies and delegations, consuls and representatives to each other's countries and to international conferences to promote and protect their interests, so can women – who are present within the sovereignty of a state but are not really represented or served by it. We can now, and should, 'speak truth unto power' and in 'another voice', rethinking the relations between these male sovereignties, while addressing the mechanisms of disparity and injustice.

An international course on gender awareness found that to be oppressed is to experience and perceive subordination, fear, hunger and vulnerability, to be unrepresented, marginalised, dependent, denied humanity, controlled, dominated, underprivileged, inferior, powerless, and therefore to perceive others as exercising power, control, superiority, prejudice, stereotypes, ideology, ambition, ignorance and a lack of respect, being maintained there by law, economic models, religion, science, language, technologies, humiliation, violence, trivialisation, total exclusion or selecting out what is 'valid', blaming the victim, economic marginalisation, miseducation, conformity, denying, devaluing, pathologising, criminalising, problematising. All these are characteristics of racial and class superiority, as well as of sexism; however, as we know from experience, many purist anti-racists, anti-imperialists, and socialists display sexist attitudes and behaviour, while denying their part in women's oppression. Women are clearly the 'last colony' to be liberated, gender the last variable to be applied, feminism among the last political movements to be recognised.

At first our diplomacy meant adding new questions to the 'other business' of that agenda but, with vigour, invention and tenacity, pushing these ever higher until they are integral to every subject, and the agenda itself is questioned. Conspicuous examples of these achievements by women's lobbies are the World Conference on the Environment and Development in Rio in 1992, and that on Human Rights in Vienna in

1993, where they transformed the language and direction of the final documents. Similar initiatives have been pursued in smaller events and institutions all over the world, 'mainstreaming' feminist concerns on an unparalleled scale, often with the support of Canadian institutions and government. In preparing for the International Conference on Population and Development in 1994, there have been unprecedented international exchanges between women, producing coherent and articulate demands[5] for action out of an event usually left to demographers, doctors and experts in 'population control'. The process has just begun, as I write, to transform the Social Development Summit, in 1994, using the issues and ideas being assembled for the Fourth World Conference on Women in Beijing.

This diplomacy is not an exercise in self-promotion by the privileged, but the coming together of many courageous individuals of all backgrounds aspiring to change the present androcentric paradigms and misogynistic realities, and to divert our futures from their man-mapped, life-threatening, exploitative paths.

These gains have not been smooth or easy; the dangers and setbacks are enormous. As I wrote in 1980, we experience daily 'obstruction, harassment and persecution',[6] ridicule, humiliation and subtle retribution for being so bold as to protest at the present patriarchal order, and we witness the regular imprisonment, wounding and murder of our friends and collaborators, and of many others not known to us. The capacity of the wealth- and powerholders to brush off the challenges of egalitarian social relations like so many specks of dust from their sleeve is indubitable. The incitement to suppress women's movements through appeals to culture, religion, and the restoration of 'normality' is a constant feature of insecure societies, destabilised by indebtedness and poverty, and of insecure politicians looking for quick allies among the electorate. Feminists and women's movements everywhere have common problems in being taken as seriously as other political movements, especially when competing for resources. The resistance to change cannot be underestimated in state and civil institutions which should be responding to the self-evidently just claims of women. Some adopt trivial modifications to present an up-to-date face to the world, without fundamental structural or philosophical reform, so that the individuals concerned retain their place in the hierarchy. If domestic decisions are made without the consent of the female citizenry, who are so rarely represented in elected assemblies or enabled to express their own opinions, then how much less are our interests involved in relations, friendly or inimical, between states?

The deliberate and casual ways in which civil servants justify inaction and the preservation of their privilege can reduce good policy to nothing.[7] Simultaneously, in the name of contemporary news values, journalists push vital stories of women's current achievements, and past history-making, out of the political space; even though the media are viewed as the defender of the oppressed, they often savage the victim if she is female. Politicians, keen to deny the systemic exclusion of women from the political process, dismiss feminism as a form of neo-imperialism or as 'interference in the culture'. Then, with no self-consciousness at all, they step into a meeting on the conditionality of 'development aid' which will blatantly alter the 'receiving culture', usually to the particular detriment of women. Hypocrisy and ignorance, bred of an education that ignored gender relations, defend personal, class and gender privilege enshrined in organisational cultures and procedures.

Feminists have been a force in international politics before – Andrée Michel, Judith Large and other authors here remind us of The Hague peace conferences, unsuccessful in their primary objectives of obliterating war but surely achieving a cross-border solidarity which had been interrupted by patriotism in the pre-war Socialist International. As surely as there must have been other unrecorded contacts and events, and as visible international women's organisations and federations were formed throughout the first half of the century, so feminists must have struggled individually and collectively in villages and towns throughout the centuries and across the world, well before the expression 'feminism' was coined by Frenchman Charles Fourier. The 15th- century writer Christine de Pisan is remembered here, too, but two thousand years earlier Buddhist nuns sought to define the political culture of their religion according to their needs, as did the Gnostics, before being suppressed. Western women know that Mary Wollstonecraft, Olympe de Gouges and other 18th-century revolutionaries exchanged ideas born of the contradictions between their lives and the revolutions around them, and that some paid with their lives.[8] Latin American feminists were vigorous in the 19th century as their countries threw off Spanish rule, but succumbed to the 'informal empire' of European commerce.[9] The anti-slavery movement in North America generated strong women, black and white (although credit usually goes to men), many of whom became the backbone of the women's suffrage movement. There are still stories to be uncovered of the millions of women throughout history who protested against rape, wars, conquest and economic exploitation.

Today, however, there are significant objective differences from the past. One is that we now have human rights, internationally agreed standards for egalitarian relations between human beings, based on common humanity rather than the privileges of property ownership, lineage, race, name and sex. These form a contract between states and peoples, as individuals and social groups, to moderate the power of the state and to mediate that of groups and individuals towards each other. They were fully respected and implemented by no government, and were weakened by their selective use in antagonistic foreign policy before the fall of the Berlin wall. Until 1993 they were under-used by women, but they justify, as no law has before, every claim that the poorest and most victimised aspire to make of the privileged and powerful, be they compatriot or foreigner. They endow us all, as no political order has before, with a universal philosophical and practical system of social, economic and political equality between men and women, in public and in private, that is not dependent on an unprovable religious authority. They are top-down instruments, and were written by leaders with the privilege of birth, class and gender, but they validate women's humanity, dignity, rights and interests as nothing has done over two millennia. As a long-term protagonist[10] of the use of human rights standards to promote and defend women's identity and rights, I must declare a particular interest in this area:

Upwards of 3 billion persons are subject, systematically and casually, to a wide range of violations because they are female. States have provided inadequate protection, although they have obligations under the UN Charter and the Human Rights instruments to promote women's human rights actively so that they may be enjoyed universally .... No state has eliminated the intermediary power of men, in public and private spheres, who thus continue to determine, often arbitrarily, how women may live and exercise their rights. The principles of free consent and selfdetermination, in public and in private, have not been promoted by states for the female gender. Thus billions of girls and women are subject to fear and many different forms of violence on a daily basis, to slave-like and servile marriages, to hunger and deprivation while over-burdened with work, to degrading treatment and to systematic economic exploitation by different agents, to sexual abuse and exploitation, all destroying their rights to health and personal security.[11]

A second difference from the past is that the UN Decade for Women 1975–85, and its follow-up, fuelled feminist internationalism and legitimated women's movements in every country of the world. The three intergovernmental World Conferences were themselves extremely significant, despite their formality and disappointments. Although government delegations tend to follow their countries' foreign policy and power-bloc priorities, rather than make commitments in the interests of 'equality, development and peace', enough consensus was found through conventional diplomacy for the Plans, Programmes and the radical 1985 Forward Looking Strategies. The International Convention on the Elimination of Discrimination Against Women (CEDAW) was adopted by the international community in 1979, and the International Declaration on Violence Against Women in 1993, both of which oblige governments to extend their promotion and protection of women's human rights in both private and public, as did the Vienna Declaration and Programme of Action in 1993. CEDAW, a major human rights instrument though rarely treated as such, has been ratified by numerous countries, but more reservations have been entered against it than against any other, often defeating its purposes.

The 'symbiotic and simultaneous' non-governmental events – the 1975 Tribune and the Forums in 1980 and 1985 – really stimulated pragmatic but passionate internationalism among feminists. Each attracted thousands of women (and some men) who, in the hurly-burly of 50 workshops a day, discussed, debated and argued about every subject under the sun, losing their innocence about global sisterhood but losing also their prejudices, replacing them with the knowledge of women's common struggle everywhere. Out of the Decade came publications, networks, international conferences, newletters, seminars, workshops, courses, each bringing in more and more to make common cause, and sending them out again with renewed courage, energy, ideas and sense of purpose. It was a period of 'bursting vituperative leaflets; from the thesis chilled for a safe passage through patriarchal academia to the cheery illustrated sheets for illiterate women, we have been making our voices heard'.[12] Since then there have been serious feminist analyses of economics, the international debt and structural adjustment programmes, debates on democracy, re-democratisation and decision-making that excludes women, scholarly discourses on women's art, books on the medicalisation of childbirth, medical ethics, and wilder slogans on technology and pornography, days of study and action on men's violence and on sharing domestic responsibilities, meetings on media, theology and the redefinition of God, training in gender awareness and planning. Scarcely a topic has been untouched.

There have been other developments. The first women lawyers in Nepal, for example, qualified and started to defend their sisters' interests; civil servants went on strike in Papua New Guinea about violence, and in Switzerland about unpaid work. Ugandan refugee women in Sudan organised public meetings on their demands; Tanzanian tea-pickers objected to their own wages being paid to their husbands. Women's trades unions have been formed in the Philippines and in the Netherlands; feminist political parties in Peru, Iceland and Britain. Bolivian highland peasant women went to Africa, Trinidadians to Nigeria, and delegations of women's ministers met four times in the Commonwealth. 'First ladies' were summoned together by IFAD to discuss rural poverty, and a handful more women have been appointed to senior positions within the UN. There have been six regional feminist 'Encuentros' in Latin America, and many occasions of regional advocacy, especially in preparation for the World Conference on Human Rights.

The Decade's legitimation of indigenous and popular feminisms across the world explained and validated to individual women their unease with the pressures upon their lives, by showing them that their problems were not peculiar. This encouraged them to identify with others, link up their dissenting thoughts, and take action. The significance of this new dual authority of internationalism and inner self-confidence is often underestimated by Western women, who have not experienced a struggle for national independence, and its betrayal, and consequently have rarely – until relatively recently – engaged with the state. In the supposedly open post-war societies of the North, where welfare politics soften critical choices and tolerate debate without engagement, there are daily trade-offs and betrayals, but they are more diffused.

Feminist internationalism

Our country throughout the greater part of history has treated me like a slave: it has denied me education and a share of its possessions. Our country still ceases to be mine if I marry a foreigner; our country denies me the right to protect myself, forcing me to pay others a very large sum annually to protect me. Let it be understood that you are fighting to gratify a sex instinct which I cannot share, to procure benefits which I will not share .... As a woman I have no country.[13]

Internationalism is, in essence, multidisciplinary, which causes its practitioners to have already crossed some of the frontiers erected in orthodox masculine study, so the internationalists observe how the macrostructures and policies affect the micro. The feminists know the personal is political. From the junction of the two can be seen the impact of the international order on the individual woman.[14]

Foreign policy is separated from domestic policy as if a different set of values and morals are necessary. This replicates the traditional separation of the public from the private, and reinforces that separation when transposed to the international-public and the national-private. Both, however, agree that women's place is physically and morally domestic. The explosion of 'the woman question' into the international public sphere sets off a chain of necessary reaction, of which policymakers would prefer not to think.[15]

Internationalism is one word for many diverse connections and actions. It is tactic, means and strategy through a myriad of acts, and is, like feminism, a philosophy of affinity, alliance and compassion, all of which disregard the imposition of nationality and frontiers. It reclaims international relations from relations between states, which do not represent or present women's interests, to relations between peoples.

In 1981, recognition of women's movements as a force on the international scene was given by the publication of *Pressure Groups in the Global System*.[16] My chapter described the diversity of priorities and ideas, and the linkages, within and between women's movements, based on the experience of the Forum and World Conference in Copenhagen that year, identifying the different forms of violence against women and the relationship of women and their unpaid work to the international economy as the most salient emerging concerns; both have been realised. At that time 'women in development' (often reduced to WID) became the formalised, and constricting, expression for feminism in international relations; while later to become almost a science, expanded into gender and development, WID too often ignored the impact of international macro-economic changes and the question of rights rather than access.

In 1984, within a paper from which the idea for this book emerged,[17] I wrote that feminist diplomacy requires women of the countries of the 'North' to take responsibility for listening to and responding to the priorities of the women's movements of the 'South', exposing the contradictions of unequal economic relations, and at least working on our own institutions to limit their damage. International debt, new technological communications, forms of production and distribution through trade and services, militarisation and the politics of energy, all therefore place themselves firmly on our agenda. Earlier, the Norwegian Council of Women had published the pamphlet *An International Women's Policy* in 1979, defining it as 'an active policy to advance the position of women all over the world in all relevant areas and by all means occasioned by international relations'. The Norwegians led the way in financing women's programmes, and the DAWN Network, whose 1985 analysis[18] has come to be identified as 'Third World' women's positions on many of these areas, although it has been superseded by books such as *Unequal Burden: Economic Crises, Persistent Poverty and Women's Work*, edited by Lourdes Beneria and Shelley Feldman.[19] Swasti Mitter's recognition of the gender dimension of the international division of labour emerged in *Common Fate, Common Bond*[20] in 1987. A special edition of *Millennium: the Journal of International Studies* focused on 'Women and International Relations'[21] in 1988. Cynthia Enloe published *Bananas, Beaches and Bases: Making Sense of International Politics*[22] in 1989 elaborating many of the linkages between the policies of her country and the systemic exploitation of women where those policies materialised. J. Ann Tickner published *Gender in International Relations: Feminist Perspectives on Achieving Global Security*[23] in 1990.

There are some reasons for caution in practice. Of these, two are 'maternalism', or indeed a surrogate liberal paternalism, from women in the North towards women in the South, and perpetual self-victimisation in the South, by adopting the male diplomatic agenda. Maternalism often imbues partnerships between North and South groups, even those that have no religious tenets. It takes on the presumptions of class and former empire, containing a superiority that can be racist and patronising and which presupposes that, for example, peasant women do not know their own priorities or how to organise themselves. Or it denies realities, for example, of educational indicators: that there are more women professional engineers in Egypt and lawyers in Turkey than of either in Britain; or of health indicators which put the most medicalised society in the world, the US, quite low for neonatal infant and maternal mortality compared to other industrialised countries. And it may deny the lagoons of poverty in the North, the adjustment policies and economic restructuring that have been taking place in European societies, Canada, the US, and are under way in Eastern Europe, all of which utilise gender inequalities and vulnerabilities, thereby increasing them.

Meanwhile, by projecting all the blame indiscriminately on the North, elite women in the South absolve themselves of their responsibilities in the inequalities within their own society, or of using their relative privilege to challenge patriarchy and to work with their compatriot women to protect them from exploitation by outsiders. It obviates their readiness to mobilise resources from their own wealthy elites, prolonging both the unequal relationship between North and South, which they deplore, and the importance of the 'donor' agencies with their transient policy fashions, putting their movements in a perpetual state of dependence on external funds. This indiscriminate blame also thwarts exploration of the commonalities between countries and solidarity actions with oppressed women in the North.

The linkages may also be reduced to guilt for an international order in which most women took no part, and from which they reap no benefit; guilt is not a creative motivation for any relationship. All of these are easily manipulated by governments and power-blocs, as they were at the World Conferences, against the interests of women themselves, obscuring the specificities of gender subordination within that international order, from which governments of South and North both gain. There are dangers, too, of rendering gender in international relations a wholly academic discipline, segregated from the daily realities of women's lives and without active outcome. Conversely, internationalism can be interpreted as 'jet-setting' and making speeches in other countries, and some do partake in just such visa-collecting. But it has far more content than conference tourism.

Thus the internationalism with which ISIS and CHANGE were founded in 1979, or Women Living Under Muslim laws in 1984, Entre Mujeres in 1990, and many other international and regional networks has a consistency which resists manipulations of self-interested states. It attempts to recognise the community of all peoples, artificially (and certainly arbitrarily) separated by frontiers and national institutions which are the outcome of masculine conflict and reward systems. As a philosophy, internationalism opposes oppression regardless of place. It spreads awareness of ideas and of practical techniques across the borders of class, ethnicity and nation, ideas that accelerate change towards egalitarian social and economic relations. Internationalism removes isolation, enabling groups and individuals to recognise that their problems are not solitary but structural. It contains respect for the 'other' and curiosity to see change rather then perpetuation of the status quo. It attempts to avoid the cultural relativism used to excuse personal bestiality and institutional cruelty, deplored in Nazi Germany but joked at in Amin's Uganda. It dislikes league tables of success or suffering, for the death by starvation of a homeless person in a rich country is not a 'better' death because of the country's overall GNP rating than the death by starvation in a resource-poor country. The knifing of a prostitute is no less painful to the victim because of her alienated social status than the knifing of a president with his political pre-eminence. The quality of democracy of a country which has millions of TV sets[24] but still effectively excludes women from active participation by many means, is not better than that of a remote village where all people participate fully, vocally and as beneficiaries of the common wealth, but which has no telecommunications.

As a tactic, internationalism is a means of offsetting the patriarchal bias of religion, nationalism and citizenship, experienced through the exclusion of women from community decision-making or democratic institutions, by using a 'higher authority' – the international human rights instruments – to outlaw barbarism and guarantee sex equalities. This endorses the moral imperative of women's movements, and legitimates them. The need for this alternative authority cannot be underestimated, for there are few other weapons available for this revolution which is in the home, the street, the workplace, among the promoters of democracy, theologians, artists, technologists, in every nook and cranny of human relations.

Perhaps it is imaginable that women could take to armed struggle against their oppression, and their oppressors. There would be many contradictions, even without resorting to the debate on the 'nature' or 'natural passivity' of the female sex, or the absence of the x chromosome. Women's armed struggle would impugn feminism as an intrinsically anti-violence movement; it would be a submission to the 'inexorability' of violence, and to the indefinite, and cost-ineffective 'solution' it offers. It would be a triumph of militarisation, rather than an alternative to it, and an impoverishing transfer of already limited resources to the already rich and influential arms suppliers, and with the limited purchasing power of women, only small numbers would be equipped, giving the state armies and gangs quick victories, whatever the courage of the combatants. Since billions of women struggle for survival already, provoking collective defeat in their name would also defeat the very essence of feminism and internationalism.

To resist and make progress against all the particular experiences and forms of oppression, women's movements need to innovate as few have before. They need to be able to propose solutions to every problem and to propose policy to fill the opportunities created by the lifting of barriers and burdens – for unfamiliar freedoms can be hard to survive without support. Gandhi's passive resistance co-existed with violence, and played carrot to the warmongers' stick, but in women's case passive resistance has to be partnered by active insistence: demonstrations, against and for issues, inspiring songs and slogans, strikes from domestic work as much as from formal employment, collective self-help and work exchange, poetry, film, pictures, participatory research, celebrations and mourning, legal challenges, consumer boycotts and buy-ins, alternative tribunals, dance, tax refusals ('No Taxation Without Representation'), naming violators, labelling crimes, friendship and comfort, counter-proposals, electoral boycotts of sexual harassers, all the means described in this book, and more. They need the capacity to mount single-issue campaigns without losing the overall aims, to flourish with heterogeneity without sinking into divisiveness, to make mistakes without self-destructive criticism, to be realistically optimistic without self-deception. They require leadership without masses of 'led', populism that is not simplistic, sophistication that is not a cynical disguise for superiority or fear, vision that is practical and to which everyone is equally entitled. The American feminist peace slogan, 'Not in Our Name', is a powerful denunciation of foreign policies devised in the 'national interest', without consent or consultation with the majority of the electorate, who benefit nothing from it. The Philippines' concept of 'illegal debt' has the same effect of repudiating international financial arrangements made by one elite with another, without benefit for most people, but with impact upon those least able to cope with it. The 'Women in Black' meet weekly in Israel, former Yugoslavia, New York, London, Amsterdam, to mourn women war victims and protest at war itself.

Through the feminist re-examination of human rights both as a philosophy and as a set of practical standards, women's relationship with the state comes under scrutiny. The worldwide failures of states to promote and protect women's human rights, so that they are enjoyed on an equal basis with men's in private and in public, must have a cause beyond mere forgetfulness. State machineries were constructed by men, for men, with a reward-system from which women do not constitutionally benefit. Carole Pateman and other political scientists, and feminist anthropologists such as Henrietta Moore have examined the history of the indirect relationship that women have with the modern state, as with the sources of authority in most traditional communities, which is mediated by men through their marital and kin relationships. Through this 'sexual contract' the state endows men with power over women through marriage, paternity and brotherhood, and maintains this power through nationality laws, taxation, social security, administrative and judicial procedures, language and technical terminology, including the use of 'the household' as an economic and political behavioural unit. The implicit and explicit favouritism of the state towards men is being challenged in some countries, notably Namibia, where women have caused the constitution to reflect their existence as autonomous persons and as a social group; there are demands for land and solutions to their economic dependency from 'grassroots' women who survived the liberation war fought through their fields and houses. Women in South Africa look to them, and to others struggling to redefine democracy, so that they do not lose out from the abolition of apartheid.

Jacqueline Pitanguy, former President of the Brazilian National Council for the Rights of Women (NCRW) and therefore a key actor in the Latin American process of redemocratisation, examines some of the practical issues of citizenship here, the shifting perceptions of other social movements towards popular feminism, and finally the failure of government to honour commitment to genuine change in the asymmetry of power among the 147 million persons within that country's vast boundaries. Such political inequality makes for inequity not only in resource distribution, but in expectations thereof: without the time and resources to create a thoroughly broad-based, popular feminist movement, the NCRW could neither break the circles of circumstantial despair among her countrywomen, nor ensure their support in the showdown with government.

Australia is probably the country with the most advanced relationship between women and the state, but, as Eva Cox demonstrates, using Carole Pateman's contract theory, it is still a relationship using the male as norm, and protecting privilege 'disguised as growth'. Female wages have risen minimally since the Second World War, and the marriage unit is still the unit of social entitlement, despite an emphasis on individualism which Eva Cox sees as keeping feminists separate, denying women recognition as a 'social group'. Eva's conclusion therefore is that the feminist dream, 'with practical recipes', is more likely to come from the theory of 'muddling through' with conflicts creating opportunities for change, rather than giving all responsibility and control to the still patriarchal state, which is intrinsically unreliable towards women's interests. There are, it seems, choiceless options open to women in their relationship with the state, which, according to the state's duties evolved after the Second World War, should be promoting our rights, without fear or favour. Indeed, I would contend that unless and until a state is actively devolving power to women, in both private and public spheres, to determine their own lives, as well as actively promoting the protection of their rights, it cannot be described as exerting good governance .

Military power, and the processes of militarisation, are addressed from different perspectives. Andrée Michel suggests that most modern Western feminists have allowed themselves to be distracted from this ultimate patriarchal reality in North–South relations, the architect of international debt and destroyer of liberation, by the side-issues of aid and development co-operation. She relates this distraction to the continuing restriction of female education to non-scientific subjects, and highlights the contrasting opportunities for women from Southern countries like Brazil, South Korea and India, which have produced feminists who challenge the models of macro-domination (although by the same token all of those countries are also now major exporters of arms). Trade in military hardware and military training, it must be said, have also been deliberately omitted from the multilateral trade treaties such as the GATT or UNCTAD, or the Lome Agreement, as if they bore no relation to public expenditure. (The massive traffic in human beings, pornography and drugs is also absent from the counting and mapping of trade. The effect is to skew figures on the transfer of resources and technology on which other calculations, such as GNP, and decisions are based, and to disguise the real power-holders as well as the devastation of local economies.)

While militarisation equips dictators and even elected leaders with the means to subjugate their citizens, military trade can trigger conflicts of which the direct and indirect victims are more often civilian than military: hundreds of thousands of lives sacrificed to maintain ruthless leaders' control and power, and since the Second World War, many times more civilians than soldiers have been killed and are being killed in today's conflicts, and one in nine persons is a refugee. Military trade also finances repressive movements; thus Andrée Michel argues, in the interests of political and market stability Western Christian countries actually finance Islamic fundamentalism, which, like the many anti-democratic dictators they supported in the past, they claim to oppose. In so doing they sacrifice women's liberation and human rights. The depth of the oppression of Iraqi or Kuwaiti women was no *causus belli* in 1990; instead 200,000 of them were sacrificed for the return of the Emirs' undemocratic control in Kuwait, and of oil to American car-owners and electricity grids.

Paula Rose outlines her campaign to deal with the reality of NATO's power. This campaign was originally one of many small products of a mass meeting of the European women's peace movement in 1983 – at which, coincidentally, I spoke on the triangular relationship between militarism, the making of debt, and female pauperisation and insecurity. 'NATO Alert' grew from a Sunday evening discussion group into a major dialogue (always punctuated by the need to find child care) between the well protected patrician power-brokers and women politicians from all over the NATO bloc, as well as the first Warsaw bloc visitor to enter NATO headquarters. It is a factual story of women's 'diplomacy': women of no special status finding within themselves the ways and means of 'speaking truth unto power'.

This is a concept which Judith Large explores, along with the necessity to scrutinise existing power structures, in her rich chapter on feminist conflict resolution. The shift of the effects of war from military to civilians has been one marked outcome of the ever higher technology of war – another being inflation – but there has been no equivalent shift of power to civil society to give or withhold consent to war and adversarial politics. So that power must be claimed and used, not as threats and bribes but to defuse conflict and replace it with alternative ways in which social groups, individuals and countries relate to one another. Women in Ethiopia are rediscovering their own traditional forms of conflict resolution, and there are hopes that they can be expanded in other parts of Africa. Increasingly feminists are redefining 'security', because, like 'freedom', most women do not find it in their daily lives. They did such redefining at the Rio Environment Conference, demanding food security and secure livelihoods; while women's peace movements turned the language of Cold War belligerence of the 1980s to demonstrate how insecure we felt in the shadow of our armed 'protection'.

Reflection on the power of different forms of media is a daily and universal occurrence among feminists. Content analysis shows a culture of both sexist imagery and blank spaces where the words and doings of women, in their own reality and potentiality, should be, although free media are regarded as the key preservers of democracy and civilised values. Both the ownership structure and the career paths in the media significantly fail to defend women's political interests within the pages of newspapers and in the features and news bulletins of television. The media connive with states by failing to expose the oppression of women and suppressing the free expression by women of their pain. To this must be added the definition and subjectivity of newsworthiness. The daily ordinariness of male violence against women, for example, merits no mention despite its accumulation and scale – gross violations of human security by any other definition; thus awareness, protest and solutions have all been suppressed. Conversely the experiences of feminist political parties in Spain, Iceland, Peru and now Britain, or of women's peace initiatives in Sudan, former Yugoslavia or Northern Ireland, are accorded no value in news terms. In Chapter 14, Anita

Anand analyses news values and describes the objectives of the Women's Feature Service (WFS), which produces feminist print news from the South, and analyses its success where others have failed. The WFS emerged from the Inter-Press Service which was formed very much in the context of the New International Information Order, declared to give 'developing countries' access to media and reduce the command of news and information by North American and European news and information networks. However, the members of the UNESCO committee which drew up a statement of NIIO purposes were themselves blind to the similar problem that the 'country of women' also has in breaking through what UNICEF has called the 'apartheid of gender'. WFS is too much of a lone voice on the international news scene, although there are numerous lively feminist media consortia, journals and newsletters within countries – *Sister Namibia* or the Mexican *Fem*, for example.

As conveyers of cultural and political values, Western media strive to create a global homogeneity which secures markets for consumer products originating in the industrialised countries; this often displaces local value added processing and manufacture, thereby disrupting the sustainability of local development and sending scarce foreign currency overseas. They expand the market for media products, too – TV shows, syndicated columns and advertisements, replete with the misogynistic culture we know so well. Ursula Paredes (Chapter 7) illustrates the purpose and conduct of a campaign in Latin America on television advertising. This employs both the International Convention on the Elimination of Discrimination Against Women and fair trading agreements to challenge the sexism of local and international advertising agencies on behalf of the wider audience of women. Political consumerism like this is a force feminists could employ more widely. By turning the 'social duties' of consumption work into a challenge to the pay and conditions of employees in the production of materials, for example, richer women could exercise power in solidarity with poorer, even reshaping the models of production or distribution. Consumers and real producers are often set at odds with one another through the intermediate actors in the international trading system. I had hoped to include chapters with alternative economic models from India and Britain; however, the time and resource constraints on women's movements meant that the development of these models has yet to be fulfilled.

Perhaps in consumer tactics lies some hope, too, for action to support the subjects of Leith Dunn's chapter on conditions and functions of the employment of women in Free Trade Zones. With the Caribbean as both playground and industrial park for the US, there has been rapid expansion of companies operating in the Free Zones, reducing their labour costs and overheads by employing women who are, as if by nature, cheap and flexible. Although many expert economists ignore the multitude of ways sex and gender are put to use in macro-economic policy, preferring to corral them in the soft social box, this is one of the more ridiculous aspects of genderblindness. For, as Leith Dunn demonstrates, gender is a strategic variable in industrialisation, as it is in economic restructuring and the effects of international debt. The Caribbean is not unique, and the Zones and the fly-by-night operations of multinational companies in other areas, such as South-east Asia and Mexico, have been the subject of writing and networking over almost two decades. In Fiji, for example, the garment industry – applauded by the European Industrial Development Fund – has begun developing similar exploitative conditions. Some unionisation has been allowed, here and there, or a women's health post started, but the dominant processes have not really yielded to the pressures for improved conditions and autonomous associations. In 1981, I proposed that multinationals employing women through subsidiaries should be subject to a Code of Practice like the six Harrison Principles for South Africa, which would modify investors' practices, rather than throw hundreds of thousands out of employment. As powerful, unelected and undemocratic actors on the international scene, but deeming themselves aloof from the international labour standards and human rights covenants, multinational corporations need to be brought into the potentially punitive framework of the law and human rights standards, and lose the protection of the states where they are based. In 1992 the proposals were adopted by the OECD-DAC,[25] although there is little sign of them being applied.

That women in the industrialised countries should know how the international economy impacts on their sisters elsewhere, as well as on themselves, is one of the arguments in Gwyn Kirk's contribution on women and the environment. She links gender subordination with the belief system of dominance, 'environmental racism', class arrogance, imperialism and destruction of the ecological system through over-exploitation of the natural resources. Although she points to only 6 per cent of the world's population using 40 per cent of the energy, Gwyn also describes with passion the maldistribution of energy, and other resources, within rich countries. The issues of the environment are not, therefore, just the survival of trees, but the survival in dignity and democracy of the humans who live among the trees, alongside the polluted rivers, and within hostile conurbations where services do not function or are increasingly being withdrawn from the poor on grounds of market reform. It is the economies of rich communities in both the rich and poor countries which are unsustainable, but the sustainability argument has been directed at the poorest and most powerless. Women, without the right to control their own bodies or to livelihoods, are

blamed for 'over-population'. This has stimulated the feminist preparations for the International Conference on Population and Development.
Gwyn Kirk also believes agendas for action should be developed that
avoid what much middle-class ecofeminism proposes, namely a retreat
into state and commercial dependency on women's free work, thereby
threatening the survival of those least able to give their time.

For, as Rose Waruhiu outlines (in Chapter 9), 'integration' into the
belief systems of the modern economy has entailed more overwork for
most of the 474 million African women. This reality reflects back starkly
on economists of the North, especially in the post-Cold War triumph-
alism, demanding answers. How can theories, models and processes
that define themselves as 'benign development' so marginalise women
that the definition cannot be sustained? African women, Rose suggests,
want more control over their own destiny by becoming political partners
rather than subordinates to their men or to the new masculine 'democratic' institutions. They want life understood and shaped from their
perspectives, in their own immediate environment, rather than through
a distant, theoretical or nationalistic lens. What has been dumped on
Africa during the past fifty years by outsiders and dictators has made
women vulnerable to religious fundamentalisms whose message is, as
many women have said, an acceptance of subordination.

The trade in young girls from Nepal to India, from the Philippines
and Sri Lanka to the Gulf States, and within Thailand, from poverty-
stricken countries of West Africa or Latin America, for example, to
Europe and North America has much to do with maldevelopment,
underpayment for raw materials, and has to do with indigenous patriarchal systems preventing women from owning land, acquiring credit
and the like. The same applies to the profit-taking by East Asian
companies from the starvation-wage employment of young women in
Bangladesh, Fiji, Mauritius, to escape the Multi-Fibre Agreement's
quotas. It also applies to places where the unconditional cancelling of
military- or elite-inspired debt still leaves the military in charge, and
the people paying the social cost.

To change the future it is necessary to retrieve the past, and use it
as evidence to challenge the current order. The histories of womankind,
and the story of the suppression of those histories, are needed to give
identity to feminist actors past and present, and also to name the
ideology of oppression. While the mainstream media self-righteously
protest at the suppression of historical events and personalities in
Eastern Europe over the past half-century of communism, they do not
denounce the eclipse of the sub-classes of all societies, especially women,
by the history of the power-holders. In *Bridging the Gap: Women's Studies
and Development*, which I edited in 1988, Rudo Gaidzwana tackled the
obscurity of the colonised. Here, Judith Zinsser's contribution (Chapter

13) on a popular women's history project in the United States is an example of a tiny local initiative grown into a national movement that gives a self-discovering pride in women's past existence, wisdom, struggle and artistry, and makes names for women in a young country more used to tales of gunslingers and sheriffs, 'men in the midst of other men'. For popular feminism to emerge, a genuinely popular sense of a past, historic substance and traceable lines of connection are necessary. Judith Zinsser observes, however, that mainstream historians have not yet begun to modify, let alone revolutionise, their perception or analysis with this enlightenment. There is still the prejudice that only men are competent to examine and interpret the past, thereby fixing their interpretations, which gain the status and strength of received wisdom, for decades. Historians obliterate all women, except handfuls of concupiscent queens and mistresses, and the achievements of the poor, of slaves and ethnic groups, outside the dominant elite, unless they assume its characteristics. Viewed from anywhere outside the US, it would seem perhaps that missing from this popular history is a critique of the misuse of economic power by successive American male political establishments, through support for agencies and corporations which exploit gender socialisation and natural resources. Were this recognised, it should bring a renewal of energy and solidarity in the struggle to reshape patriarchal political economies worldwide.

For this reason, the re-entry of Japanese power on to the international scene through economic expansionism, which 'grows by discriminating' and is the 'root cause of human rights violations', is addressed by Yayori Matsui. From a vanquished country, with a militaristic past denounced in the international courts, Japan has risen to become the richest nation in the world, but the methods, means and motives are open to question, in particular by indigenous feminists. Using her position as a journalist, Yayori Matsui has been able to observe and criticise the rapid extension of management systems (to many Western industrialists the subject of admiration and envy) fostered by Overseas Development Assistance, through East Asia, creating opportunities for Japanese commercial interests and indebtedness for the poor, whom ODA is intended to help. She examines the links between women of Japan itself and its neighbours through this seamless industrial culture which ruthlessly utilises gender and the environment as an infinite resource – a process against which women are fighting back. She also traces the political and policy sequences of war responsibility, racial prostitution both in the past and today, remilitarisation and the Gulf war. It always requires courage to bear witness to the ugliness of power, especially when one's country is, by man-made indicators, successful in the world community. For such commitment is not comfortable, and only narrow political channels exist through which to present the challenge.

The outcry against the daily insecurity caused by male violence against women is the most universal occurrence of the past fifteen years. Many consider that there is an active, hot war against women as a social group rather than as specific persons, being waged by individual men to defend the order of collective male privilege and female subordination. Ginny NiCarthy, formerly editor of the *International Network Against Violence Against Women Newsletter*, outlines the phases of recognition of the issue from denial to helping the victims, from naming the crimes to naming the perpetrator. She reminds us that the expression 'violence against women' is a crime without a criminal, a violation of human rights without a violator, centring on the victim and even perpetuating the culture of blaming *her*. Without perpetrators, and without a social context, there is nobody and no syndrome to prevent, treat or punish, or make restitution to the victim. Ginny NiCarthy, like other activists for women's human rights, also reworks the language: torture and terrorism are both weapons in the war against 'the country of women', although for 'conventional' human rights protectors and the media, the use of the words are restricted to the direct actions of, or against, the state. Yet pimps torture prostitutes to make them return to their jobs, husbands torture wives for not fulfilling their 'domestic duties' in servile or slave-like marriages from which there is no legal, social or economic exit. Many women fear entry into the public space, where they should be able to enjoy and exercise all their rights, because of the terrorism and intimidation awaiting them. In 1990 the first Women's Conference on Security and Co-operation in Europe (CSCE), held in Berlin, concluded that violence in various forms was 'a crime against humanity', a crime equal to the Holocaust. The draft American Convention on Violence Against Women represents the years of suffering, protest and innovation throughout Latin America made into potential law. The Declaration on Violence Against Women adopted by the UN General Assembly in 1993 is a clear signal that such violence is unacceptable. 'Zero Tolerance' campaigns are spreading across continents. The position of Special Rapporteur on Violence Against Women is to be created in 1994 by the UN Commission on Human Rights as a result of many different sources of advocacy. No longer can an Under-Secretary of the UN itself say that violence 'is not an important issue for Third World women'.

As actions in other parts of the world mark 25 November, the Latin American Day Against Violence Against Women, and convert it into an International Day of Action, so it is worth reflecting on the resurgence of International Women's Day, 8 March, in the past twenty years, from a neglected commemoration of the repression of women trade unionists before the First World War, to a day of action and regeneration. International Women's Day is now the most widely celebrated day in the world. It is marked in countries of all religions, all ideologies, all races and all 'levels' of development; it is commemorated in tiny Pacific islands, large cities, desert areas and rich wheatbelts, in offices, factories, universities and amongst independent women's groups. It reflects the growing strength of the women's movement, a strength made out of rich diversity but with unity expressed through the universal celebration of this day. These international days bring us together, providing a focus for our often lonely efforts, and being, at the same time, both symbolic and practical manifestations of the culture of feminist internationalism.

Although cultures are in constant change, they present the most difficult areas for feminist action. People crushed by poverty, loneliness and insecurity, both male and female, are persuaded by dictators and charismatic leaders to defend often repressive cultures to give themselves the individual and collective courage, and identity, to face up to or fight the despair of unmet expectations, economic domination or the ideology of material consumerism. All societies need non-material values to give them coherence, but all cultures are characterised by male domination and female subordination which may be used as the 'social glue', rather than being an incidental symptom. Male control of the female becomes more and more significant in the search for a political identity that will be heeded by the power-holders. It requires women to express submission in order to 'belong' to, or to 'deserve' the protection of, the community. Modern fundamentalist expressions of religions exemplify this, turning the submission of women into an intrinsic character of the community. Material examples are where Christian or Muslim humanitarian relief agencies demand conversions, adoption of the appropriate dress code and other cultural practices, before giving food. Women's obedience is also both to the sexual and reproductive demands of their 'partners', which negates the concept of marital rape and freely chosen pregnancies, and to their male family members' disposal of their energy, creativity and work. Thus women connive in their own oppression in order to survive.

One belief system, which specifically requires acts of violence against the female sex to uphold cultural traditions at the cost of life and health, is addressed by Olayinka Koso-Thomas (Chapter 8). Female genital mutilation (fgm) has been the experience of perhaps 80 million women and girls living today, many perpetuating it through their own daughters and granddaughters in obedience to community authority which they feel too powerless to question, let alone challenge, without the support of a converse authority. Yet there are now campaigns, led by courageous African women, with prescribed lines of action necessary in the many countries where the practice is rooted. These forward-looking prescriptions could be adapted, perhaps, to eradicate other deeply held belief systems which control women's sexuality or economic power, without creating a vacuum to be filled by new man-made, women-victimising 'traditions'. For there have been many examples of women's movements making gains for women as a social group, but then governments claw back in other ways, and male individuals and groups demonstrate their insecurity by employing new restrictions. The rapid commercial expansion of both violent pornography and 'bodyism', the destructive cult of conformity to certain models of beauty, so prevalent in North America and Europe, have been cited by feminists as exemplifying this.

My own concluding chapter covers some of the tactics, aims, actions and achievements of CHANGE, 'speaking truth to power'. We generated 'gender awareness' and 'mainstreamed' women in national and international institutions before the expressions were coined; our aims included 'the human rights and dignity of women and publicising their abuse whether by state, commercial interest or individual'. Our work has been characterised by the skilful use of scarce resources, like that of many others in feminist movements, while we see waste and corruption all around. CHANGE is by no means alone in the scope of its adventures, for there are many international women's networks, although most have more limited or specific mandates, derived either from their location, inclination or decision-making structure, or from the fashions of their donors. The process of advocacy is continuous, and the serious advocate never assumes a small gain to be an irreversible triumph. Coalitions are the bridges which build the connections and the synthesis between seemingly diverse interests in order to challenge the inherited order and to create new options. Most of the people in whose interests we take up these actions will never know who gave of their time, passion and intelligence to try to tackle the forces that dominate them. This is the Diplomacy of the Oppressed.

Notes

1. Speech at the first International Conference on Teaching and Research Related to Women, Montreal, 1982. Judith Astellara is a Chilean sociologist, and former refugee, at the Autonomous University of Barcelona, Spain.

2. In *Women, Development and Empowerment*, Pacific Women, 1987.

3. From a participant at the 1986 Women's Studies Summer School in Spetses, Greece.

4. *Some Questions on Feminism and its Relevance in South Asia*, Kali for Women, 1986.

5. Women's Voices '94, *Women's Declaration on Population Issues*, International Women's Health Coalition, 1993.

6. The wording was introduced into a statement to the UN by NGOs at the 1980 World Conference for the Decade for Women.

7. See the catalogue of miseries in *Women, Political and International Development: The Bureaucratic Mire,* edited by Kathleen Staudt, Temple University Press, 1990.

8. See especially Sheila Rowbotham, *Women in Movement,* Routledge, 1993.

9. See, for example, Marta Zabaleta, *Myths, Dreams, Women in Argentina,* CHANGE, 1993.

10. First of all, *Of Violence and Violation: Women and Human Rights,* CHANGE, 1986.

11. Georgina Ashworth, *Changing the Discourse: a Guide to Women and Human Rights,* CHANGE, 1993.

12. 'An International Evaluation of the UN Decade for Women', special issue of *Women's Studies International Forum,* 1985, Vol. 8, No. 2, Pergamon Press.

13. Virginia Woolf, *Three Guineas,* Virago edition, 1991.

14. Georgina Ashworth, Introduction to 'An International Evaluation of the UN Decade for Women'.

15. Georgina Ashworth, 'A Glimpse of the International', in *The Invisible Decade: UK Women and the UN Decade,* eds. Ashworth and Bonnerjea, Gower, 1985.

16. Edited by Peter Willetts, Frances Pinter, 1981.

17. 'Towards a Feminist Foreign Policy', a paper given to the Mediterranean Women's Studies Summer School, Spetses, 1986; a preparatory version was given to the International Relations Centre, London School of Economics, earlier that year.

18. Caren Grown and Gita Sen, *Development Alternatives With Women in a New Era,* reissued in 1987 as *Development, Crises and Alternative Visions,* Monthly Review Press, 1987.

19. Westview Press, 1992.

20. Pluto Press, 1987.

21. London School of Economics, 1988.

22. Pandora Press, 1989.

23. Columbia University Press, 1990.

24. This is one of the indicators in the Human Freedom Index which UNDP used in the *Human Development Report 1990* and which I have critiqued in *Women and Human Rights,* OECD-DAC, 1992, in as yet unpublished papers (e.g. North-South Institute, Canada, and the Development Studies Association) based upon that, and to a lesser extent in *When Will Democracy Include Women?,* CHANGE, 1992.

25. *Women and Human Rights: A Policy Paper,* OECD-DAC, 1992.

2

Feminist Conflict Resolution

Judith Large

'War begins in the minds of men' is a commonplace in academic circles regarding international relations or the analysis of international conflict. An admirable quote, intended to steer the student's gaze away from purely military or strategic indexes to a clearer definition of the perceptions and psychology behind terms like 'the national interest'. But it does not go far enough: ('war begins in the minds of men') a logical conclusion to the sentence would say where war ends – in the bodies of men, women and children. As we approach the end of the twentieth century, those bodies accumulate. We live in complex, highly differentiated times; conflicts proliferate and spiral at a pace bewildering to numbed observers and fatal for their participants – usually residents of less developed countries. Yet the ways of studying international conflict and, more important, the ways of dealing with it are still largely confined to masculine thought forms, which will not be suitable for the next century.

It has been estimated that to date in this century about 100 million people have been killed in wars. In the First World War, 95 per cent of casualties were soldiers. In the Second World War, 56 per cent of the dead were civilians, mostly women and children.[1] With the proliferation of violent conflicts and internal wars since the end of the Cold War, estimates of civilian casualties now range between 86 per cent and 90 per cent of war deaths worldwide. But the human cost of war does not stop with death statistics. Refugees and displaced persons now number more than 20 million. The relationship between civil conflict and famine is painfully evident in countries such as Ethiopia, Somalia, Sudan; severe malnutrition has devastated the population of Iraq, where prior to the sanctions maintained since the 1991 war, 70 per cent of all food was imported. The picture is not complete without those other consequences of armed conflict: destruction of the natural environment, and physical and psychological disablement of the human infrastructure.

Environmental damage may be blazing islands due to the US nuclear testing blasts. The disintegration of the human habitat – ruination of the essential social fabric, as in Beirut, Belfast or Basra – can mean: no personal security or livelihood; no basics, such as drinking water or sanitation; no provisions; no services; no resources; no shelter. Herein lies the completion of a vicious circle: it is amid such war-torn environments that the seeds of social conflict and the violence of despair take root.

'Conflict resolution' has implications different from those of judicial settlement or of one side subduing the other by superior violence. At its most basic, resolution attempts to deal with the issues in dispute at source, rather than looking to 'impartial' authority structures or resorting to a fight. Hence the reticence of one commentator on South Africa even to use the term, given the comprehensive levels of change implied, preferring the semantics of 'accommodation' or 'management'.[2] In resolution, the 'source' of a dispute is taken to lie in attitudes as much as in structures or institutions. This is a tall order, as anyone dealing with interpersonal or domestic violence will realise. It is in the personal sphere that resolution was first attempted – in counselling, affirmative action groups, non-adversarial divorce proceedings, or neighbourhood mediation schemes. It is the approach of this chapter that values must change in order to tackle the diverse structural sources of any given violent dispute. Violence itself cannot bring about change without generating emotions of hostility, even if it can shake up the structures involved. The same applies to the coercive halting of violence.

The domestic initiatives mentioned above were taken during and after the 1960s, a decade of social upheaval in much of the North, manifested in many anti-authoritarian demonstrations, and in the rise of the new feminist movement. One view of social psychology (backed by ancient myth as much as by modern empirical research) holds that co-operative and relational thought processes are classic feminine forms of consciousness while hierarchical and linear approaches are more masculine. ('Feminine' and 'masculine' are here seen as organising principles of thought; individual men and women are capable of either or both approaches.) Yet it would seem that neither academic nor practitioner in the field of international relations allows for any gender affiliation to conflict resolution theory.

John Burton, for example (a pioneer in challenging 'power politics' as a main analytic framework) acknowledges that, 'it was not until the early 1960's that there was any effective challenge to the normative and authoritarian approach of classical theory'.[3] But he identifies the source of such a change as the sphere of industrial relations, and the incentive as increased productivity. Consider the following use of language as Burton describes new approaches to decision-making which 'focused attention on the advantages of cybernetic or steering and reactive processes, rather than on unadulterated power and hierarchical approaches'.

Similarly, a New Zealand academic visiting the international relations department at the University of Kent in 1990 presented a paper on the evolution of New Zealand's contemporary (holistic and enlightened) judicial and political policies on the environment, the nuclear question, and approaches to conflict. He was startled, but in complete agreement, when it was put to him that his complex graphs failed to account for value exchange between Maori and white women, followed by the women's movement's influence on male establishment outlooks. Maori women had passed on their own view of the earth as a living entity, with caring and nurturing as priorities over domination, mastery or control.

The problem of affiliation highlights questions of legitimacy and power. On a global scale the dilemma has been well described, in this case by a man, Lloyd Etheredge:

> That international politics is a world of men is a central and probably con-sequential fact; one that may illuminate underlying sexual dynamics, and one that is important to the extent that males are more inclined than women to seek strength, power, activity, dominance, competitive achievement; such qualities make them more fearful of others and more predisposed to unleash violence. In truth I do not know if hope is a realistic stance. Men may have the capacity to be rational, generous, and mutually cooperative, but as we face a world in which nuclear weapons and conventional armaments prolif-erate, it is sobering to know that the world in which they proliferate is a world of men.[4]

There will be those who object that to divide thus by gender is too simplistic. They will point to Iranian women soldiers in the Iraq-based Liberation Army of Iran, to Tamil Tigress cells, or to US Army women fighting in the Gulf or helping to invade Panama. It may have been Margaret Mead who called warfare a social invention, they will say, but it was Margaret Thatcher who galvanised a cabinet into fighting a war with Argentina. Fair enough. But next to these points loom some very large normative questions.

Firstly, in two of the most collectively traumatic events for the West-ern world this century – the Nazi holocaust and the development and use of nuclear weapons for mass murder and destruction – project dominance and control by men is well documented.[5] Secondly, both these events were enhanced by the overtly masculinised Western science which today gives us cluster bombs, Stealth, Cruise, Smart and instant images of technological domination. I am thinking of computer images of targets being hit, counterposed to nature. The former has been associated with masculinity and the latter with femininity. In each case it has been claimed that human progress requires that the former achieve domination of the latter.

> And the day to day world we live in is so permeated by scientific rationality as well as gender that to non-feminists and perhaps even some feminists the very idea of a feminist critique of scientific rationality appears closer to blasphemy than to social criticism as usual.[6]

So it is in the social sciences, where current paradigms create mechanistic frameworks: 'realism', 'structuralism' and 'pluralism'. From realism we have the classical reactive view of power politics. Structuralism lays bare the economic skeletons which pluralism fills out with the flesh of social organisation. While constructive as theoretical tools, each can become reified to the extent that we study the paradigm and not what is actually happening. The system will be identified but not the arms dealer, as lamented recently by J. K. Galbraith. He points out the relentless flow of weapons of destruction from affluent countries to poorer ones, and the subsequent slaughter and social dislocation. Economics as a discipline has 'rarely addressed itself to the military power; frequently this has been accepted as inevitable, a given factor'.[7] The micro-economics of a particular firm is one thing, the use of its product for devastation three thousand miles away is quite another. We focus on results and end-products with a 'valuefree' view of processes. For fear of blame or complicity we fail to trace the thread of unintended consequences. For much of academia, proactive consequential thought is not considered rational enough. And even here, as in the scientific and political communities, a power structure emerges. Repressive tolerance meets the feminist voice.

If, however, we accept the proposition that gender-associated traits are acquired behaviour rather than innate tendencies, then there is also increased scope for change in learned methods and approaches to conflict. The Seville *Statement on Violence* (UNESCO, 1991) argues, for example, that the technology of modern war has exaggerated traits associated with violence both in the training of combatants and the conditioning of general populations. There is no genetic disposition towards warfare; it is not a feature of every society. Yet we take organised political aggression as given. The critical view does not deny severe conflicts of interest, nor opposing goals, but argues for a transformation of process away from destruction. Particularly in the post-cold-war context of increasing socio-political disintegration and the emergence of questions of ethnicity and identity, the utility of war must be sharply questioned. Historical grievance and conditions of scarcity can combine in volatile ways.

In former Yugoslavia, where this combination exploded violently, groups of citizens organised to attempt conflict resolution in the midst of crisis. In practical terms (often following bombardment and the partition of land) this meant cultivating and applying skills in:

analysis of the parties in their locality and their stated positions and/or needs and fears;

communication, listening to individuals and groups, dispelling rumour and propaganda, enabling safe dialogue and confidence-building meetings;

negotiation and mediation for the process of civic organisation, viability and the building of a resource base; and

strategy for specific action or projects, particularly in the realm of human rights (for example sit-ins to prevent the eviction of minorities), relief work with refugees, educational and therapeutic work with veterans, the war-wounded, and children.

Such skills must be adapted to be culturally appropriate in any given context. In both eastern Slavonia (Croatia) and northern Vojvodina (Serbia) it has been seen as important to understand and counteract the emotive use of symbolism as an adjunct to the mentality of war.

Such groups cannot function in isolation (witness the tragic demise of comparable peace and multicultural initiatives in Sarajevo owing to external interference and war). Creative international networking is essential for moral and practical support. Essentially their work is about community building, responsible empowerment, and the transformation of a militarist culture into a culture of potential for active peace. The term 'active peace' (or positive peace) is drawn from work by Johan Galtung and Adam Curle, in which peace is not just the absence of war but a condition in which social justice and respect for human rights prevail. In negative peace may be found severe structural violence, inequality or social repression, even if no outright war is evident. Peace groups work on several levels – individual, grassroots, civic and regional. The backdrop to these initiatives are daunting state structures, often complicated by warlordism, protection rackets and criminal paramilitary activity.

Power structures require scrutiny if conflict at various levels is to be understood. They do not always entail coercive superiority or dominant strength, but may be intricate patterns of dependency. Say my wage packet depends on an arms contract. A foreign regime is dependent on those weapons for waging war and controlling its population. Firms in my country are dependent on the other state for natural resources, the other state depends on that market, or foreign imports, or credit. Meanwhile I depend or rely on management to take decisions, they in turn look in part to government policy. The cycle manifests itself in countless ways.

We may further break down the nature of power by looking at the social currencies or forms of influence at work here. Consider factors such as the holding of a particular expertise or desired skill, control of resources, shared goals or the building of a group identity. These apply to the example above as they might to personal relationships.

Power as a generally perceived term, however, incorporates a number of concepts such as force, legitimacy and authority. One feature of women's social position is that they may have a nominal political position (they vote; they pay taxes) but lack force, legitimacy and authority. To look at potential for conflict resolution it may be that we cease measuring by 'power' and 'role' and look instead at intersections between 'the social, economic, political and ideological spheres of social life in such a way as to build up a picture of women as particular kinds of social individuals within particular social formations'.[8] Women are social actors involved in social strategies, with short- or long-term aims. Some of these strategies will be conscious, activist organising. Others may be unconscious or relatively subtle.

Conscious attempts at organising may include participating in struggles to overcome injustice or structural violence – conflict chosen as a means to a better end. 'The advocacy of revolt must be in inverse relation to the possibility of reform.'[9] At various times in history the women of El Salvador, Vietnam or Angola, for example, have had far fewer options for bringing about social change than the women of the United Kingdom or the Netherlands. (No blanket judgement of individual or group strategies is intended here.)

Let us rather consider the scope of militarism as a culture in its own right, and the massive infrastructure involved: decision-makers, politicians, weapons designers and producers, the armed forces themselves – all these are social actors on whom we are meant to confer tremendous authority. Sometimes this authority is challenged: the Hague International Women's Conference of 1915, anti-war movements, the US 'sanctuary' movement for the sheltering of illegal refugees from violence in central America, the women's peace camp at Greenham Common in England, CHANGE, Cruise Watch or the Campaign Against the Arms Trade and related activism. But people-to-people initiatives and 'second track' diplomacy are seldom given any credit for change; we are meant to believe that the 'powers that be' are the only powers that are. Traditional first track diplomacy represents hierarchical political leadership and as such appears functionally to be both masculine and exclusive, for example Margaret Thatcher and Ronald Reagan taking personal credit for the end of the cold war! The 'second track' (NGOs, special advisory groups, trade and business, professional/interest networks such as physicians, artists, mothers etc.) deals with nurtured relationships and is inclusive.

It follows then that conflict resolution theory itself can be turned into special techniques to be applied at special workshops organised largely by male 'experts' (yet another domain of male specialists). At the same time, at grassroots level, men and women caught in militaristic spirals attempt to find their own alternatives. They work out of their own indigenous cultures, sometimes with support from outside sources: Oxfam, the Mennonite schemes, Quaker Peace and Service – involvement by empathy. Like the eye of a storm, women may be seen making their own statements in the midst of severe repression and violence: 'Women in Black' in Belgrade, the Anti-War Campaign in Croatia; the International Women's Peace Initiative, formed after the Iraqi invasion of Kuwait, active during the Gulf war; Mothers of the Disappeared in Chile, Argentina, and Sri Lanka; the Mothers for Peace in Northern Ireland and the former Soviet Union. They seek in their own ways (citing a Quaker phrase) to 'speak truth unto power'.

At its simplest, militarism has two basic requirements: attitudes and armaments. Attitudes almost stopped the US Congress (in a close vote) condoning the use of force to compel Iraqi withdrawal from Kuwait. The continued existence of the cold war arsenal and newly developed high-tech weaponry (plus US strategic long-term interests in the Middle East) overrode any alternative tactics. The question of who built the Iraqi war machine in the first place is continually ignored in the light of renewed arms sales and exports to the region. It is difficult to imagine the long-pent-up pain and bitter memories of Serbs and Croats erupting into full-scale militarised violence without the easy availability of weaponry and hardened attitudes towards territory and ethnicity. The same may be said of Beirut.

Politicians, notably at the much-hyped 1991 G7 meetings in London, have made sweeping pronouncements on 'global' arms control; at the same time US dealers contracted to sell US$4 billion worth of arms to Middle Eastern countries. Neither the politicians nor the dealers are current or prospective victims of these wares. It is time that these deals were perceived as overtly misogynistic. Where are the female exporters of sophisticated torture equipment to dictatorships the world over? Where are the groups of uniformed women, to be reductionist, who rape men?

While the above are not readily evident, there is female complicity in militarism. It goes beyond the level of girl soldiers to those personal intersections mentioned above. The arms dealer, the torturer and the general all have personal lives and many have female partners. Genuine agreement and support for a militaristic stance is one thing. But what of the residual effect of centuries of patriarchal dominance in the realm of defence and security? What of unconscious 'he knows best' attitudes and denial of tacit involvement? When do unconscious social strategies have their own cumulative results? Put rather differently, given those centuries of (Western) male dominance, how many women have opted for strategies of conflict avoidance rather than challenging institutionalised violence? Compliance, like resistance, may be seen as a strategy – part of ongoing negotiations within class or gender relations: 'Knowing when to give in is an integral part of knowing how and when to resist, if you happen to be poor and weak.'[10]

When women resisted the values of their men in Nazi Germany or in nuclearised America, as often as not the means were withdrawal of service rather than open political confrontation. 'Not speaking', refusing to cook or have sexual relations, withdrawing domestic labour – all have a limited utility, meant to put over a message without cost or harm to the messenger. In their own ways they are statements which defy dependency. There is increasing anthropological evidence to suggest that some women use withdrawal as a strategy for survival. Many choose to work around the state rather than to work with it:

> ... evidence suggests that women's politics has often been concerned with evasion and avoidance, with complex strategies of resistance and compliance. Perhaps women have tended to work outside the state because they have always been marginalised within it.[11]

Perhaps the state as a political form represents masculine values and a degree of mystified vested interest with which they choose not to compromise. The same withdrawal and side-stepping of official channels may be seen in other recent organising – notably that concerned with peace, the environment or human rights. On the one hand this bodes well for continued people-to-people contact, and for retaining qualities of empathy, listening and dialogue when dealing with differences. On the other hand it begs the question of authority structures as they stand. This raises the vital issue of appropriate forms of confrontation. The feminist believing in empowerment and social justice walks a tightrope between the compromise of an aggressive stance against militarism and the need to retain values that are proactive and healing rather than reactive and destructive.

Above all the issue must be reclaimed by women – one need only look back to the 1915 publication, *Militarism versus Feminism* to realise that from the outset conflict resolution has been a feminist concern. Popular myth would have us believe that the vote, contraception or equal pay have been sole traditional aims. Our social histories need to rediscover individuals like Berta von Suttner, whose campaigning work and 1889 book, *Die Waffen Nieder* (English title, *Lay Down Your Arms*), launched the debate on de-militarisation in Central Europe and was instrumental in the establishment of the Nobel Peace Prize and subsequently the International Court of Justice in The Hague.

Traditionally allocated the tasks of nurturing and caring, women's scope for contributing to attitude-formation is considerable, if it could be valued as such. And the more these tasks are shared by men (for their own education), the better. Armaments and lethal hardware have their origins somewhere. The intellectual divide between their manufacture and their potential use is the same divided thinking that divorced the split atom from any responsibility for Hiroshima. What Jonathan Kozol refers to as Western schizophrenic 'fragmentized reality'[12] can be overcome. A women's group in rural Gloucestershire, for example, refuses to accept 'Islam' and 'the West' as towering entities external to their lives. They invite Muslim women from the nearby city for discussion and dialogue and sharing. They are anticipating possible conflict arising from differences, and are working against this in a proactive way. It is a small, local initiative. In both the short term and the long term it may matter a great deal.

'Top-down' peace-making procedures (Versailles, Camp David, Lancaster House conferences, etc.) involve power elites and the promise and delivery of resources or rewards by the mediator. They can deliver new institutional frameworks, sometimes, but they only scratch the surface of feelings, ideologies and conditions which motivated the violence originally. Personal advocacy for reconciliation, moral and physical support for the rebuilding of lives, and new definitions of 'security' are essential for genuine conflict resolution. Some contribution is within the reach of every feminist, of every individual, who chooses to be involved.

Not many of us have the opportunity to mediate directly in militarised disputes. Most of us have the scope for questioning how one social context adversely affects another, through political interference, domination, exploitation or neglect. We also have immediate surroundings which reflect wider issues on a personal scale – be they race relations, housing, environmental management or domestic violence. Withdrawal as strategy is one thing, but passivity is quite another. Feminist conflict resolution will entail challenges – confrontation, discourse, caring, even conflict itself, to ensure that the world's victims of militarised disputes receive the attention they deserve. In one way or another we are all part of the whole. Arms and wealth have brought diplomatic recognition and status in the past; only the feminist approach will ensure a future diplomacy for the oppressed.

Notes

1. Frank Barnaby (ed), *The Gaia Peace Atlas* (London, Pan Books, 1988), p. 98.
2. H. W. van der Merwe, 'South African Initiatives', in Mitchell and Webb (eds), *New Approaches to International Mediation* (New York, Greenwood, 1988), p. 184.

3. John Burton, 'The History of International Conflict Resolution', in Azar and Burton, *International Conflict Resolution* (Brighton, Wheatsheaf, 1986), p. 44.

4. Lloyd Etheredge, from 'A World of Men: The Private Sources of American Foreign Policy', quoted in Brian Easlea's *Fathering the Unthinkable* (London, Pluto Press, 1983).

5. See Easlea, op. cit., and Claudia Koonz, *Mothers in the Fatherland: Women, the Family and Nazi Politics* (London, Jonathan Cape, 1987).

6. Sandra Harding, *The Science Question in Feminism* (Milton Keynes, Open University Press), p. 19.

7. J. K. Galbraith, 'At the Mercy of the Military', the *Guardian*, 6 August 1991, p. 17.

8. Henrietta Moore, *Feminism and Anthropology* (Cambridge, Polity Press, 1988), p. 134.

9. Keith Webb, 'The Morality of Mediation', in Mitchell and Webb, op. cit., p. 27.

10. Moore, op. cit., p. 180.

11. Ibid., p. 183.

12. Jonathan Kozol, *Illiterate America* (New York, Plume Books, 1985), p. 191. See also Vandana Shiva, *Staying Alive*, (London, Zed Books, 1989).

3

Militarisation of Contemporary Societies and Feminism in the North

Andrée Michel*

Up to the present day, and without notable exceptions, feminist writings in Northern industrialised nations have not addressed the processes of militarisation and the structures which generate them, either as a mode of development which affects the situation of women, or as patriarchal structures elaborated solely by men. Feminist writings do not present the militarisation of contemporary societies as an obstacle to the realisation of the ideals sought throughout the International Women's Decade: equality, development and peace. Many Western feminists focused their writing more on the theme of equality than on that of development, and women peace activists only rarely proclaimed themselves feminist.

Feminists of the Western world have deciphered and identified the oppression of women by the patriarchal state, but generally they have done so in a selective and limited manner. They have identified the national state as: a sexist legislator responsible for the legitimisation of violence towards women in the field of civil, penal, social and fiscal rights; a sexist employer who carries out gender-based discrimination in the workplace; a sexist tax-collector who penalises prostitutes while sparing pimps, clients and brothel-keepers. Yet they remain silent when their national state proves to be a sexist agent in the distribution of budgetary resources, offering enormous sums to the men in the defence sector while allotting small amounts to sectors in which the majority of workers are women (education, health etc.).

This situation has come to pass as if feminists had limited the analysis of patriarchy and of sexism to the relations between the sexes, either on

---

* translated by Pamela A. Genova

an inter-individual scale or in very limited contexts (family, work, political life, etc.). They have forgotten the analysis of the gender relations present at the heart of the structures and procedures of militarisation which have, if not generated, at least legitimised, developed and amplified to an extreme degree the violence of men towards women. Disarmament between states is not supported by feminist groups; in the same way, they do not examine parliamentary debates which, when it comes to voting on national budgets, distribute state funds to many different social partners. This distribution can never be neutral from the feminist point of view.

As a result of this approach, the national states of Western societies have been brought, under the pressure of women's movements, to formulate legislative changes and to take positive measures in favour of improving women's hitherto limited priority. There has been some emphasis on problems concerning the equality of sexes (juridical, economic, social and political equality) and concerning some forms of violence towards women (wife-beating, rape, sexual harassment, incest, excision, etc.). Yet these states systematically ignore the forms of violence towards women resulting from militarisation, since these national states are the principal architects of that militarisation, and pressure from feminists has not yet been able to reach them on this point.

It is therefore necessary to examine the various sociological factors that have contributed to this selective analysis of the patriarchal system within the Western feminist approach, factors that have also contributed to their tardiness, compared with the more comprehensive analyses of Third World counterparts. Among the more decisive factors of these findings, we can identify, first, the differential socialisation between the sexes; second, the lack of analysis by feminists of a sexist model of militarised development imposed on Southern countries; and third, such a model for Northern countries.[1]

The dichotomy of gender-based education in the West

The Western feminist movement has always been deeply influenced by writings, theoretical and otherwise, of feminist authors and researchers, whether freelance or linked to a university, foundation or research institution. Western female students have always been particularly oriented towards literary studies, social sciences (history, linguistics, anthropology, psychology, education, communication, religion, etc.) and the arts. These women have been much less prepared, however, to decipher the sexism present in the world's contemporary political and military organisations, because they still represent such a small percentage in those fields of study (economics, political science, etc.) which would allow them to approach such subjects with a critical eye. As is true in the case of present-day France, the increase in this percentage still represents a phenomenon too recent to have a measurable impact on contemporary feminist thought.

Indeed, in France, where the percentage of female students at university level surpasses that of male students (51 per cent in academic 1982–83), such figures must be considered in the light of the particular fields of study which attract higher numbers of women. For example, statistics from 1973–74 show 66 per cent of women in literary disciplines, while in 1982–83 their number rose to 67.8 per cent of students in those fields. In economics, for the same periods of reference, women represented 28 per cent and 42 per cent respectively.[2] Moreover, the attrition rate is much higher for women than for men, especially in disciplines which have recently attracted more female students. In 1980, for example, women represented 45 per cent of all students in the first two years of economics at the university level, while in the final stage of the programme they made up only 24 per cent.[3]

But even at the core of their orientation towards the humanities and social sciences, there is a dichotomy between masculine and feminine centres of interest. If, indeed, during the 1979–80 academic year, women obtained between 40 per cent and 58 per cent of all doctorates in languages, modern literature, classics, psychology, ethnology and anthropology, it is also true that this percentage falls to 18 per cent in geography (a science often qualified by the phrase 'a science of war'), 17 per cent in philosophy and 16 per cent in sociology,[4] disciplines which would permit a more complete understanding and articulation of the feminist problematic in relation to the macro-economic phenomena of militarisation.

The gender-based dichotomy of university education is even more striking in Quebec, as is evident in the following statistics which compare percentages of women students at all levels of university study in various domains within the Quebec system of higher education.[5]

	1976	1983
Linguistics	70.8%	72.9%
Psychology	54.9%	68.9%
Political Science	27.1%	33.3%
Economics	17.1%	26.3%

Even today the number of female students in scientific disciplines in Quebec is quite low, in spite of the progress made between 1976 and 1983 in those domains which would allow women to understand more completely the patriarchal nature of the 'development' of their society and of Third World societies.

As for those women who have succeeded in obtaining positions as teachers within the university system, their numbers are generally concentrated at the bottom of the professional hierarchy. In 1979, they represented 14 per cent of all positions in humanities, compared to only 9.5 per cent in political science and 7 per cent in economics. These percentages are too small to allow these women to guide students, both male and female, in questioning the legitimacy of such issues as nuclear rearmament, the economics of arms sales, and the foundations of economic development. In 1985, the percentage of women teaching at French universities in all disciplines combined reached 25 per cent, the average in European countries, not strikingly different from the rates of 27.5 per cent in the US and 24 per cent in Canada.[6] In sum, the weak participation of women in higher education, their lowly positions in the university hierarchy and their specialisation in certain domains represent major factors which keep women from articulating the paradigm of militarisation in contemporary societies.

The situation is more promising in certain Third World countries where the percentage of women teaching at university level is higher than in so-called developed countries. Women represent 38 per cent of all university teachers in Latin America and the Caribbean islands: 43 per cent in Brazil, 40 per cent in Cuba, 33 per cent in Argentina, Nicaragua and Panama.[7] Moreover, while the percentage of female university teachers in North America and Europe is the same for public and private institutions of higher learning, the percentage in the latter reaches 55 per cent in Latin America.[8] The same is true in Asia, where many countries show high numbers of women teaching at university level, compared to percentages in Northern countries: 53 per cent in the Philippines, 38 per cent in Mongolia, 31 per cent in Lebanon, and so on. Further, university disciplines show much less gender bias, in the case of both students and professors. Doubtless this factor helps to explain why the macro-economic and political problems of the militarisation of contemporary societies are much more often the object of feminist writings in Southern countries than in the North. In any event, such questions are not portrayed as a taboo subject for feminist thought.

Another differentiation between masculine and feminine roles in the realms of research and reflection may be illustrated by the following statistics describing the participants, both male and female, in an interdisciplinary conference on the American military-industrial complex, held in the United States in October 1985: only 22 per cent of all participants were women, and only 11 per cent – two women out of the 18 – were conference speakers.[9] Of these two, one was connected to a department of social sciences while the other was a peace activist. Among the male conference speakers, only five out of the 16, less than one-third, were from social science departments. One was a peace activist, while the others worked in university disciplines traditionally labelled masculine, where it is possible to acquire the necessary information and concepts to be able to situate the military at the heart of social and economic development. As a consequence, the scientific specialisations and professional qualifications of Western women, feminist or not, prepare them poorly not only for research on the agents and processes of militarisation, but also for the identification of the agents and processes of the patriarchal system. On the contrary, these women are much more capable of deciphering sexism and the domination of women by men in the domains of grammar, linguistics, literature and art than they are in the political, economic and military organisation of the world.

Absence of Western feminist analysis of a model of strongly militarised development imposed on Third World countries

Nations in the South have already adopted a model of strongly militarised development, as is illustrated by the type of development seen in newly industrialised countries (Brazil, South Korea, India, Argentina, etc.), where a high percentage of production focuses on arms manufacture, and where an equally high percentage of exports is constituted by arms sales.

This aspect of development is, however, rarely mentioned in the feminist critique of development, wherein analysis is generally limited to Third World countries, as if the Northern countries do not themselves follow the same logic of economic, militarised development. The literature of Northern feminists on 'women and development', of which the most celebrated work is that of Esther Boserup,[10] vigorously denounces the perverse effects of 'development' on women of the Third World. Yet this literature does not introduce as an object of analysis the model of militarised development of the authors' own countries, as if this mode of development was above all suspicion. Perhaps it is because these authors, isolated in a Eurocentric or Americo-centric perspective, accept such a model unquestioningly as intrinsically valuable and representing the global norm. Incidentally, this perspective is also that of multinationals and large international financial institutions.

Other critiques by Western feminists of the mode of development in the Third World are equally ambiguous, since they do not allow for an identification of the deep-rooted mechanisms established by Northern countries, with the participation of Southern states, mechanisms which result in a negation of basic needs: the transfer of savings from Southern countries into Northern banks; the financing of white-elephant projects while basic infrastructure (potable water, sewerage systems, centres for

public health and family planning, etc.) fail miserably; the unfair economic exchange wherein the technology of Northern countries is bought
at high prices, while natural resources are purchased at low prices; the
mechanisms of aid and of Northern protectionism; the military *coups
d'état* instigated or supported by the West in order to put into power
corrupt leaders devoted to Western interests; and the arms sales which
put countries into debt and eventually lead to interminable, bloody
civil, frontier or international wars. Feminist inquiry too often remains
at the level of the description of sexist projects of development particular
to the Third World. Rarely does it question the dominant patriarchal
model which governs North–South exchanges.[11]

Of course, there is no lack of Northern feminist critical writing on
the postulates of Western economics and the systematic misrepresenta-
tion of women's work, both formal and informal, in labour statistics
and in evaluation of the Gross National Product. Indeed, there do exist
feminist proposals to replace inadequate economic indicators by more
pertinent factors, such as time-budgets which give a more complete
idea of the contribution of Third World women to production and
familial consumption than do the garbled statistics delivered by most
national and international institutes. From this finding, feminists moved
to the denunciation of sexism in national and international agencies
that eliminate Third World women from the elaboration, decision,
application and evaluation of development plans. But they have not
questioned the political, economic, financial, military and cultural domination of Southern countries by those of the North as an essential
factor in the global decline of women into poverty.

When we integrate militarisation into the model of development
spread by the West throughout Third World countries, we cannot help
but realise that it is the women of these countries who pay the highest
price in the process of militarisation and in military operations. The
two following examples will illustrate this point.

UNICEF calculated that in 1981 military spending in sub-Saharan
Africa rose to 11 per cent of the total budget of the entire sub-continent,
while spending reserved for health made up only 5 per cent, and for
education, only 16 per cent.[12] As a result of the African debt due to
arms sales, the International Monetary Fund and the World Bank
policies, supported by the agreements of Lome IV, required that African
governments make drastic cuts in public expenditure. These cuts fell in
realms such as health and education, obviously a devastating move in
a sub-continent where two thirds of all women are illiterate, and fewer
than one woman in two is helped in childbirth by a medical aide or
traditional midwife. The fertility rate per woman is the highest on the
planet (6.6 children per woman), and family planning services reach
only 10 per cent of all African women of child-bearing age.[13] This is a

catastrophic situation which compromises the future of African girls above all others. It is they who make up the majority of the unschooled, since the traditional response of poor families in debt is to keep their girls out of school. What one study has shown in Tanzania is true throughout sub-Saharan Africa: 'People decided to educate boys only, thus renewing the colonialist tradition of giving girls fewer opportunities for a future education.'[14]

Military operations always penalise women and children more seriously than men, as the 1991 Gulf war proved yet again. The most recent report issued by the United Nations Development Programme (UNDP) shows that 'the cost of ten days of the Gulf war would suffice to vaccinate all the children in the world over the next ten years against all diseases which are controllable through vaccines'.[15] But the effects of the Gulf war do not concern only children. Demographic studies carried out for more than 30 years in large European and American institutions have shown the strong correlation between infant mortality and the fertility of women. The higher the infant mortality rate, the more pregnancies and births, a fact which becomes clear in societies where women want to have a sufficient number of surviving children to ensure that they and their husbands will be taken care of in case of injury or old age. As a result, military spending, because of its claim on immense resources − for the profit of the arms merchants − prevents a reduction in the infant mortality rate and has a direct influence on the situation of Third World women. The higher the infant mortality rate, the more intense the fatigue of women brought on by the number of pregnancies and the amount of domestic and educational tasks to complete. The lower the rate of infant mortality, the fewer children these women have, and they would thus be freer to improve their education and their health. Moreover, the fewer children there are in a family, the more likely it is that young girls will be allowed to go to school, instead of staying at home to look after their brothers and sisters while the mother works. Thus the cycle would be broken: the illiteracy of girls, the high fertility rate, poverty, misery, famine, all represent core elements in a vicious circle, the progression of which could be reversed.

Sanctions, which represented an economic war against Iraq both before and after the military war, struck Jordan directly. For Jordan, the flow of refugees and the halting of commerce with Iraq represented a loss of US$3.6 billion in 1991, as well as the disappearance of 50,000 jobs. According to a recent UNICEF report, the results of the war already imply the malnutrition of 250,000–300,000 children and the increase in the number of babies weighing less than 2.5 kilos at birth from 5–10 per cent before the war to 30 per cent after the war.[16] It is clear that such a situation could only bring an increase in the infant mortality rate and cause a regression in mothers' conditions. The

UNICEF report also shows that tens of thousands of women either pregnant or of child-bearing age are threatened by disease and by a high maternal mortality rate.[17] In a country where 'the rate of literacy, education, and access to health services and clean water are among the highest in the world, and in many cases approach rates in the industrialised states of the world',[18] one Jordanian woman remarked that because of the Gulf crisis, '... we are becoming like the populations of Africa: thin, poor, sick and dying.'[19] Again,

> ... because of the Gulf war, families can no longer allow themselves to spend the few dinars needed to offer their children basic scholarly materials such as pencils, notebooks, compasses and sports clothes. Many families are forced to use money which would normally go towards buying food for the education of their children. They are obliged to sell furniture, jewellery, heating equipment, clothes, anything of value. Not everyone succeeds in his endeavour, and some families succumb to economic pressure and send their children out to earn money in the streets rather than sending them to school.[20]

It is the girls who pay the highest price, as is illustrated in one neighbourhood, where the girls go to school only part-time, because in the morning or evening they must share their uniforms with the daughters of other families.

In Iraq, where the United States systematically carried out a war of destruction against institutions and equipment essential to daily life (for producing potable water, distributing electricity and operating the sanitation system), carried it out so effectively that the country was set back more than 50 years, it is easy to imagine the fatigue, disease and anxiety which befall the women who are caretakers of daily life and who tend to sacrifice their own essential needs to those of their children.[21]

Since the time when the Western model of development, based on militarisation and the unfair distribution of natural resources and income, displayed its failure to the poverty-stricken masses in the Maghreb, the Middle East and African countries, there has appeared a new danger threatening women: the increase in religious fundamentalism. Once fundamentalism succeeds in taking power, such as in the Sudan, its presence is visible through the restoration of archaic religious laws and customs directly affecting women. The implicit male sexist logic which functions through fundamentalism can be read as follows: since the Western model of economic development depletes the resources which go to the popular masses of the Third World, why not isolate women from access to these resources by enclosing them in houses, keeping them from paid labour, from the consumer market, from political functions, in fact from everything that might constitute the beginnings of their emancipation? The rhetoric used to carry out this racket against women asserts that the traditional model offered by archaic religion and customs may succeed where the Western model has failed. Should we then be surprised that the most staid supporters of fundamentalists, who corrupt Muslim societies from Morocco to Pakistan, exist in the oil monarchies of the Gulf? Is it not logical that the vassals of the West, who place oil revenues into Western banks in order that this money will help Western development, fear the anger of the poverty-stricken Arab masses, and thus turn this anger towards women by financing fundamentalist structures? The racket against women operates therefore through fundamentalism. It is set forth as a solution to nations frustrated by the West's own racket, established as an international economic system at the heart of North–South relations. Through the alliance of Western countries with the oil monarchies of the Arabian/Persian Gulf, such as obtained during the Gulf war, it is the West which ultimately acts as the support for the Muslim fundamentalists it professes to combat. This fact should enrich feminist thought, since the fundamentalism of so-called democratic Western countries follows the same sexist economic logic. It aims at sending women back to the kitchen and isolating them in reproduction, leaving open to men a job market which is shrinking daily.

The absence of Western feminist inquiry into the model of development imposed on Northern countries by the dominant classes

I have shown elsewhere[22] how the West made use of the entire arsenal of grants for students and interns, international conferences and colloquia, the media and the overwhelming Western preponderance of scientific and economic publications combined to 'socialise' the future intellectuals and leaders of the Third World, to sensitise them to the priorities and values of a militarised form of development. This socialisation is the same for intellectuals of both sexes in the developed world during their years at primary and secondary schools, and at public and private universities and civilian or military institutions. From these schools emerge upper- and middle-class women and men who will constitute the future leaders in the political, economic, military and cultural spheres of the developed world. Thus, across the frontiers of developed nations, a vast system of complicity between members of the scientific/military/industrial complexes is established, capable of shaping public opinion in order that it supports the interests of these complexes.[23]

Even if these complexes compete in the arms market, they coalesce easily amongst themselves, and with their vassals, when the privileged classes of the developed world are threatened by a rising regional Third World power. Western feminists do not escape any more easily than does the Third World 'elite' from the intensive socialisation by which the 'brain-washing' dominates the media and all levels of Western education. Their education, which emphasises the humanities at the expense of political and economic science, does not furnish them with the conceptual apparatus necessary for critical analysis of a strongly militarised model of development. For this militarisation is present, not only within systems of production, arms sales and military coups, but also at the very heart of economics and politics.

In fact, it is enough simply to read the daily economic press to realise that problems of production and consumption are presented in terms of fierce competition. The strongest, who are often the most competitive, the smartest, the most malicious and even the most dishonest, must win. In spite of the myth of regulation by the market, the strongest are not always 'the best', but often those who succeed in overwhelming their adversaries through corporate agreements, the work of lobbies pressurising states or international organisations, the practice of 'dumping', and even sheer fraud. Thus we speak of the 'economic' war in every domain: the war of motor vehicles, of electronics, of information, of soya and of pigs, of wheat and rice, pitiless wars in which the strongest, least scrupulous of competitors usually wins.

Militarisation was a crucial force during the period 1970–85 through military spending at the core of national budgets, and in arms sales and production in the traditional economic indicators (GNP, GDP, commercial balances, etc.), even though the role it plays is generally underestimated – in order to avoid alarming the public. Statistics from major research institutions and international organisations reveal that, worldwide, one-quarter of all credit destined for research and development, and one-quarter of all researchers and engineers, are occupied in military research: 70 per cent in the United States, 60 per cent in the former USSR, 50 per cent in Britain and 33 per cent in France, compared to 13 per cent in Germany and 5 per cent in Japan.[24]

The power of this model of development originates in the fact that it discovered how to gain legitimacy in public opinion, with both sexes, by deploying certain myths corresponding to Western expectations of progress, comfort, security, and work, to mention only the most obvious. It is essential that Western feminists now uncover the underlying mystifying and sexist nature of these myths.

A recurring theme of the partisans of militarisation, who hope somehow to justify or lighten the effect of the loss of millions of human lives due to wars, is that military research and war have allowed for scientific and technological progress, by updating, for example, the medical technology which contributes to human comfort. The supporters of this view are not, however, capable of furnishing sufficient proof to uphold their thesis, since there exists only a minute number of cases documented in reports published by defence departments. Already in 1980, however, it was estimated that ' ... in the past 30 years, had the total dollars we spent on military research and development been expended instead in those areas of science and technology promising the most economic progress, we would probably be today where we will find ourselves arriving in the year 2000'.[25] Indeed, much research has shown the near failures of the techniques and of the research on civil industries (industries in which most women work, as we will see further) conducted by the military. Japan and Germany, deprived of the potential to make nuclear weapons, have dominated the world through their industry, particularly in the realm of high technology (electronics, computers, etc.). In Britain, the research of Mary Kaldor, Margaret Sharp and William Walker has shown that military research does not systematically encourage civilian-oriented research.[26] It has been proved that the 55 per cent of French electronics that goes towards armaments can rarely be adapted to civil industry, while ' ... all the international specialists believe that the development of this sector is being conducted, and will continue to be conducted, for the public at large and not solely for military ends'.[27] Thus in 1988, the French trade deficit with Japan and the 'four dragons' – Taiwan, Korea, Hong Kong and Malaysia – in the field of electronics reached FF20 million.[28] Civil aeronautics represents another striking example, for

> ... there are only a few shared aspects in the definition of civil versus military planes. The experience gained by Dassault in small military supersonic planes has practically no use whatsoever in the development of Concorde by the Aerospatiale group ... . Even in the domain of electronic equipment, and particularly in that of flight patterns, the needs and necessary performance of civil and military materials are too vastly different to allow for significant comparison.[29]

In the United States, the Defense Secretary admits that 90 per cent of the colossal budget reserved for military research '... can have absolutely no effect on civil industry'.[30] This exclusive appropriation of resources has brought about great losses for American industry on the domestic market. While in 1978 American industry controlled 75 per cent of the domestic electronics market, in 1986 it controlled only 25 per cent of the same market, as a direct result of a major increase in military research, implemented by the Reagan administration.[31] Northern countries where military industry has developed at the expense of civil industry (USA, ex-USSR, France, Britain) are also the countries where 'de-industrialisation' has been extremely damaging. It has upset the commercial balance of industrial exchange and exhausted the sources of jobs, since it is civil industry that determines the creation of most positions of service work, the realm where most women work.

The myth of 'security', excessively guaranteed by militarisation, is easy to refute, especially in reference to the situation of civilians and of women. Past wars have shown that as a result of technological progress

> ... irrespective of the outcome of wars, the prime losers have been the civilians whom the military is supposedly protecting. Whether through direct war actions or indirect starvation, civilians constitute a rapidly growing share of war victims: they accounted for 52 per cent of all deaths in the fifties, and 85 per cent in the eighties. It is without exaggeration that economist Kenneth Boulding says 'National defense is now the greatest enemy of national security.'[32]

That which can be asserted about the civilian situation is doubly true for women, who represent the predominant percentage of those raped, forced into refugee status, slaughtered defencelessly or prostituted in the course of military operations, as American research on the Vietnam war has very clearly shown.[33]

It has been asserted that because of nuclear deterrence since 1945, France was not ravaged by a third world war, but France had had no bomb during the period of peace from 1870 to 1914. We must search for a more logical explanatory factor. The unique experience of Europe, torn apart by two world wars, led the Western nations and the then USSR to the decision cynically to plan the export of war into Third World countries, rather than allowing it to remain in their own territories. This stance prevailed in spite of the misleading rhetoric of the 'cold war', an alibi invoked to legitimise the arms race in public opinion.[34] Westerners and Soviets sent war to Third World countries through intervening states, ethnic factions, guerrilla groups, and so on. At present, there are 13 civil wars in Africa alone which are ruining an already ravaged continent. Is it because 'security' in the developed world does not seem to be threatened that so few feminists speak out against arms sales to Third World countries, arms sales which are the necessary consequence of the production of those arms which are not utilised in Northern countries? Obviously one cannot examine the problem of arms sales without also considering the production of those arms, in the recent past closely linked to the alibi of the 'cold war', today related to other 'enemies'.

The security of women in developed countries is necessarily dependent on the existence and effective running of public services (particularly education and health) which guarantee jobs for them, since a high percentage of employment for women falls into these sectors. But their security also depends on the infrastructures women utilise when they bring up children and simultaneously carry on a professional career. It has been shown in the United States how, under the Reagan administration from 1981 to 1985, military spending was financed in part by budget cuts in the realm of services destined for poor women. This situation is particularly striking in a country where, according to the statistics of the National Advisory Council for Economic Opportunity, if the proportion of single-parent families headed by women continues to grow at the same rate that it did from 1967 to 1979, the poor population in the year 2000 will be exclusively composed of women and children.[35] Quite recently the powerful American Medical Association addressed a memorandum to President Bush asking him to take urgent measures to guarantee minimum medical coverage to the 33 million poor Americans who now have no recourse to medical insurance.[36]

To have a well paid, permanent professional position, which guarantees social benefits (protection against sickness, injury, unemployment and retirement), is the best way for women to protect themselves against the uncertainties of marriage, the unexpected fluctuation of the economy and the domination of men. The myth of the creation of jobs due to military production, a myth taken up by all the spokesmen within military–industrial complexes, has only rarely been the object of study in the critical work of feminists, who are themselves victims of this dominating myth. The claim is that if arms production factories were to be closed, tens of thousands of workers would suddenly find themselves unemployed. But the inverse question is never formulated in feminist theory: how many positions could be created in civilian production and services, if this domain were to receive the support now directed at defence? Moreover, which gender inevitably profits the most from positions created within the military?

Economists have already responded to these two questions with well documented arguments. In the United States, the calculations formulated by Nobel prize-winners such as Leontieff, by research institutions, by representatives of Congress and by state agencies have all arrived at the same conclusions: twice the amount of money is necessary for military production compared to civilian production.[37] The reason for this is simple: sophisticated Western arms production uses a great deal of capital while saving on labour costs. The materials used are extremely expensive (rare metals, special alloys, new materials, etc.), while the manufacturing processes of high technology (automation, robotisation, etc.) demand very little human labour, and the few men needed must be very highly qualified and therefore well paid. In the United States, the manpower of the defence industry is composed of 59 per cent engineers and managers, compared with only 30 per cent in civilian industries. American women, like their counterparts in other developed countries, prefer to develop their qualifications and carry out their professional goals in the fields of health and education, rather than in that of engineering, where they now fill less than 5 per cent of the positions. It is obvious which gender benefits from the creation of new positions in military industry, as well as which gender suffers from the lack of available positions in civilian industry, owing to the increase in military production. These findings were calculated in the United States with great methodological rigour by economist Marion Anderson and her associates. She has shown that between 1981 and 1985, 1,146,000 projected positions in civilian industry were repressed, as a direct result of an increase in funding destined for defence, an increase, incidentally, higher than the inflation rate itself. In consequence, the creation of jobs in military industry cannot compensate for the loss of jobs in the civilian domain. Moreover, Anderson has also shown that 80 per cent of the lost positions would have been those for women, and that in general women are the hardest hit by such policies, for the following reasons:[38]

- The workforce in the American military industry is mostly male; women make up only 9.5 per cent.
- The erosion of the revenue of couples as a result of increased taxation generated by military growth has caused American consumers to cut back on the purchasing of durable goods, that is products from those industries where the workforce is composed mostly of women, deeply hit by unemployment in times of economic slump.
- Even those non-durable goods industries such as textiles, food and other services, where a large percentage of workers are women, have been affected by the rise in military industry. Anderson has detailed the loss of jobs for women in this sector between 1981 and 1985: 11,000 jobs in textile factories; 95,000 jobs in food services; 288,000 jobs in secretarial work and other office positions; 5,500 jobs in health care, particularly in nursing. At the same time, only 2,160 women had obtained positions as engineers in aero-astronautics, for example.

By destroying Third World economies through excessive arms sales, Northern states have also damaged the job market in their own countries. Indeed, the World Bank estimates that one-third of the debt paid each year by developing countries to developed nations is a direct result of the purchase of military equipment.[39] One US senator has estimated that in 1988 the Latin American debt had cost the United States more than one million jobs, for Latin American countries had invaded the North American market with their exports in order to gain enough capital to pay off that very debt. Inversely, North American exports to Latin America had collapsed. In fact, '… in economies with no growth, money that goes for interest is not spent on imports'.[40] Feminists in Western countries need to keep these facts in mind when their governments announce plans to continue to sell arms to Third World countries. Who will pay the bill? Women before anyone else; those of the Third World, of course, but also those of the developed world.

Developed countries, such as the United States, Britain and France, are also those where, in spite of the presence of women in the job market, the notion of a dual society has very aggressively been established. Two job markets coexist simultaneously in these countries. The first is constituted by full-time, well paid jobs, which guarantee insurance and other benefits. The second market embodies precarious positions, generally part-time, poorly paid and without benefits. As if by chance, the first job market is directed first at men (who find these favourable conditions particularly in military laboratories), while the second market is reserved for women. In Britain, where 50 per cent of the funding reserved for research and development goes to the military, the percentage of women working part-time jumped from 4 per cent in 1951 to 44.5 per cent in 1987, while the figures for male employees in the same period rose from 0.3 per cent to 4.6 per cent.[41] In the United States, women hold 52 per cent of temporary positions and 84 per cent of part-time positions. Moreover, the percentage of women working part-time within the totality of women's positions has increased with startling speed: from 14 per cent in 1975, it rose to 21 per cent in 1982.[42] In France, where a law concerning military spending projects an extra cost of US$444 billion to modernise the defence system over a period of five years, 22 per cent of women work part-time, while only 3.2 per cent of men hold such positions.[43] Research has revealed that in those three countries part-time work does not represent a choice by women but rather a constraint imposed on them by the job market.

The militarisation of Western societies, far from benefiting women, only widens the professional and social gap between the sexes. It has resulted in a dual model of society in which the worsening of social inequalities, unemployment and poverty provoke frustration and aggression not only towards immigrants but also against women, the objects of increasing violence. Such feelings are also stirred up by fundamentalist movements, which find their constituencies among the poorer social classes.

Fundamentalism in all its forms, whether Muslim, Jewish, Catholic, Protestant, Hindu or any of the innumerable sects now developing, responds to the most archaic expectations of the masculine psyche, through the support of such notions as the exclusion of women, the return to traditional norms denying women the right to work and the control of their bodies, in order to isolate them in the traditional roles of wife, mother and servant to the founders of these movements.

The first feminist voices documented in writing, particularly since Christine de Pisan, have brought to women a message of demystification, a refusal of the myths, prejudices and stereotypes employed by men to legitimate their domination and exploitation of women. Feminists, often without realising they were feminists, have worked for centuries towards a rejection of the traditional distribution of masculine and feminine roles justified by men, who take recourse in such arguments as the infallibility of the divine word, proclaimed by the three monotheistic religions, or the pretext of biological differences concerning procreation. Northern feminists are thus well prepared to examine the patriarchal myths and structures which continue their repression in Western notions of family, work, mass media, culture and general discourse. Yet feminist critical approaches to the structures and myths of development too often make an abstraction of North–South relations and of the myths of development in the feminists' own societies. Their critique is conducted as if it concerned only the development of the world economy in a limited region of the planet, that is, in Southern countries. However, the priorities, postulates and approaches of the South are usually based on models taken from the North. In short, they denounce the negative consequences of development on Third World women, but they avoid challenging the development of Northern countries, as if this model was not consubstantially connected to the militarisation of the economy and to North–South relations.

It seems unthinkable, for example, that Northern feminists would abandon to the World Bank the task of denouncing the fact that ' … military spending is much too high in developing countries and the majority of investments serve neither to reduce poverty nor to encourage economic growth'.[44] Yet feminists do criticise the politics of 'structural adjustment' of the International Monetary Fund and the World Bank, a political model structured in such a way that it not only forces Third World countries to pay interest on their debts, but it also penalises women more than any other group. When we consider that one-third of the sums paid out by Third World countries is destined to reimburse those countries' military spending, would it not seem appropriate to examine from the outset the model of militarised development of the most powerful Northern countries, a destructive model which acts as a prototype for the Third World?

It is impossible to trust the World Bank and Northern countries when they state their supposed desire to restrict and control arms sales to the Third World. First of all, on what grounds can one refuse to offer to other countries that which they esteem to be useful and necessary for their own defence, except of course those of considering oneself the strongest nation, the 'protectors' of the entire world? Indeed, as long as the West continues to arm itself with highly sophisticated weapons, the desire of the Third World for those same weapons will continue.[45] Secondly, it is foolish to attempt to force others to believe that one's goals are to restrict and control arms sales to the Third World while continuing to produce those arms. This reflects the law of escalation, which applies to the production of arms as much as to any other product. The profits transferred by Southern countries into Northern banks through arms sales represent a 'necessity' for the North.

I have identified the major factors which cause reticence in feminists to decode the patriarchal system and its violence against women, hidden by the militarisation of the world economy. To summarise these factors, they are as follows:

- the lack of university study by feminists, since they are still so new to the fields of economics and international relations;
- feminists' timidity faced with the prospect of throwing off the traditional yoke of sex roles, which has reserved for men a near-monopoly of the identification of priorities in economics, North–South relations and strategies to assure national security.

It is now certainly time for Northern feminists to recognise the inherent sexism of masculine definition and identification of national economic and military priorities. In the vast enterprise of demolishing myths that awaits feminists, they will discover great support and considerable potential. The support will come from Third World feminist enquiry, where feminists have integrated into their critique a holistic dimension, lacking in Northern feminism. The DAWN manifesto represents the most striking example of this perspective.[46] The potential is embodied in the preference of Northern women for non-violent solutions to international crises and conflicts. Not only is this preference for non-violent solutions enormously different from that of men, but it has also been maintained with remarkable consistency and is to be found in all Western countries where opinion polls are conducted regularly.[47] But simply because women, victims of the violence of men, refuse violence more often than men as a solution to a conflict, it does not necessarily follow that they will then actively demand that their governments handle international problems through negotiation instead of military force. Preferences and opinions remain isolated from action. Yet it is the duty of Northern feminists, empowered by their own potential, to come to an agreement on equal standing with Southern feminists, to be able to respond to the expectations of the poorest women on the planet. They need to identify alternatives to the present model of development, which is based not only on the oppression of women, but also on the violence of unequal relations between the North and the South, on the dynamics of militarisation and debt. Aided in these goals by the least sexist of men, feminists should initiate from the outset a form of inquiry which should allow for the construction by women of a better world, where a diplomacy of the oppressed would replace the violence of the oppressors in the solution of conflicts.

Notes

1. For lack of more appropriate terminology, I will use the expressions 'Northern countries' and 'Southern countries', countries of the centre opposed to those of the periphery, developed countries opposed to those of the Third World. I am however aware that all such terms are not really adequate.

2. CNIF–INSEE, *Les Femmes en chiffres*, Paris: Centre National d'Informations des Femmes et Institut National de la Statistique et des Etudes économiques, 1988.

3. Ibid.

4. *Etudes sur l'accès en France des femmes à l'enseignement et à la formation scientifique et aux carrières correspondantes*, Paris: UNESCO, October 1981, ED–81/WS/136.

5. Francesco Arena, 'Présence des femmes en science et technologie au Quebec', in *Des femmes dans les sciences*, special no. of *Cahiers de recherche sociologique*, Vol. 4, No. 1, April 1986 (L'Université du Quebec à Montréal).

6. *Etudes sur l'accès en France des femmes* op. cit.

7. *Enquête sur la représentation des femmes dans l'enseignement superieur, la recherche, la planification et la gestion de l'éducation*, Paris: UNESCO, March 1987, ED–87/WS/8,181 pages.

8. *Enquête sur la représentation des femmes* op cit.

9. *The Military-Industrial Complex: Eisenhower's warning thirty years later*, an interdisciplinary conference on the economic, political, social, rhetorical and technological implications of the military-industrial complex. Corvalis, Oregon, Oregon State University, 13–15 October 1988.

10. Esther Boserup, *Women's Role in Economic Development*, New York: Saint Martin's Press and George Allen, 1970.

11. A remarkable exception can be found in the Northern feminist association WIDE *(Women in Development Europe)* whose members do not hesitate to question their own model of development.

12. UNICEF, *Un avenir pour les enfants d'Afrique*, New York: UNO, 1985.

13. UNICEF, *Un avenir*, op. cit.

14. Ruth Meena, 'Women and the Debt: the Tanzanian experience', in VESO, Noord-Zuid Campagne, Utrecht (The Netherlands), 1988.

15. 'La pauvreté tient plus aux erreurs politiques qu'au manque d'argent', *Le Monde*, 24 May 1991.

16. UNICEF, *Jordanian Children in the Eye of the Storm*, Amman, 1991.

17. Ibid.

18. Ibid.

19. Ibid.

20. Ibid.

21. *Rapport sur les besoins humanitaires au Koweit et en Iraq au lendemain de la crise*, United Nations Security Council, 20 March 1991, New York. S/22366.

22. Andrée Michel, (ed), 'La Militarisation et les violences à l'égard des femmes', *Nouvelles questions féministes*, No. 11–12, Winter 1985, pp. 5–28.

23. Andrée Michel, 'Le complèxe militaro-industriel, la crise du Golfe et la démocratie en France', *L'Homme et la Société*, 1–2, No. 99–100, June 1991, pp. 197–212.

24. Michael Renner, 'Enhancing Global Security', in *State of the World 1989*, ed. Lester Brown et al, New York, London: Norton, pp. 123–53.

25. Ibid.

26. Mary Kaldor, Margaret Sharp and William Walker, 'Industrial Competitiveness and Britain's Defence', *Lloyds Bank Review*, October 1986.

27. L'Economie du Militaire', *L'Economie en Question*, No. 17, June 1981.

28. *Le Monde*, 22 March 1989.

29. Pierre Marion, *Le Pouvoir sans visage*, Paris: Calmann-Levy, 1990.

30. Alain Arnaud, 'La logique de l'armement, source de declin', *Le Monde diplomatique*, July 1990.

31. Ibid.

32. Michael Renner, 'Enhancing Global Security'.

33. Kathleen Gough, 'The War Against Women: Prostitution in Vietnam', *Manushi*, No. 1, November 1984.

34. André Gunder Frank, *Political Ironies in the World Economy*, University of Amsterdam, Department of Economics, Research Memorandum No. 8423, July 1984.

35. Teresa Amott, 'Race, Class and Feminization of Poverty', *Socialist Politics*, No. 3, April 1985.

36. *International Herald Tribune*, 15 May 1991.

37. Harold Freeman, *Towards Socialism in America*, Cambridge, Mass: Schenmann, 1982, 2nd edition.

38. Marion Anderson, Michael Frisch, Michael Oden, *The Empty Pork Barrel: The Employment Cost of the Military Buildup, 1981–1985*, Lansing, Michigan: Employment Research Associates, 1987.

39. 'BIRD Pede Ao 3 Mundo Final de Gastro com Armas', *Jornal do Brasil*, 29 September 1989.

40. Senator Bill Bradley, 'Third World Debt Costs US Jobs', *Transatlantic Perspectives*, No. 17, Winter 1988, pp. 13–14.

41. Colette Bernas, 'La Societe duale: discours et pratiques patronales', *Annales de l'Université de Savoie*, No. 12, (Chambery: 1989) pp. 115–31.

42. Joan Smith, 'The Paradox of Women's Poverty: Wage-earning Women and Economic Transformation', *Signs*, Winter 1984, Vol. 10, No. 2.

43. CNIF–INSEE, *Femmes en Chiffres* (Paris: 1988).

44. 'El Banco Mundial Condicionara las ayudas a la reduccion de los gastos militares', *El País*, 28 April 1991.

45. Andrée Michel, 'Le Nucléaire au Brésil: Comment s'y prendre pour endetter un pays du Tiers Monde', *Damocles* 42, January–February 1990, pp. 19–21.

46. Gita Sen and Caren Grown, *Development Crisis and Alternative Visions: Third World Women's Perspectives*, London: Earthscan, 1988.

47. Marjorie Lansing, 'The Gender Gap in America on the Force Dimension', *Third International Interdisciplinary Congress on Women*, University of Dublin, 6–10 July 1987.

4

War Against Women

Ginny NiCarthy

'As a woman,' said Virginia Woolf, 'I have no country. As a woman I want no country. As a woman my country is the whole world.'[1] Virginia Woolf was not alone. Other women would like our country to be the world – a world without man-made barriers to our autonomy and peace. But we are reminded, daily, that it is the assumed privilege of men to decide how humans will live or die on this planet. Like it or not, the boundaries of 'our' countries are created by men. Regardless of voting rights in some nations, real political and personal power remains in the hands of men. The structure confining us is patriarchal, but the word is too abstract, too impersonal, to indicate the various and nefarious means men use to control women – their needs, choices, and lives, individually in each nation and internationally – and to keep that control.

Foeticide to Femicide

'Violence begins early and at home', wrote Canadian Barbara Roberts,[2] quoting figures from the US National Conference on Child Abuse and Neglect in 1981, which showed that one out of four girls in the US is sexually assaulted before she reaches the age of 18, while other studies show one in three. For too many females, violence begins even before birth and ends with femicide – the murder of women. Ultrasound technology and amniocentesis now enable a doctor to identify whether a foetus is male or female, which translates for some prospective parents to 'desirable' (male) or 'expendable' (female). The preference for the male sex over the female is reflected in many ways, from subtle signs and symbols to outright violence throughout life. In India and China, significantly more male foetuses are chosen to live. As many as 99 per cent of foetuses aborted in some Bombay clinics were female.

A UNICEF report found that 'a quarter of the 12 million girls born in India annually are dead by the age of 15, many of them victims of

neglect, discrimination and sometimes infanticide because of their sex
... . [A]lthough girls are born biologically stronger, 300,000 more of
them die each year than boys ... .'[3] The World Health Organisation
reports that in many countries, girls are fed less, breast-fed for shorter
periods of time, taken to doctors less, and die or are physically and
mentally maimed by malnutrition at higher rates than boys.[4] Pregnant
women and their foetuses suffer malnutrition because of food taboos
enforced for pregnant women. Fewer girls than boys go to school,
UNICEF says, because 'the tyranny of the household takes over a girl's
life as soon as she can perform the simplest task'.

At the other end of some women's lives is 'femicide', a word coined
in the 1980s to describe murders of women simply because they are
women, or because they dare to define for themselves what it means to
be a woman. In the past thirty years, the incidence of femicide has
grown enormously. In Montreal, Canada, Marc Lepine stormed into
an engineering classroom, ordered male students to leave, and turned
his semi-automatic rifle on 14 women engineering students, killing them
all. He was more explicit than most males who commit femicide, calling
the 14 women he murdered 'feminists' and 'viragos'.[5] 'In 1990, in Italy,
some 200 women were murdered in circumstances absurdly classified
by the mass media as "sexual crimes of passion, of jealousy".'[6] In
Washington State, USA, the bones of dozens of young women were
found over a period of several years in a wooded area, murdered, police
think, by the 'Green River Murderer', a man never found. Most victims
of the 'Green River Murderer' were young women prostitutes or women
assumed to be prostitutes. Feminists have protested against the sluggish
investigation, which they attribute to bias against the presumed lifestyle
of the victims. In India, Bangladesh and Pakistan, in 1987 alone, 8,906
men burned their wives to death, claiming they were suicides or
accidents.[7]

A teacher called the dormitory of St Kizito boarding school in Meru,
Kenya, a 'death chamber' after 360 high-school men forced their way
in to rape 71 of their fellow students. In the process of their mass
assault, 19 women were suffocated or trampled to death as they huddled
in fear of the men's attack. It was apparently the killings that called
worldwide attention to this event, incidentally exposing the ordinariness
of rapes committed by high-school men against women students in
Kenyan boarding schools. A woman teacher said, 'The boys didn't
mean any harm. They just wanted to rape'. Rape is said to be a
common way of boys expressing their frustration when they cannot get
what they want.[8]

These headline events are picked almost at random. Every day in
virtually every country of the world where men devise and enforce
the criminal codes, women are murdered. News of these murders is

considered worthy of publication, or not, depending partly on the colour and lifestyle of the victim or perpetrator. When stories are published, the reasons for some of these murders are said to be unknown, so they're dubbed 'senseless'. Others are said to be 'caused' by failure to pay adequate dowry (India), or the 'deranged' state of the killer (Montreal, Washington State) or jealousy (Italy). But the factor that puts each woman most at risk of murder was just that: she was a woman.

Silence and denial

In between foeticide and femicide is an array of horrors perpetrated against women because of their gender. When recorded, estimates are that 40–80 million women are battered by male partners. Many crimes of violence, or legal forms of exploitation and coercion, are directly related to the perpetrator's unwillingness or inability to distinguish between power and sex. Sex demonstrates power; power is sexy. Subordination is 'weakness', even when maintained by law, custom, religion, culture and economics.

Throughout history some women have protested against battering, rape and other violent crimes. Many have gone unrecorded. Among the unsung heroines was twelve-year-old Hauwa Abubakar of Nigeria, who gave up her life rather than live with the man her father married her to four years earlier. Her husband was old enough to be her grandfather. Three times she ran away, and three times she was sent back by her father, who owed the man dowry money. 'Sold' is more accurate than 'married off'. The third time she escaped and was sent back by her father, her husband 'chopped off her legs and genitalia with an axe and Hauwa Abubakar died'.[9]

More often, women have buried the violations under a blanket of shamed forbearance and denial. Some women blame themselves for not speaking out sooner, even when they had little choice. It is true that 'the strongest prisons are built with walls of silence',[10] but there are times when denial of reality – the silence of the mind – enables survival in that prison. No person can tell another when is the time to deny, and when the time to shout one's outrage from the rooftops. The price of resistance is high. Even to name the crimes can be terrifying.

First stage of the movement: naming the crimes

We have found 'that voice among others like ourselves', that Audré Lorde wrote of,[11] and in twenty years it has grown into an international roar. In 1970 we only whispered the words 'rape' and 'incest'. Whispered, because we had been persuaded that 'those' things only happened to 'other' women, the ones who were strange or bad anyway.

Whispered, because most of us had been told the violations were our own fault. Whispered, because the perpetrators warned us not to tell anyone what they did to us, if we wanted to live. We did not even have names for many of the violations against us until the 1970s. We could lament, cry, scream, but we could not articulate our informed rage about them, nor organise against these crimes, while they were, literally, still unspeakable.

Now we have made the crimes speakable. Separately and together, in villages, cities, provinces, states, countries and then, finally, in international forums, we have called them intolerable. In the early 1970s, women began to speak aloud the forbidden words, 'rape' in the US, and 'wife-beating' in Britain, where Erin Pizzey opened the first shelter; in Canada, India, Australia, New Zealand. We said the most dangerous and radical of words: 'It was not my fault'; 'I am not the one to blame'. In the US, the truth gradually emerged that the man who rapes is rarely the monster, the stranger, leaping from the bushes; more commonly it is a man we know, an ordinary, 'sane' man. In England it became apparent that some of the most dangerous men were those who had sworn to love and honour 'until death us do part' and whom women had promised to 'obey'. For the next twenty years women in one country after another would continue to learn, including how death often parts women from their violent husbands. It would be a number of years before we would discover how commonly rape is part of the pattern of battering, and to name it 'marital rape'. It would take still more years for laws in some US and Indian states, and in a few other countries, to recognise marital rape as a crime. In Britain it took until 1991. Additional time would pass before we recognised and named the 'acquaintance rape' and the 'date rape' as pervasive forms of male violation of women.[12]

1975: a turning point

In 1975, publications began to proliferate about crimes against women, especially after the United Nations International Women's Year conference in Mexico City. At that conference the official UN Report made only one set of recommendations about violence against women. It suggested steps to improve trials of rapists, and – much more radically, for its time – it recognised marital rape as a crime. The simultaneous NGO conference, 'The Tribune', raised women's consciousness about numerous issues. Grassroots women compared notes on reproductive freedom and the politics of battering and rape. Rape crisis centres had begun to be established during the previous few years in US cities.

In the cities of India women marched, demonstrated and began their own investigations of 'suicides' and 'accidental' deaths of brides in kitchen fires. The payment of dowry had already been outlawed, but feminists continued their protests against its illegal practice. Demands for dowry payments gave an excuse for men to harass – and sometimes murder – their wives.[13] By 1975, Women's Aid, the British coalition of refuges for battered women, brought a more political perspective to woman abuse than the one presented by the shelter's founder. In 1976, the International Tribunal on Crimes against Women took place in Belgium. Women from over 40 countries testified about numerous forms of violence against them. The workshop on violence against women, the largest of the conference, inspired a number of women to establish shelters for battered women in their home countries.

By 1976, we named 'sexual harassment' in the United States, which was later called 'Eve teasing' in India. We said we would no longer accept it as an inevitable part of the environment. We said we wanted it to stop. Like other forms of woman abuse, we could never have predicted the pervasiveness or effects of sexual harassment on women throughout the world. Now we are far more aware. Mexico: 'The Mexican Federation of Womens Trade Unions reports that 95 per cent of women workers are victims of sexual harassment.' USA: 'Forty-two per cent of female (federal) employees ... reported being sexually harassed at work ... (during the two years prior to the survey (1981)).' India: '... a coalition of women's organisations in Bombay demanded "ladies only carriages" in mass public transit after serious incidents of sexual harassment of women commuting to and from work.' More women in the 12 countries of the European Community complained of sexual harassment than of sex discrimination in their employment.[14]

In 1977, Senegalese writer Awa Thiam noted that interest had begun to surface in stopping excision and infibulation in some African countries. Worldwide, 65–75 million women are victims of some form of genital mutilation. She recognised that these practices were viewed by 'traditionalists' as purification ceremonies and rites of passage. But she insisted on naming them differently: 'Whatever other people may claim,' she said, 'what [the victim] experiences is a "mutilation".'[15] It would be another five years or more before many African governments would take action to discourage or outlaw such practices, or the Inter-African Committee be funded to combat the practices.

In 1978, 128 women from 13 Western countries met in Amsterdam at an international conference on battered women, and agreed that 'women being battered is rooted in an international acceptance of the subordination of women'.[16] In 1977, the Asian Women's Association was formed to defend Korean and Thai women against Japanese sexual exploitation. In 1979, Kathleen Barry described the international traffic in prostitution as the 'sex colonisation' of women. She said, 'forced prostitution and forced marriage, which includes wife battery, veiling, arranged marriages, and polygyny, confirm the subordination of all colonised women'.[17] In 1981, 250 Latin American feminists gathered to exchange ideas at the first Encuentro Latinoamericano y del Caribe, held in Colombia. Two years later, Peru hosted a second conference, where double the expected 300 women participated; they have been succeeded by others, always growing in numbers; the last was held in Argentina.

Throughout the 1970s, international publications on women's issues covered violence against women. Feminist analysis of battering, rape, pornography and incest proliferated in books, films, role plays and pamphlets. Some researchers compared patterns of violence towards women cross-culturally. Knocking down the 'prison-walls' of silence showed us more similarities than we imagined in the victimisation of women in otherwise extremely different cultures. The commonality of our reactions – first shame and denial, then sorrow and sometimes guilt, followed by anger and action – made some of us begin to believe that women live in one 'country'.

In the women's rape crisis centres, health clinics, feminist newspaper offices, law collectives, bookstores and battered women's shelters, women described what men had done to us. We listened to each other. Then we told our stories again, to other women and to the public. We exchanged information about studies reporting how many girls had been forced to have sex with their fathers, step-fathers, uncles, brothers; how many girls were forced into marriage in various parts of the world, forced or driven by poverty into prostitution, or forced to undergo genital mutilation; how many women were battered, killed by husbands, raped; how many murders were claimed to be suicides or accidents. And how many memories of our own humiliation and violation each of us had suppressed. We did not want to admit we were compiling a version of 'body counts', the casualties of war against us. They were not just numbers to us; they were wounded, vibrant, live women. Or dead and mourned sisters.

While we soaked each other's gashes, sat in emergency rooms, listened and talked, we learned that women needed jobs, lawyers, medical care, child care, money to pay for all these services, group support from peers and a host of other goods and services typically required for people coming out of war zones. Out of our awareness of those needs we began to organise to stop the war against us.

Naming the perpetrator

When we took the important step of naming the violent acts that women endured, the terms we used – sexual harassment, marital rape, dowry murder, sexual mutilation – *implied* there was a perpetrator. But the phrases did not specifically state that a *person* had done something to another person. Even more rarely did we say that the person who committed the crime was a man. In reporting figures from research, we rarely used words like 'fathers', step-fathers', 'husbands', 'boyfriends', 'men' or 'man' to indicate who had committed the violation. The most common formula for speaking of these violations by (mostly) men remains much the same today. We continue to say, 'these women were raped', 'Maria was beaten', rather than to mention the doer.

We can see a significant difference when we reverse the word order, so that those who commit these acts are clearly the subjects. Currently we say, 'in the United States a woman is raped every six minutes, and a woman is battered every three minutes'. Suppose instead we say, 'in the United States a man rapes a woman every six minutes, and a man batters a woman every three minutes'. Another example: 'in India, eight out of ten wives are the victims of violence, either domestic battery, dowry-related abuse, or, among the least fortunate, murder'. Suppose we say, 'in India, eight out of ten husbands batter their wives, and, in the extreme, murder them'. These changes make us focus on the violent person who committed the crime. They give us a clue about where to look for the cause of the problem. This does not mean – necessarily – that every man is suspect. It means there is something about a world-wide culture of male dominance that encourages or allows violence, especially sexual violence and humiliation of girls and women. But, as Georgina Ashworth wrote, 'all men benefit from the silence'.[18]

To compound this same type of misleading language, we commonly say 'battered woman', pronouncing it as almost one word – 'battered-woman' – to describe the victim of the man who battered her. This usage has political ramifications, since it leads us to focus on the woman and divert attention from the man who batters her. This can rather quickly lead us away from thinking about what someone did. Psychologists, police officers, individuals, jurors, researchers wonder what kind of woman this 'batteredwoman' is,[19] centre their questions, and those of the public, primarily on 'why she stays', 'what kind of women get battered', rather than on who does the battering and why, and what to do about it.

Does stating a subject, a violator, come too close to giving us a picture of reality? Is it too painful to face the fact that the religious leader,[20] therapist or father we appeal to for guidance, or the brother or cousin we love and trust may be the one to smash his fist into his wife's face on a fairly regular basis; or – uninvited – intrude his tongue, hand or penis into some part of our bodies we consider our own?

The words 'rapist' and 'batterer' contain semantic difficulties also. They imply a particular character type, one totally different from 'normal' men. A 'rapist' or 'batterer' is not someone we expect to find planting his garden next door to us, sitting next to us at religious services, at a political demonstration, or riding home on the village bus after a hard day's work; working with us on a legal case or in a factory. But women do work, eat, sleep, study and live next to these men every day of their lives

Are we afraid that we will be labelled 'man-haters' if we state that husbands/fathers/men/boys committed *x* violations against women – most of them their wives, daughters, step-daughters, nieces or sisters? Or afraid that if we fully face who the perpetrators of these crimes are, we will become man-haters'? The miracle is that very few of us hate men, as a generic category. But whenever we say out loud *who* rapes, *who* batters, *who* kills for dowries, *who* forces children into marriages, *who* arranges businessmen's tours for sex with nine-year-old girls, *who* stones women for not dressing as the torturers deem proper – when we name these perpetrators as men, we are accused of being man-haters. The listener prefers to 'cut out the tongue of the messenger' rather than face the emotional and social consequences of the message.

Perhaps we would also like to deny that many men turn away when women are tortured or beaten. There are some 'conscientious objectors' in the war against women, who protest against the war, and do what they can to stop it; but more visible action and leadership are needed. Men and their female supporters will protest that not *all* men do these things; they do not believe we know that. We also know that some women aid and abet these crimes. We acknowledged above that boys and men are sometimes victimised.

1985: another turning point

In 1985, approximately 14,000 women managed to beg, borrow, save and earn enough money to travel to Nairobi, Kenya for what was billed as the End of the UN Decade For Women. We came from virtually every country in the world. This time we understood each other more readily than we had ten years earlier. As the end of the conference approached, more and more women knew it was not the 'End' at all. For Jamaican women's theatre company SISTREN had started street theatre on different forms of violence; WAND had identified incest as a major hidden issue; Nepalese lawyer Silu Singh had drawn an advice book for illiterate women fearing being battered; Papuan women had gone on a day's strike to draw attention to the violence against them; courses had been arranged in Canada for the violators; US courts were ordering counselling for violent men; refugee workers had named the awful sexual violence against women refugees – 70 per cent of the total; European trade unions had taken action on sexual harassment; CHANGE and others had begun making violence against women in all its forms a human rights issue.[21] We knew we would keep our new-found worldwide connections alive, through networks, newsletters, organisations, personal and professional contacts. Many went home to start more political organisations, shelters, newsletters, action groups and crisis lines to deal with all kinds of regional, local and international problems of violence against women. The UN Centre for Humanitarian Affairs began work on violence against women officially, even counting its economic cost. The Commonwealth produced important handbooks for its 44 menber states. The Asia and Pacific Development Centre's women's programme linked the issues to health. The Third World Movement Against Women's Exploitation (TW–MAE) had begun to protest against prostitution and militarisation in the Philippines.

The price of resistance

The price we pay for our nonviolent resistance to violence and sexism is commonly called a 'backlash', but it is time to find a new word to describe men's reactions to our organising, for the retaliatory violence is grossly disproportionate to our protests. We need a word that conveys the viciousness of some of the attacks and the complexities of individual and organised men's campaigns against women.[22] Male reprisals for our legal reforms, demonstrations, boycotts and occasional destruction of property sometimes have been swift, violent, illegal and precisely targeted. Grassroots women's bookshops, newspapers, shelters, abortion clinics and other centres in the US have been devastated by break-ins, arson, damaged vehicles, destroyed property. An activist was nearly run over, and women working at an Indian women's centre in Canada were charged with child neglect after they started community action. Thirty women and three children at the National Workshop of Peasant Women in Colombia were stripped and abandoned without food for 48 hours. Other women activists have been raped and murdered.[23] These attacks were so immediate and sharply targeted, it was obvious what triggered the retaliation.

Sometimes the actions against women are diffuse, legal, well organised, well financed, and even couched in the language of protectiveness. US President Ronald Reagan, in the guise of protecting the unborn, in the so-called 'Mexico City Policy' adopted at the second World Population Conference, prohibited US assistance to any private foreign clinic providing abortion services, which included counselling, referral or education.[24] These funds, which one powerful man decided to control, provide 40 per cent of world funding for abortions. Millions of women who say they want legal abortions – some of them pregnant from marital or other rapes – will be forced to bear children they cannot adequately care for, or to risk backstreet abortionists with whom the fatality rate is so high. 'An estimated 50 million abortions, half of them illegal, are performed around the world each year, resulting in the deaths of as many as 200,000 women.'[25]

Other assaults may or may not be directly related to women's political action. They can be pre-emptive strikes, in case women are thinking of claiming their rights, as is often the case when husbands assault their wives. In other instances women serve as conveniently established targets, receptacles for men's anger and frustration over aspects of their lives they cannot control.

Images of male power flood every aspect of the mass media. The confluence of violence and sex in much pornography is only the most gross, dramatic version of daily fare. The visual assaults include advertising images of muscled men who strike menacing or protective poses, while simpering childlike women gaze at them adoringly. Video games and films of child sex abuse are distributed throughout the world, as are rape and pro-nazi video games. Comic books such as the Japanese 'Rape man' ride waves of popularity. Movies that glamorise rape are in high demand for export from the US throughout the world. The Canadian film, *Not a Love Story*, examined the culture of violent sexual hatred that the US exports just across its borders, from a film industry bigger than Hollywood: that producing violent pornography. A pornographer interviewed says, 'no man wants equality with women; of course the growth of my business reflects this'.

'Her body's beautiful so I'm thinking rape; shouldn't have her curtains open so that's her fate,' are lyrics from a 'Geto Boys' popular album in the USA.[26] 'Acha Iniuwe Dogodogo Siachi', or 'Even at the risk of death, I will not give up the girls', runs a new 'AIDS acronym' in Swahili in Nairobi, Kenya.[27] Is this 'backlash'? Or 'just' symptomatic of the helplessness felt by so many 'young people' as the world's problems become more evidently massive and seemingly inescapable? US sociologists and psychologists 'explain' violent images in MTVs and rock/punk music. They are the results, they say, of disaffection, divorce, residues of the Vietnam War, child abuse, mothers going 'out to work' that influence the purveyors of the 'youth culture'. But too often these 'experts' overlook the fact that most of the violence and fantasised violence in music and video is perpetrated by and consumed by men – at the peril of women. And girls have similar experiences as their male age-mates coping with divorced parents, and so on, while they are subjected more often to incest, rape and battering, with which they cope in markedly different – mostly non-destructive – ways.

In the coming years we can expect more backlash, as women insist on their fair share of the available benefits of the earth and the decision-making that determines how they are distributed. Women need to cultivate an attitude of scepticism about the findings of the 'experts' –

a kind of soft backlash – that can distract us from remembering the lessons we've learned. We must not forget:

- It is, by and large, men who commit crimes of violence against us.
- Laws that encourage or permit the violations to continue are man-made.
- Media that glamorise violence and make it sexy are, by and large, controlled by men.
- Destructive portrayals of women's lives are not merely individual aberrations.
- They are part of a political culture of men dominating.
- They are permitted by powerful men.
- They are planned.
- Many are consciously designed to demonstrate power over women.
- Violence is the ultimate proof of power.
- Violence against women is political.
- It is not trivial.

Violence against women is not 'trivial'

As Charlotte Bunch wrote,

> Abusing women physically is a reminder of this territorial domination and is sometimes accompanied by other forms of human rights abuse, such as slavery (forced prostitution), sexual terrorism (rape), imprisonment (confinement to the home), or torture (systematic battery).[28]

Women's issues are still considered trivial, compared to 'real' problems; life-threatening dangers of impoverished, war-torn people, especially in the 'Third World'. Women are told that their 'private' and 'personal' positions cannot compare with the serious problems of dictatorships, imprisonment, revolution, torture, mass deaths, poverty and terrorism. If this were true it would have to mean that when a woman is tortured by a soldier as well as a husband, she does not notice fear and pain from her husband. Or it implies that a woman living in a democracy should focus on that privilege, rather than protesting about her husband's control of her. In spite of the enormous output of educational materials on battering and rape in the past twenty years, the public cannot seem to grasp the extent or depth of women's suffering from these 'trivial' crimes. A major part of our educational campaign must be to continue working to get this point across to the international public, as well as to our communities.

Dictatorships. Women in many parts of the world are told exactly who they may, or must, have sex with. Sex outside marriage may be a crime for a woman, not a man, and women may be subjected to family ostracism, imprisonment, stoning or death if they deviate from that norm. In 'enlightened' countries, a rape victim must often endure humiliation and publication of her past sexual history, which – because she is a woman – is treated as a source of shame.

In most countries a husband may, without reprisal, tell his wife whether she can leave the house, where she may go and how long she is allowed to stay. Madlyn, like many North American women – women 'free of dictatorships' – was forcibly kept from seeking safety for herself and her child. When she tried to sneak out of the house, her husband held a gun at her head all night. Maria, a citizen of a Central American democracy, was permitted by her husband to attend university, but he accompanied her to class every day to see that she did not speak to other men. Women are commonly told what to wear, whether to be sexy, and how sexy; whether or not they may drive a car, own a house or keep the money they earn. Sometimes the distinction between the national dictatorship and the marital/co-habiting one is invisible. If these women do not live under dictatorship, what are we to call it?[29]

Revolution, racial oppression. In South Africa, Nicaragua and numerous other countries, women have learned 'that freedom for women does not come automatically from struggles for democracy, national liberation or socialism. The struggle for women's freedom must be a special struggle'.[30] Revolutionary men still batter their wives, and the struggle for the 'liberty of man' often means exactly that. Is battering by a revolutionary man not as painful as from another man?

Torture. Although rape is the 'torture of choice' for soldiers and interrogators in national struggles, it is also the choice for many men in the person-to-person political struggle against women's rights, including in marriage. But there are other forms of torture as well. They include, for instance, an Irish husband who doused his wife's 'naked body with gasoline and then danced around her, flicking matches', and a man who 'poured a kettle of boiling water over the vagina of [his] wife, just before she went into childbirth labour'.[31] Countless cases of fathers, step-fathers and other male (and some female) relatives torture children by forced or coerced sexual activities, as well as psychological terror and physical beatings. Do these forms of torture not maim and terrorise?

War. Women and girls are murdered for unknown 'reasons', in the favelas of Rio de Janeiro.[32] Girls, ages 10, 11 and 12, chained to their beds in a Thai brothel, die when the brothel is burned and they cannot escape. Serial murders; dowry murders; murders in the course of rape; murders by irate, possessive husbands: if this is not war against women, what shall we name it?

Poverty. 'The question, "what is your greatest problem?" The unnervingly frequent answer, "my husband beats me".' 'Unnerving', because the questioner, Lori Heise, researching for Worldwatch, has not even intended to investigate interpersonal violence. She expected to hear about other serious problems from these women, who 'daily have to walk four hours to gather enough wood for the evening meal, whose children commonly die of treatable illnesses, whose security can be wiped out with one failed rain'. They are the poorest of the poor, yet they were worried about violence in their lives. 'Battering, mutilation [and] murder [are] still pervasive against many women' around the world, says Heise.[33] Is it assumed that hunger and malnutrition give immunity to the pain of a beating?

Terrorism. Women of every kind, all over the world, live with the knowledge that there is no safety, no haven for them at work, on the streets or in their homes. A Canadian study of 961 schoolgirls, grades 6–13, found 'consistently high levels of anxiety about rape, and sexual and physical abuse'.[34] The headline violence against women is the drama. But fear of men invades the daily lives of women, frequently capturing mind, emotions and physical space. Fear is the air we breathe, the water we swim in, as women living in the 'country of men'. Terror respects no age, class or race, no geographical boundaries.

Connections

One of our major tasks in this movement against violence is to make connections between many kinds of oppression, both violent and not violent. This is not to say there is something inherent in men that 'causes' them to target women. Nevertheless, any problem-solving technique calls for, first, naming the problem, and then looking for the cause or causes. Something about the conditioning, training and defining of maleness encourages contempt for women, an assumption of power over them and a belief that sexual violence is the most viable form of exercising that power. Sports, war, violence against women (and men), sex and economics are intertwined in men's sense of pleasure and power.[35] The manifestations of socialised maleness – that is sex/power – in law, music, film, literature, medicine, education and employment are often claimed to be accidental. But we have seen the retaliation when women bring the pattern of our oppression to the attention of men. The miracle is that this cultural conditioning does not 'take' for all men. Not all of them support governmental male control of women. Some are even conscientious objectors in this war against women.

Our work is to create a world with *less* violence. Less cruelty, discrimination, fear, humiliation and hatred. Our style is to do it non-violently and – whenever possible – with love in our hearts. We do not want to become the people our sisters warned us about. Elizabeth Janeway says,

> ... the weak ... have to learn to be *brave in a different fashion*. For there is indeed a kind of courage that is very familiar to the weak: endurance, patience, stamina, the ability to repeat everyday tasks every day, these are forms of courage that have allowed generations of the governed to survive without losing ultimate hope ... . But for decisive action, something else must be added: bravery, daring, risk-taking in public. These, to the weak, seem beyond their means; this is the courage of the powerful ... . Women have also been given a specific role, that of supporter, whose duties are absolutely opposite to the role of initiator.

Nevertheless, we are acting powerfully. We are being daring. We are initiating. We take it a step at a time, learning as we go. We cannot say exactly what our next steps will be. Perhaps courage takes a touch of madness. The current system enables men to decide which marriage, sex and birth control laws are in the (male) states' interests. It enables men in control to determine what employment, if any, women will be permitted, and often how much they will be paid. Man-made policies also regulate which forms of resistance against male violence and control are permitted.[36] In spite of massive obstacles, women have got laws and customs changed, even where men seem to have a stranglehold on law-making positions. Women organise within and across continents, and internationally: in the Pacific islands they 'individually and collectively' disapprove of violence against women and agree on strategies for taking action against it.[37] Women from the Asia–Pacific region agreed at a 12-country workshop in China that the worst aspect of being female is fear of male violence. Polygamous marriage in Africa is viewed by women organising against it as 'a means of obtaining cheap labour and a great exploitation of women by men'.[38] At a meeting between Canadian and Chilean women, 300 health workers from Argentina recommended 'changes in legislation to typify domestic violence as a crime ... '.[39] It is true that it took enormous energy to make these gains. It is also true that we can never afford to be complacent. Our successes require eternal vigilance, to guard against them slipping away. But each year more women in more villages, cities, countries and international organisations hear the naming, add to it, work for legislation, achieve positions of some power.

Rather like Sisyphus, we are condemned to keep pushing the boulder up the mountain. Innumerable boulders, rocks, torrents of pebbles, roll, hurtle, rain down on us from atop the mountain. They kick up a lot of dust, too, that interferes with clear visibility. Our vision sometimes gets so blurred we imagine the powerful may be right: that we have reached 'post-feminism'; that we should not have tried to change things at all, or that most of our problems are solved, and only require individual solutions. This is a special hazard for women in the West. Each woman is admonished to inch her personal rock up the mountain, oblivious to the torrent descending collectively on her sisters.

The idea that socio-economic problems can be most effectively solved individually prepares us to accept research claiming all kinds of things for women. To the extent that there is truth in any of these claims – and there may be some – the solutions are social, not individual. They are not just women's problems. They affect men as well. So we must look through the clouds of dust and scrutinise the work of every reporter and scientist – male, female, feminist, non-feminist – with healthy scepticism. Elizabeth Janeway points out that questioning authority is called by the powerful, 'mistrust ... which leads on to *disloyalty*'. She advises us to nurture our mistrust when we are faced with what seems false. She entreats us not to be sabotaged by the powerful's redefining of our healthy scepticism.

Criminologist Elizabeth Stanko has this advice, in relation to relying on the criminal justice systems for achieving justice: 'We need to establish a new definition of the risk of danger. Rather than associate violence with our times in public places, we should think of risk as related to how often we find ourselves in the presence of others who have more power ... . The challenge of the 1990s will be to find mechanisms to alleviate the dangers accompanying unequal power.'

Notes

1. Virginia Woolf, *Three Guineas*, quoted in Off Our Backs, 'Country of Women' column.

2. Barbara Roberts, 'Peace Studies and the War Against Women: a survey of research', paper for the Canadian Peace Research and Education Association Annual Meeting, June 1982, mimeo.

3. From *The Lesser Child: The Girl in India*, a report prepared for the government of India to mark South Asia's Year of the Girl Child (1990), quoted in *Women's Health Journal*, No 1, 1991, p. 11. 'The ratio of men to women in Indian society continues to widen in favour of men. In 1901, there were 972 women to every 1,000 men. By 1981, the ratio had dropped to 933. In some states, the figure dips to the mid 800s.'

4. Sundari Ravindran, *Health Implications of Sex Discrimination in Childhood: a review paper and annotated bibliography*, WHO/UNICEF, 1986.

5. 'Viragos Take Back The Night', *Off Our Backs*, February 1991, p. 6.

6. 'Women in Black Build Worldwide Solidarity', *New Directions For Women*, May/June 1991, Country of Women Section, p. 2.

7. Quoted in Stephanie Solomon, 'Wife battering: A global issue', honours thesis, The Centre for Global Issues and Women's Leadership, Rutgers University, p. 21.

8. 'Kenyans Do Some Soul-Searching After the Rape of 71 Schoolgirls', Jane Perlez in the *New York Times*, 29 July 1991.

9. Hannah Edemikpong. Letter to *INAVAW News*, Summer 1989, p. 9.

10. Janice Mirikitani, 'Prisons of Silence', in Gloria Anzaldua, *Making Face, Making Soul*; Haciendo Caras, San Francisco: an aunt lute foundation book, p. 199.

11. Audré Lorde, from 'The Transformation of Silence into Language and Action', quoted in *Off Our Backs*, April 1991, p. 9.

12. Englishwoman Diana E.H. Russell made marital rape a reality to any women when she published *Rape in Marriage* (Macmillan) in 1982.

13. Madhu Kishwar and Ruth Vanita (eds), *In Search of Answers: Indian Women's Voices from* Manushi, London: Zed Books Ltd, 1985. See also Stephanie L. Solomon, op. cit.: 'The practice of giving dowry has been illegal in India since 1961, and Dowry Harassment has been a punishable offense since the 1980s ... . The issue of the Dowry Death was first exposed in the mid 1970s.'

14. Roxanna Carrillo, 'Violence Against Women: An Obstacle to Development', pp. 3, 9. Available from Center for Women's Global Leadership, Douglass College, 27 Clifton Avenue, New Brunswick, New Jersey 08903, USA. Diana E.H. Russell, 'Sexual Exploitation: Rape, Child Sexual Abuse and Workplace Harassment', Beverly Hills, Sage Library of Social Research, Vol. 155, p. 270.

15. Awa Thiam, *Black Sisters Speak Out*, London, Pluto Press, 1978.

16. Susan Schechter, *Women and Male Violence*, Boston, South End Press, 1982. See also Perdita Huston, *Third World Women Speak Out*, New York, Praeger, 1979, for interviews with women in Sudan, Egypt, Sri Lanka and Mexico. Educated women said they wanted a modification of marriage rights and inheritance, polygamy and divorce law.

17. Kathleen Barry, *Female Sexual Slavery*, New Jersey, Prentice Hall, 1979, p. 181.

18. *Of Violence and Violation: Women and human rights*, CHANGE, 1985.

19. See Sarah Lucia Hoagland, *Lesbian Ethics*, Institute for Lesbian Studies, Palo Alto, California, 1988, for further discussion of these linguistic twists.

20. A study by the United Methodist Church's General Council on Ministries found 77 per cent of its clergywomen reported being harassed, 41 per cent by church colleagues or other clergy. 'Approximately ten per cent of psychotherapists responding to surveys acknowledge having sex with at least one patient, many of them admitting to sexual involvement with more than one patient.' *INAVAW News*, Winter 1989, p. 7.

21. All these instances are from information collected before the End of Decade Conference, at conferences and from publications. Violence had been a major issue in many of the 45 or so workshops held daily during the 1980 Copenhagen 'Forum', parallel to the full UN Conference (Ed.).

22. Susan Faludi, *Backlash: The Undeclared War Against American Women*, New York, Crown Publishers, Inc., 1991.

23. 'Resistance #8: Native American Women/Boycott Stores', *INAVAW News*, Spring 1991.

24. *Women's Health Journal*, July–September 1990, p. 18.

25. Worldwatch study quoted in *Toronto Globe and Mail*, 16 July 1990, Toronto, Canada; *Women's Health Journal*, July–September 1990.

26. *Ms*, November–December 1990, p. 89. *INAVAW News*, Winter 1990–91, p. 10.

27. 'AIDS: Africa's Family Disease', *Newsweek*, 16 September 1992, pp. 42–3.

28. Charlotte Bunch, 'Women's Rights as Human Rights: Toward A Re-Vision Of Women's Rights', *Human Rights Quarterly*, #12, 1990, p. 490.

29. From Ginny NiCarthy, *The Ones Who Got Away: Stories of Women Who Left Abusive Partners*, Seattle, Washington, The Seal Press, 1987.

30. 'Women and the African National Congress', *WIN News*, Spring 1991, p. 57. Excerpt from the women's journal, *Speak*, P.O. Box 45213, Mayfair, 2018 Johannesburg, South Africa.

31. From Robin Morgan, *The Demon Lover*, New York and London, W.W. Norton, 1989, p. 315.

32. Ibid., p. 311.

33. 'The War On Women', from *INAVAW News*, Summer 1989, p. 2, reporting on an article of the same title from the *Washington Post*. See also *Worldwatch Papers*, March–April 1989, for original article.

34. Stephen Hume column, *Vancouver Sun*, 1991. See also studies of fear, especially related to women, in Elizabeth Stanko, *Everyday Violence*, London, Pandora Press, 1990, and M. Gordon and S. Riger, *The Female Fear*, New York, Free Press, 1988.

35. See Rosalind Miles, *Love, Sex, Death, and the Making of the Male*, London and New York, Summit Books, 1991.

36. See Cynthia Gillespie, *Justifiable Homicide*, for a discussion of the 'reasonable man' self-defence.

37. From *Tk Blong Ol Meri Newsletter*, special issue, published by World YWCA, Box 3940, Samabula, Suva, Fiji. Excerpted as 'Violence Against Women in the Pacific' in *WIN News*, Winter 1991, p. 46.

38. Letter from Hanah Edemikpong, *INAVAW News*, Summer 1989, p. 9.

39. From *INAVAW News*, Winter 1990–91, excerpted from *Women's Health Journal: Latin and Caribbean Women's Health Network*, #18, p. 16.

5

Women Resist Ecological Destruction[1]

Gwyn Kirk

Women form the backbone of grassroots organising around ecological issues worldwide. Well known examples come from the Chipko (tree-hugging) movement in India, the Kenyan women's Green Belt movement, Micronesian women working in communities devastated by atomic testing, US women organising against toxic dumping, Native American women's research on toxicity in breastmilk, and many projects in Asia, Africa, and Latin America promoting sustainable agriculture. Women are also central to anti-militarist work in many countries, campaigning against US bases and military prostitution in the Philippines, for example, or the build-up of nuclear weapons at Greenham Common in England.

The basic issue is survival. It is estimated that some 40,000 children die each day, mainly in Africa and Asia, from malnutrition and a lack of clean water, while these continents export food and other cash crops to the rich countries of the world.[2] Indeed, those of us living in the US, who make up 6 per cent of the world's population, currently consume 40 per cent of the world's resources. The legacy of colonial maldevelopment, current loans, and increasing militarisation worldwide means that most Third World countries are chronically, and increasingly, in debt to First World governments and banks.[3] The wide gulf between rich and poor nations parallels wealth differentials between elites and the majorities of the populations of poor countries, and between the mainly white middle classes and the poor in North America and Western Europe. Military budgets have risen in virtually every country, to a staggering total, with arms sales a major export for many industrialised countries.[4] The majority of the world's poor are women. Their poverty, together with the prevalence of routine violence against women – battering, rape, incest, trafficking, sex tourism, military prostitution, and so on –

amounts to no less than a war against women, of global proportions. Dominance of people over the non-human environment means widespread environmental destruction, as evidenced by air and water pollution, a depleted ozone layer, global warming, acid rain, and so on – by now a familiar list, and an integral part of capitalist as well as state-planned economies.

The purpose of this chapter is to identify common frameworks which inform women's perspectives and activism around ecological issues, despite the very different life situations that women find themselves in. Women's engagement in ecological concerns comes from varied experience, but through their close material connection to the non-human environment, women in the Third World (poor countries, as well as poor women in the US) are at the cutting edge of resistance to ecological destruction. We environmentalists and ecofeminists in North America and Western Europe have much to learn from them as we develop our agendas to tackle the source of much environmental degradation: the unsustainable, highly militarised economies of our own countries. In writing this, I am very aware of my identity: a white, college-educated teacher, sometime community activist, originally from Britain, now resident in the US. I am mindful of what Adrienne Rich calls the 'politics of location',[5] the particularity and limits of my experience, and that the very examples I am able to draw upon depend on personal connections or accounts published in English.

Given the limitations of space, this work is necessarily schematic. My key concern is to show how gender, race, class and imperialism are connected to ecological destruction, and that effective analysis and activism need to be informed by a broad, integrative perspective. I see three major frameworks for women's analysis and activism around ecological issues: development, environmental health and anti-militarism. There are obviously points of overlap among them, but they can also be usefully distinguished. I draw on examples from rural and urban settings, and from North America and Western Europe, as well as Third World countries.

Women and development

The world of agricultural development agencies, multinational corporations and many governments is dominated by notions of development and progress, where large-scale, chemically-dependent, capital-intensive, mechanised agriculture, usually producing cash crops, is the model to be promoted and funded. A growing literature on women and development thoroughly critiques this approach on a number of counts: it emphasises cash crops at the expense of viable subsistence agriculture; it excludes women, who are major agricultural producers, from much development policy-making; it promotes ecologically unsound agricultural practices; it impoverishes rural people and adds enormously to their daily burden of work for survival.[6]

The external debt incurred by Third World countries as a result of development loans and 'aid' packages has increased dramatically in the past 20 years or so. Pressure to produce cash crops comes from development agencies and funders such as the World Bank and the International Monetary Fund through structural economic adjustment policies, whereby timber and cash crops, which earn foreign exchange, take precedence over subsistence agriculture in an attempt to reduce spiralling external debts. In addition, socially useful government programmes, never adequate to begin with, are drastically cut back, with severe consequences for women and children.[7]

Women make up 80 per cent of the farmers in Africa, where subsistence agriculture is almost exclusively women's work. They are the main users of water in agriculture and forestry, as well as for domestic purposes, and carry it each day, sometimes several miles. Women are also responsible for finding fuel – wood, crop residues, and manure – also a time-consuming and often arduous daily task. While some women are involved in cash-crop production, the division of labour by gender, and the gender bias of many development projects means that men produce most cash-crops, and receive the income from them. Cash-crops compete increasingly with subsistence agriculture for available land, labour and water. Women still have to provide food for their families, which often means farming more difficult land, and walking further and further for firewood and water. Ironically, this may mean that women who well understand ecologically sound practices are themselves pressured into farming steep hillsides, for example, or cutting trees for fuelwood, thus worsening soil erosion and flooding during heavy rains.

Women's role as primary agricultural producers in Third World countries gives them direct experience and understanding of ecological issues.[8] Vandana Shiva details the links between ecological destruction and imperialism. She shows how deforestation in India began under the British, who colonised the forests and reduced 'this primary source of life into a timber mine', replacing the earlier oaks with more commercially valuable pine. She sees the Western model of economic development as profoundly patriarchal, a process which turns sources, whether forests, seeds, or women's bodies, into resources, which have value only when placed in a system that produces profits.[9] Sustainable agriculture does not do this, but respects the integrity of all living parts: earth, water, seeds, domestic animals, people's knowledge of cultivation, their skills and labour.

Many subsistence farmers oppose development that is not sustainable, and struggle to maintain or initiate ecologically sound agricultural practices, which often draw on longstanding cultural traditions. The very successful Chipko movement, in which rural women opposed commercial logging in the Himalayas by hugging trees, is an example of the former.[10] The National Council of Women of Kenya's Green Belt Movement is an example of the latter.[11] Started in 1977 by biologist Wangari Maathai, this programme was initiated and promoted by women as a solution to the diminishing supplies of fuelwood in rural Kenya. Its wider aims are to develop the knowledge and self-confidence to enable people to take part in sustainable, not destructive, development.

There are thousands of small-scale, ecologically sound development projects in the Third World, many of them organised by women.[12] Such projects have their counterparts in the US, particularly on Native American reservations, in inner cities and in rural areas. These include Native American economic development projects, women's economic projects in rural and urban areas, and community gardening in inner cities, often initiated by people of colour or ethnic minorities in the US.[13]

In the Tierra Amarilla land grant area of northern New Mexico, for example, a Chicano economic development project has among its objectives environmental protection, cultural revival and conservation, workplace democracy, and social justice, and thus links a range of struggles which are usually separate.[14] Ganados del Valle/Tierra Wools is a workers' co-operative of 20 people which owns some 3,000 head of sheep, and produces high quality, hand-woven rugs and clothing, and organic lamb. The weavers design and undertake their own work, uniting mental and manual labour. The project has developed large flocks of Churro sheep, a hardy breed well suited to local conditions, which was nearly extinct, as commercial ranchers favoured other breeds. This area has been farmed by Chicanos for many generations. There is a longstanding tradition of sharing water, and of collective responsibility for maintaining irrigation ditches. Pastures are diverse, comprising a range of grasses which mimic native grasslands. As ethnobotanists, women know the back country in great detail because they go there at different seasons to gather herbs for medicinal purposes. Sociologist and activist Devon Pena sees the significance of this project as an intersection of environmental struggle and ethnic self-determination, linking the protection of culture and environmental diversity, and utilising ethnoscientific knowledge. He argues that land-based Chicano culture can be considered an endangered species, given the pressures for assimilation into Anglo-American economic life and values, and the objectification of 'the other' through tourism, one of the few economic opportunities for Chicanos in the south-west of the USA.

Alan Durning argues that such small-scale projects are 'our best hope for global prosperity and ecology'.[15] There are many of them and a need for many more, though Gita Sen suggests that the next problem is how to scale them up without destroying them. Women in industrialised countries should know much more about what women in poor countries are up against, particularly the impact of structural/social adjustment policies imposed by our governments, the World Bank and the IMF. We should take up this issue in our countries and engage in public debate about the debt crisis. We should also understand that our militarised, oil-dependent economies are the least sustainable, with the largest deficits of all. The Thatcher and Reagan/Bush administrations imposed severe social adjustment policies at home, reducing public spending on health, education, social welfare, housing and so on in the UK and the US, as a direct cost of high military budgets. This has widened the gap between rich and poor, but also has the greatest impact on women and children. On an international level the wealth of industrialised countries is bought at the expense of Third World poverty and degradation. The challenge for people from rich nations is to 'live simply so that others may simply live' without romanticising poverty, imposing a philosophy of denial, or assuming moral superiority.[16]

Women and environmental health

Environmental health provides another framework linking women and ecological issues.[17] The effects upon health of environmental degradation are becoming increasingly recognised by workers, community activists, and health professionals. Wealthier, middle-class people are able to buy 'good environment' to some degree, by owning land and property which give them controllable space, relative security and safety, peace and quiet perhaps, and good accessibility to city services or the countryside. Even the very wealthy cannot buy complete immunity from pollutants, as toxic substances seep into water, food and air, but they are less affected by toxic waste dumps, workplace hazards ranging from chemicals to visual display terminals, the extensive use of pesticides by agribusiness, and radioactive contamination from nuclear power plants, weapons manufacturing and testing.

Women and children are 'ecological markers' with regard to toxins, and show signs of disease earlier than men do, either due to low body weight, as in the case of children, or because their bodies are 'unhealthy environments' for their babies. In the US, many women are campaigning against toxic pollution in a movement significant for its class and racial diversity. Typically, they get involved because they become ill themselves, or through caring for a sick relative. Women piece together the information needed to find the source of the illness, publicise their findings, and take on agricultural or industrial corporations and city agencies responsible for the contamination. An umbrella organisation, the Citizens' Clearinghouse for Hazardous Wastes (CCHW), founded by Lois Gibbs in the early 1980s, provides resource materials and news of local activism.[18] It publishes reports on legal and scientific aspects of such campaigns, community organising and movement-building. Of particular interest is *Empowering Ourselves: Women and Toxics Organizing*, which came out of a CCHW women's conference, in recognition of the crucial role women play in this movement.

Toxic waste disproportionately affects lower-income neighbourhoods. Ground-breaking research initiated by the Commission for Racial Justice of the United Church of Christ mapped the overlap of toxic dumps, incinerators and sewage treatment plants with communities of colour. The correspondence is so striking that Ben Chavis, Executive Director of the UCC Commission for Racial Justice, coined the term environmental racism, linking poverty, unemployment, poor housing and health, with a degraded physical environment: social justice and environmental justice.[19] This research is challenging environmental agencies and major environmental organisations which keep poor people uninformed and/or unheard.

Speaking of the work of the West Harlem Environmental Action Group in New York City, just one of the hundreds of environmental justice organisations in the US, civil rights lawyer Vernice Miller emphasises the need to incorporate environmental issues into the human rights agenda. 'A determination has been made that we don't breathe clean air, a determination made outside our communities.'[20] While people of colour have been active against pollution for years, Miller argues, they do not think of it in terms of the environment, which they associate with white people saving whales and trees. She points out that environmental justice is about saving people in communities of colour. Similarly she criticises feminists. Reproductive rights means health care for communities of colour, not just abortion, as it is so often defined by white US feminists. West Harlem Environmental Action Group has not been well supported by white feminists or white environmentalists, and Miller argues for the need for dialogue around issues of race and class with the objective of finding common ground to unite currently fragmented movements. Carl Anthony, among others, argues that African Americans should be environmentalists because the economic system which destroys redwood groves or the Amazon rainforest, for example, is also killing inner-city areas.[21]

Environmental racism also has its international dimension, as evidenced by the Union Carbide disaster at Bhopal, India, and the export of garbage – some of it toxic – from Western Europe and North America to Third World countries. There are plans for US landfills in Micronesia, to add to the landmass and as an income-earner, and some Native American reservations are under similar pressure to buy their way out of poverty by importing garbage from US towns and cities.[22]

A Native American women's initiative concerning environmental health is the Akwasasne Mother's Milk project, started in the early 1980s by midwife Kasti Cook.[23] Akwasasne, 'the land where the partridge drums', home of the Mohawk Nation (near Rooseveltown, NY), is affected by severe chemical pollution flowing through the Great Lakes system, as well as from nearby industries. Akwasasne women became concerned that by eating local vegetables, fish and other wildlife, they might be exposing their babies to toxic pollution through their breast-milk, and questioned whether they should continue breastfeeding. Despite the economic cost, they decided to stop eating locally produced food – garden produce, fish and small game animals – and carefully to monitor their situation. Recent analysis of breastmilk samples shows that their situation is not as bad as originally feared but it still gives no cause for complacency.

Another example from the US concerns the United Farm Workers' campaigns against the extensive use of pesticides in commercial fruit and vegetable production.[24] For some years the UFW has been calling for a boycott of Californian table grapes to protest against the fact that farm workers, particularly women and children, suffer severe health effects due to pesticide exposure. Such produce is not good for consumers either.[25] Middle-class parents in the US were very effective in getting the pesticide Alar banned because it damaged children's health. Much more needs to be done to build alliances between farm workers, many of whom are Chicanos, and consumer groups.

As with agribusiness, many industrial workplaces are hazardous environments where toxic production processes are routine. This issue has received considerable attention in the US in the context of foetal protection policies, where women are seen in terms of their reproductive potential rather than as people in their own right. For example, a Supreme Court decision in April 1991 barred Johnson Controls, an automobile battery manufacturer, from keeping fertile women out of high-paying jobs involving exposure to lead. Some feminists hailed this as a victory for equal rights, and in a sense it is: 'the right to be treated equally badly'.[26] The decision did nothing to address the fundamental question of hazardous workplaces, regardless of gender. Men's reproductive systems are also affected by toxins, as has been officially accepted in some extreme cases such as exposure to the defoliant Agent Orange during the Vietnam war, and to radioactivity in nuclear plants, as at Sellafield in England.

Infertility is looked upon as a personal failing to be remedied by treatment, even though infertility treatments have a spectacularly low success rate so far, and involve a range of invasive reproductive technologies. They are expensive, and aimed at middle-class women in the context of widening individual choice. The question of why so many people are apparently infertile, and how this relates to environmental and occupational hazards is rarely asked. Feminist critiques of reproductive technologies should raise this issue more forcefully than they currently do.[27]

A related issue concerns women who give birth to deformed babies due to their poisoned environment. An extreme example of this involves women from Micronesia in the western Pacific, who have been campaigning for years against the catastrophic effects of atmospheric nuclear weapons tests conducted by the British, French and US governments in the 1950s and early 1960s.[28] Whole islands have been irradiated, and soil and drinking water contaminated. Some women give birth to 'jelly-fish babies' without skeletons, who live only a few hours. Other children survive despite severe illnesses caused by radiation. People from the Pacific see the decision to test nuclear weapons in the atmosphere over their lands as imperialist and racist. During agreements to end the UN Trusteeship of Micronesia in 1969, the then US Secretary of State, Henry Kissinger, said, 'there's only 90,000 people out there, who gives a damn?'[29] Pacific women link their struggle for survival to a struggle for political independence. They are angry at us, the women of Britain, France and the US, for our ignorance of their situation, and, by implication, of our nations' histories regarding nuclear testing.[30] They urge us to formulate a feminism that focuses on racism and imperialism as well as gender.

Indeed, the experience of Chicana farm workers, of women campaigning against toxic pollutants in workplaces, neighbourhoods and reservations, all challenge white, middle-class feminists to incorporate issues of race and class, as well as gender, into an analysis of ecological destruction.

Anti-militarism

Women working for a nuclear-free and independent Pacific think of radioactive contamination not only in terms of health, they are also anti-militarist. They have been living with the effects of nuclear war for the past 40 years, so it is little wonder that they criticise the largely white peace movements of North America and Western Europe which, in the 1980s, talked of a possible future nuclear catastrophe, either not realising or not acknowledging that such a catastrophe had already happened in the Pacific. Indeed, through the process of producing nuclear weapons – mining the uranium, developing weapons-grade plutonium, assembling and testing the warheads – militaries are the world's major polluters, producing what, in the context of the US, ex-President Nixon called 'national sacrifice areas'.[31] Community organisations in the US have been campaigning for years against nuclear processing plants and dump sites, which leak radioactive particles into the air and groundwater, in the name, ironically, of national security.[32]

Examples of anti-militarist actions by feminists are the Women's Pentagon Actions in the US, in which several thousand women gathered at the Pentagon to protest against military priorities and the vast resources allocated to them.[33] These actions, taking place in November 1980, 1981 and 1982, pointed out the connections between military violence, male violence against women and children, racism, and the rape of the earth. Greenham Common Women's Peace Camp in England started in 1981, and was still active in September 1991, ten years later.[34] Greenham inspired dozens of other peace camps outside military bases, factories making weapons components, bomb-assembly plants, and military tracking stations in North America, Western Europe, Australia and New Zealand. Thousands of women associated with the peace camps participated in campaigns of nonviolent direct action. These protests were imaginative, colourful and assertive, with powerful artistic and ritual elements, and usually organised in a decentralised way, emphasising each woman's individual responsibility. In 1987, women gathered on Mothers' Day to protest against nuclear testing at the Nevada test site, the first women's action to be held there. Such actions combine a deep concern for a life-sustaining future with political confrontation, qualities that also characterise US women's tax-resistance actions on 15 April each year, when tax resisters give money to local projects rather than paying federal taxes, 60 per cent of which is used to finance the military.

Like women in Belau, who have been crucial in the campaign to retain their country's nuclear-free constitution – incidentally the only one in the world – against political and economic pressure from the US to use Belau as a naval base, women in many countries protest against the presence of US military bases. As well as housing highly dangerous weapons of mass destruction, they also distort neocolonial economies, and in the Philippines, South Korea and Okinawa, for example, bring militarised prostitution, drug trafficking, sexually transmitted diseases and AIDS.[35]

Dominance over 'the other' – whether women, people of colour, or non-human nature – is the key mechanism underlying militarism, sexism, racism and the destruction of ecological systems. Another kind of anti-militarist work involves healing the many splits which separate individuals and communities, helping people to see dehumanised 'others' as equally human. Examples include: anti-racist dialogue projects; caring for each other's children in the turmoil of civil war, as Singhalese and Tamil women did in Sri Lanka; and Palestinian and Jewish women in Israel seeking ways to meet and talk in a war zone.

One such project which started with the aim of building the

conditions for dialogue is Partnership (Shutafut), founded by Palestinian and Jewish women in Israel in 1978. They initially developed three-day workshops for Palestinian and Jewish school students, with two professional co-ordinators, one Arab and one Jewish. These workshops were successful in developing among the students a feeling of belonging to a united group, but this quickly evaporated when they went back to their separate schools. This led the organisation to undertake projects in mixed neighbourhoods and to work with parents and teachers as well as students, looking for common projects that everyone could work towards. Since then the organisation has become more involved on an overtly political level, challenging the Israeli government to enter into dialogue with the PLO.

Partnership's experience suggests some basic principles for dialogue:

1. the need for self-confidence, without which we cannot share ourselves with others;
2. using the same concepts and criteria for talking about other people's experience as we apply to our own;
3. looking for similarities in life experiences;
4. the importance of understanding fear, and dealing with it to break the vicious circle it sets up;
5. the importance of being future-oriented, not blaming the other community or dwelling on what has happened in the past;
6. finding a common objective, however limited, that a divided community can work towards.[36]

In North America and Western Europe, women's active opposition to militarism is not currently as strong as it was in the 1980s, though the Gulf war prompted renewed activism. Many women have moved on to other issues – environmentalism, or violence against women, for instance. The way issues are framed is crucial in terms of who will be involved. Over the years, Greenham women recognised connections between militarism, poverty, racism, sexism, hunger and unemployment, and have worked on many interrelated projects: campaigning against cuts in the British National Health Service, against apartheid, pornography, violence against women, and the stockpiling of food in Western Europe to keep prices high while so many people in the Third World die of starvation. Fundamental connections between militarism and the oppression of women were emphasised, but racism and class oppression were often overlooked. This was one of the reasons that the women's peace movement did not develop beyond a certain point. Like the women from the Pacific, women of colour in the US and Western Europe also challenged women's peace movements for their whiteness and racism, and this issue divided both the Women's Pentagon Action and the Greenham networks.[37]

The peace camp started as a protest against the siting of US nuclear cruise missiles at Greenham Common in England. Under the terms of the 1987 Intermediate Nuclear Force Treaty they have been withdrawn. Women still active at Greenham are now campaigning for the de-militarisation of what used to be common land. Focusing on the way the land was simply annexed by the military has helped Greenham women make connections with others who have been dispossessed of their land in the interests of military domination: Native Americans, Australian aborigines, Pacific peoples, and so on.

Connecting theoretical frameworks

These three issues – development, environmental health and anti-milit-arism – provide somewhat overlapping, somewhat disjointed frameworks, where women's connections to ecological issues are fundamentally material, through their roles as farmers, providers for their families, workers in toxic workplaces, women opposed to violence and militarism, and so on. These perspectives all incorporate race, class and imperial-ism, as well as gender.

By contrast, much US environmentalism is limited in approach, with an emphasis on green consumerism, and conservation of endangered species.[38] Nature is often seen as a virgin, feminised wilderness – vul-nerable, innocent, weak – and protecting 'her' draws on old macho militaristic iconography.[39] At the same time, wilderness is not thought of as indigenous people's land but as a place for city dwellers' recreation. Through lobbying, public education and direct action, important steps have been taken to begin to tackle environmental problems, but many environmentalists appear to have no theory of the state, economics, or the social roots of, for example, population growth.[40] They talk of 'the problem of overpopulation', particularly in the Third World, as a central concern. Framing the issue this way is ideologically loaded, has racist implications, and obscures several key issues: the varied cultural and economic reasons why people have children; the inverse relationship between women's status and family size; the political reasons for starva-tion and hunger; the skewed distribution of wealth on an international level, where industrialised countries consume so much of the world's resources.[41] Social ecology, developed primarily by Murray Bookchin, incorporates an anarchist critique of capitalism and the state that links domination and hierarchy in human society to the destruction of non-human nature, but it has often overlooked gender.[42] Much green, and bioregional thought and organising tends to overlook issues of race and class.

Linking feminism and ecology is also problematic. A key insight of US ecofeminism is the connection between the oppression of women and the oppression of nature.[43] For some this connection is biological,[44] for others it is a result of social conditioning. The term ecofeminism refers to a confusing range of perspectives, and many feminists reject it as intellectually incoherent, essentialist or synonymous with goddess worship.[45] Women of colour argue that it prioritises gender over race and class. There is an enormous gap between much US ecofeminist writing and grassroots activism around ecological issues. Ecofeminism is an irrelevant framework for many activists, stuck at the level of abstract ideas with no material basis and no sustained political practice. Many women working on ecological issues do not consider themselves feminists at all, and may not have an explicit gender perspective.

I see the material frameworks outlined above as a more useful way to understand women's activism around ecological issues worldwide. The central idea connecting them is the way white-centred, Western patriarchy creates 'otherness' – in women, people of colour and the earth – to be objectified, dominated and used. This allows us to see how the oppression of women, racism, economic exploitation and the ecological crisis all interconnect.

Principles of ecological feminism

1. Link the domination of women by men, people of colour by white people, non-human nature by human beings, and so on, under-standing that the connection between ecological sustainability and social justice is structural, not just a campaigning strategy based on coalitions of different groups.
2. Include the experience and perspectives of women dealing with ecological issues as a matter of survival – subsistence farmers in the Third World, as well as working women and women of colour in North America and Western Europe.
3. Frame issues in ways that include women of different backgrounds and experience, so as to enable women to work together across race, class and national lines.
4. Move from a framework of oppression to a framework of resistance.
5. Oppose personal and military violence.
6. Oppose capitalism and militarism, recognising the linear expansionism of market economies as fundamental to the ecological crisis; and racist, classist, sexist social institutions, while also recognising the devastating environmental consequences of state socialism, for example in Eastern Europe, the former Soviet Union and China.
7. Develop a politics of opposition and resistance as well as a politics of reconstruction and hope.

Agendas for action

These principles give rise to extensive agendas for action. I see two fundamental questions for feminists in industrialised countries who are concerned about ecological issues. How do we stop our governments and corporations from continuing to harm people in Third World countries, particularly women and children? How do we make our economies sustainable? Women in the Third World offer us trenchant critiques of First World models of development, science and technology, driven by an exploitative economy which puts profits before human needs. They are struggling not to be 'decoupled' from ecological practices, to use appropriate technology, and to draw on longstanding ethnoscientific knowledge. Some grassroots environmentalists in North America and Western Europe have a similar approach, as I suggested above.

An ecological feminism in industrialised countries should be involved with sustainable agriculture and restoration ecology; genetic engineering as it applies to the production of seeds, plants and animals, as well as human reproduction; health, in the broad sense of well-being; structural/social adjustment policies of our own governments; violence against women in all its forms; militarism and the culture of violence it generates and requires, and so on.

This means challenging existing industrial and agricultural production processes which involve the routine use of toxic substances, excessive packaging and waste, the pollution of the surrounding environment as well as the workplace, and the oil-intensive transport of goods over great distances so that consumers can choose from a wider range of products, however similar. Given that the majority of people live in urban areas, this agenda also involves making cities more sustainable.

Many recent publications on green cities emphasise health and environmental problems: air pollution, automobile congestion, urban sprawl, energy overconsumption, toxic pollutants, deterioration of the physical fabric of the city, and the absence of open space.[46] These problems are seen in terms of current technologies and the physical design of cities. Though mention is sometimes made of social, economic, cultural and political obstacles to bringing about change in urban areas, the emphasis is often on new or revamped architectural designs and transportation technologies. A more compelling approach to urban environmental change incorporates the land-use planning concerns mentioned above, but also draws attention to other critical aspects of urban survival – affordable housing, toxic wastes, environmental health in the workplace and the home, violence and personal safety. The people organising around these issues in urban neighbourhoods are, more often than not, women who understand through daily struggles the connections between deteriorating physical environments, economic inequality and racism. Women have a history of involvement in urban politics: campaigning against bad housing conditions, high rents, unsafe streets, lead in gasoline, toxic dumps, and so on. For these activists social justice and equity are central, and altering the built environment is only one aspect of their agenda for change.[47]

An ecological city must be one which sustains life within its borders while not simultaneously eroding it outside (in rural areas or in other parts of the world). 'Sustaining life' means providing for the basic physical necessities – housing, food, clean air and water, health, security, livelihoods and education, making public transport really viable, drastically reducing oil consumption and developing renewable energy resources, changing zoning regulations to reduce commuting and to make neighbourhoods safer, and opposing the drug trade.

This agenda also means questioning what constitutes valid knowledge and who can claim authority and expertise. It includes the 'kitchen-table science' of women piecing together information about polluters and the ethnoscience of women farmers in the Himalayas. It requires research which is of interest and value to activists and policy makers, rather than abstract academic feminism, increasingly co-opted by patriarchal notions of scholarship. It needs organisations and contexts where working relationships between activists, researchers and policy makers can develop.

Clearly, what I am outlining here is both a long-term agenda and something which is already happening in small ways through many local projects. Such a broad perspective may seem utterly daunting, given the basic contradiction between exploitative economic systems and a world without violence or environmental destruction, but many women are grappling with these issues and making changes. Local, regional, national and international women's networks, admittedly small and rather fragile, currently link activists, researchers and policy makers around development, environmental health and anti-militarism. Doubtlessly, these need expanding and strengthening. As Asoka Bandarage points out, 'solidarity between women is tenuous' and divisions of race, class, nationality and ethnicity tear at the unity that brings women together.[48] There is a need for greater dialogue between women from rich and poor countries, but, as Chandra Mohanty argues, this needs to move from a politics of solidarity – implying support for others in struggle – to a politics of engagement, where we are in struggle together.

Resources

This list emphasises national organisations in industrialised countries working on issues outlined in this chapter.

North America

Center for Third World Organizing, 3861 Martin Luther King Jr Way, Oakland, CA 94609. *The Minority Trendsletter.*

Citizens' Clearinghouse for Hazardous Wastes, PO Box 6806, Falls Church, VA 22040. Newsletter: *Everyone's Backyard.*

Commission for Racial Justice of the United Church of Christ, 105 Madison Ave, New York, NY 10016.

MS Foundation/Women and Economic Development Institute, 141 Fifth Ave, 6-S, New York, NY 10012.

National Women's Health Network, 1325 G St NW, Washington DC 20005.

Nationwide Women's Program, American Friends Service Committee, 1501 Cherry Street, Philadelphia, PA 19102. Newsletter: *Listen Real Loud.*

Radioactive Waste Campaign, 225 Lafayette St, New York, NY 10012.

Urban Habitat c/o Earth Island Institute, 300 Broadway, San Francisco, CA 94133. Newsletter: *Race, Poverty and the Environment.*

Women's Foreign Policy Council, 845 Third Ave, 1 5th floor, New York, NY 10022.

WorldWIDE: World Women in Environment, 1250 24th St, NW, 4th floor, Washington DC 20037. Newsletter: *Directory of Women in the Environment.*

Women and Environments, 736 Bathurst St, Toronto, Ontario M5S 2R4, Canada. Journal: *Women and Environments.*

Western Europe

Change, PO Box 824, London SE24 9JS, UK.

Feminist Network of Resistance to Reproductive and Genetic Engineering (FINRRAGE), PO Box 2019 03, D-2000 Hamburg 20, Germany.

Womankind, 122 Whitechapel High Street, London El 7PT, UK.

Women's Environmental Network, Aberdeen Studios, 22 Highbury Grove, London N5 2EA, UK.

Women-Environment-Sustainable Development, contact Irene Dankelman, Netherlands IUCN Committee, Damrak 28-30, 1012 LJ, Amsterdam, Netherlands.

Women Working for a Nuclear-Free and Independent Pacific, c/o Jan Symington, 52 Salisbury Rd, Crookes, Sheffield S10 IWB, UK.

Australia, New Zealand

Women's Environmental Education Centre, 147A King St, Sydney, NSW 2000, Australia.

Pacific Concerns Resource Centre, PO Box 3148, Central PO, Auckland, New Zealand.

Notes

1. This chapter draws on the Ecofeminism course I first developed at Colorado College. I want to acknowledge my debt to students and colleagues there, to the many people whose work I cite, to Ynestra King, Lin Nelson and Devon Pena for stimulating discussions about these ideas, to Molly Andrews and Georgina Ashworth for their help and encouragement, and to the countless women active against ecological destruction around the world.

2. War Resisters' League, 339 Lafayette St, New York, NY 10012.

3. A note on terminology, as all the commonly-used shorthand terms are problematic. First World/Third World is embedded in a framework which assumes the

superiority of North America and Western Europe, though Charlotte Bunch partly sidesteps this problem in talking about the Two-Thirds World, emphasising the fact that the majority of the world's population lives in the so-called Third World. The language of economic development which ranks countries as 'developed', 'undeveloped', 'underdeveloped' or 'developing' assumes a unitary view of development and progress following the industrial capitalism of Western Europe and North America. This is addressed somewhat by the term 'maldevelopment', which refers to the role of industrialised countries in extracting raw materials from their (former) colonies for the benefit of the colonial powers. Dividing the world into hemispheres of political influence – West and East – is also a simplification; similarly North and South. Comparing countries also masks inequalities within them, so that one can also talk of the Third World within the First World.

4. See, for example, Helen Collinson, *Death on Delivery: The Impact of the Arms Trade on the Third World* (London: Campaign Against the Arms Trade, 1989) from 11 Goodwin St, London N4 3HQ; Ruth Leger-Sivard, *World Militaries and Social Expenditures, 1990* (World Priorities Inc., PO Box 25140, Washington DC 20007).

5. Adrienne Rich, 'Notes Toward a Politics of Location', *Blood, Bread, and Poetry* (New York: Norton, 1986) pp. 210–31.

6. See, for example, Esther Boserup, *Women's Role in Economic Development* (New York: St Martin's Press, 1970); ISIS Women's International Information and Communication Service, *Women in Development: A Resource Guide for Organization and Action* (Philadelphia: New Society Publishers, 1984); Maria Mies, *Patriarchy and Accumulation on a World Scale: Women in the International Division of Labour* (London and NJ: Zed Books, 1986); *Women: The Last Colony* (London and NJ: Zed Books, 1988); Gita Sen and Caren Grown, *Development, Crises, and Alternative Visions: Third World Women's Perspectives* (New York: Monthly Review Press, 1987); Vandana Shiva, *Staying Alive* (London and NJ: Zed Books, 1988); *The Violence of the Green Revolution: Ecological Degradation and Political Conflict* (London and NJ: Zed Books, 1991); Ted Trainer, *Developed to Death: Rethinking Third World Development* (London: Green Print/Merlin Press, 1989); also titles in note 7.

7. For details of structural adjustment and external debt, see, for example, Susan George, *A Fate Worse than Debt* (London: Penguin Books, 1988); Cheryl Payer, *The World Bank: A Critical Analysis* (New York: Monthly Review Press, 1982); *Lent and Lost: Foreign Credit and Third World Development* (London: Zed Books, 1991); Aida Fulleros Santos and Lynn F. Lee, *The Debt Crisis: A Treadmill of Poverty for Filipino Women* (Quezon City: Kalayaan, 1989); Jeanne Vickers, *Women and the World Economic Crisis* (London: Zed Books, 1991).

8. See Irene Dankelman and Joan Davidson, *Women and Environment in the Third World: Alliance for the Future* (London: Earthscan, 1988).

9. Vandana Shiva, *Staying Alive* (London and NJ: Zed Books, 1988).

10. See, for example, Anita Anand, 'Saving Trees, Saving Lives: Third World Women and the Issue of Survival', in Leonie Caldecott and Stephanie Leland (eds) *Reclaim the Earth: Women Speak Out for Life on Earth* (London: The Women's Press, 1983) pp. 182–88; Vandana Shiva, *Staying Alive* (London and NJ: Zed Books, 1988) pp. 55–95.

11. See, for example, *The Environment Magazine*, March/April 1990, pp. 42–3; Maggie Jones and Wangari Maathai, 'Greening the Desert: Women of Kenya Reclaim Land', in *Reclaim The Earth*, pp. 112–14; Wangari Maathai, 'Foresters Without Diplomas', MS Magazine, March/April 1991, pp.74–5; *The Green Belt Movement: Sharing the Approach and the Experience* (Nairobi: Environmental Liaison Center International, 1988).

12. See, for example, Marilyn Carr (ed) *The Barefoot Book: Economically Appropriate Services for the Rural Poor* (London and New York: Intermediate Technology Publications, 1989); Sue Ellen M. Charlton, *Women in Third World Development* (Boulder and London: Westview Press, 1984); Development Alternatives with Women for a New Era (DAWN), *Alternatives,* vols. I and II, from Change, PO Box 824, London SE24 9JS; Irene Dankelman and Joan Davidson, *Women and Environment in the Third World: Alliance for the Future* (London: Earthscan, 1988); Ann Leonard (ed) *Seeds: Supporting Women's Work in the Third World* (New York: The Feminist Press at The City University, 1989); Walter V. C. Reid, 'Sustainable Development: Lessons from Success', *Environment, vol.* 31, no. 4, May 1989.

13. See, for example, the special issue of *Native Self Sufficiency,* 'Women and Economic Development', vol. 9, nos. 1 & 2, 1987, published by Seventh Generation Fund for Indian Development, PO Box 10, Forestville, CA 95436; Rachel Bagby, 'Daughters of Growing Things', in Irene Diamond and Gloria Orenstein (eds) *Reweaving the World: The Emergence of Ecofeminism* (San Francisco: Sierra Club Books, 1990) pp. 231–48; Sam Bass, *To Dwell is to Garden* (Boston: Northeastern University Press, 1987); Tom Fox, Ian Koeppel and Susan Kellam, *Struggle for Space: The Greening of New York City 1970–1984* (Washington DC: Island Press); Mark Francis, Lisa Cashdan, Lynn Paxson, *Community Open Spaces: Greening Neighborhoods Through Community Action and Land Conservation* (Washington DC: Island Press).

14. See, for example, Donald Dale Jackson, 'Around Los Ojos, Sheep and Land are Fighting Words', *Smithsonian,* April 1991, pp. 37–47; Devon Pena, *The 'Brown' and the 'Green': Chicanos and Environmental Politics in the Upper Rio Grande,* paper presented at the 32nd Annual Meeting of the Western Social Science Association, Portland, April 1990; Maria Varela, 'Ganados del Valle/Tierra Wools: An Experiment in Sustainable Development, Cultural Revival and Workplace Democracy', *New Scholar,* special issue on Chicano Studies and Ecology, August 1992.

15. Alan Durning, 'Grass-roots Groups are Our Best Hope for Global Prosperity and Ecology', *Utne Reader* July/August 1989, pp. 40–49.

16. See, for example, F. E. Trainer, *Abandon Affluence* (London: Zed Books, 1985); Paul L. Wachtel, *The Poverty of Affluence* (Philadelphia & Santa Cruz: New Society Publishers, 1989).

17. See, for example, Lin Nelson, 'Women's Lives against the Industrial/ Chemical Landscape: Environmental Health and the Health of the Environment', in Kathryn Strother Ratcliff et al (eds) *Healing Technology: Feminist Perspectives* (Ann Arbor: University of Michigan Press, 1989) pp. 347–69; Lin Nelson, Regina Kenen, Susan Klitzman, *Turning Things Around: A Women's Occupational and Environmental Health Resource Guide* (Washington DC: National Women's Health Network, 1990) from 1325 G St NW, Washington DC 20005.

18. For details see Robin Lee Zeff, Marsha Love, and Karen Stults (eds) *Empowering Ourselves: Women and Toxics Organizing* (Arlington, VA: Citizens' Clearinghouse for Hazardous Wastes, 1989) and the CCHW newsletter, *Everyone's Backyard.*

19. Charles Lee, *Toxic Wastes and Race* (New York: Commission for Racial Justice of the United Church of Christ, 1987).

20. Talk entitled *Communities of Colour and Environmental Justice,* given at the 18th Scholar and Feminist Conference, 'Women, the Environment and Grassroots Movements', Barnard College, New York, 13 April 1991.

21. Carl Anthony, 'Why African Americans Should Be Environmentalists', *Earth Island Journal,* Winter 1990, pp. 43–4.

22. See, for example, Hilary French, 'Combating Toxic Terrorism', *World Watch*, Sept/Oct 1988, pp. 6–7; Diana Johnstone, 'Western Developmental Overdose Makes Africa Chemically Dependent', *In These Times*, vol. 14, No. 2, 8–14 November 1989, pp. 9–10; Clinton Cox, 'Black Communities Are Being Dumped On', *City Sun*, 18–24 April 1990, pp. 8, 12; 'Toxics and Communities of Color', special issue of *The Minority Trendsletter*, Center for Third World Organizing, vol. 4, no. 4, Summer 1991 (from 3861 Martin Luther King Jr Way, Oakland, CA 94609); report on proposal to ship US garbage to Ebeye island, ABC Primetime Live, 6 December 1990, segment on Micronesia, entitled 'Paradise Lost'.

23. See, for example, Katsi Cook, 'A Community Health Project: Breastfeeding and Toxic Contaminants', *Indian Studies*, Spring 1985, pp. 14–16; Katsi Cook and Lin Nelson, 'Mohawk Women Resist Industrial Pollution', *Listen Real Loud*, vol. 6, no. 3, Summer 1985 (Nationwide Women's Program, American Friends Service Committee, 1501 Cherry St, Philadelphia, PA 19102); Lin Nelson, 'The Place of Women in Polluted Places', in Irene Diamond and Gloria Orenstein (eds) *Reweaving the World: The Emergence of Ecofeminism*, (San Francisco: Sierra Club Books, 1990) pp. 173–87.

24. See, for example, Laura Pulido, 'The United Farm Workers Union and Environmental Politics', in *New Scholar*, special issue on Chicano Studies and Ecology, no. 14, August 1992; a documentary film, *The Wrath of Grapes*, is available from United Farm Workers of America, PO Box 62, La Paz, Keene, CA 93531.

25. See, for example, Lawrie Mott and Karen Snyder, *Pesticide Alert: A Guide to Pesticides in Fruits and Vegetables* (San Francisco: Sierra Club Books, 1987).

26. Miranda Spivack, 'Johnson Controls: Unanimous Ruling, Multiple Effects', *MS Magazine*, May/June 1991, p. 92. See also Joan E. Bertin, 'Fix the Job, Not the Worker', *Los Angeles Times*, 27 November 1989; Jeanne Mager Stellman and Joan E. Bertin, 'Science's Anti-female Bias', *New York Times*, 4 June 1990, p. A23; Kathy Pollitt, 'Fetal Rights: A New Assault on Feminism', *The Nation*, 26 March 1990, pp. 409–18.

27. See, for example, Gena Corea, *The Mother Machine: From Artifcial Insemination to Artificial Wombs* (San Francisco: Harper and Row, 1986); Gena Corea et al, *Man-made Women: How New Reproductive Technologies Affect Women* (Bloomington: Indiana University Press, 1987). For critiques of genetic engineering in animals and plants, see *Women: Genetic Engineering Is Your Business*, available from Jean Grossholtz, 10 Jewett Lane, S.Hadley, MA01075; Vandana Shiva, 'The Rest of Reality', *MS Magazine*, November–December 1990, pp. 72–3; also published as 'Land, Women and Bio-Engineering', *Edges*, vol. 4, no. 1, 1991, pp. 31–3; Michelle Stamworth, *Reproductive Technologies* (1988); Nadine Taub and Sherill Cohen (eds) *Reproductive Laws for the 1990s* (New York: Humana Press, 1989).

28. See, for example, Susie Cohn, Frances Connelly, Joan Grant, Fran Willard, *Pacific Paradise Nuclear Nightmare* (London: Campaign for Nuclear Disarmament, 1987); *WIN* special issue, 'Nuclear Free Pacific', August 1982; Women Working for a Nuclear Free and Independent Pacific, *Pacific Women Speak: Why Haven't You Known?* (Oxford: Green Line, 1987); *Half Life: A Parable for the Nuclear Age* (1986) a film by Dennis O'Rourke.

29. Quoted in *Pacific Women Speak, p.* 5; original citation Donald Henry, *Micronesia: Trust Betrayed* (New York: Carnegie Endowment for International Peace, 1975) p. 98.

30. *Pacific Women Speak* has the subtitle *Why Haven't You Known?* The Partial Test Ban Treaty of 1963 stopped most atmospheric nuclear tests, though France still tests in the Pacific. Britain and the US use the Nevada Test Site, 60 miles north of Las Vegas.

31. Cited by W. Churchill and W. 'No Nukes' La Duke, 'Radioactive Colonization and the Native American', *Socialist Review*.

32. See, for example, John Birks and Anne Ehrlich (eds) *Hidden Dangers: The Environmental Consequences of Preparing for War* (San Francisco: Sierra Club Books, 1989); Jon Christensen, 'The Bombing of the West', *High Country News*, vol. 23, no. 8, 1991; *Deadly Defense: Military Radioactive Landfills* (New York: Radioactive Waste Campaign, 1988); Minard Hamilton, 'The Hot War: Radioactive Contamination in East and West', *Peace and Democracy News,* Winter–Spring 1990; Stephen J. Hedges, 'Bomb Makers' Secrets', U.S. *News and World Report* 23 October 1989, pp. 22–8. Seymour Melman, *Profits Without Production* (New York: Knopf, 1983); *The Demilitarized Society* (Montreal: Harvest House, 1988); *The Permanent War Economy* (New York: Simon and Schuster, 1985); Joni Seager, 'Making Feminist Sense of Environmental Issues', *Sojourner,* February 1991; Seth Shulman, 'Toxic Travels: Inside the Military's Environmental Nightmare', *Nuclear Times,* Autumn 1990, pp. 20–32.

33. The Unity Statement of the Women's Pentagon Action is published in Leonie Caldecott and Stephanie Leland (eds) *Reclaim the Earth* (London: The Women's Press, 1983) pp. 14–19; also Lynn Jones, *Keeping the Peace* (London: The Women's Press, 1983). See also Ynestra King, 'All is Connectedness', *Keeping the Peace;* 'The Eco-Feminist Imperative', *Reclaim the Earth,* pp. 9–14.

34. See, for example, Alice Cook and Gwyn Kirk, *Greenham Women Everywhere* (Boston: South End Press, 1983); Barbara Harford and Sarah Hopkins, *Greenham Common: Women at the Wire* (London: The Women's Press, 1984); Gwyn Kirk, 'Our Greenham Common', in Adrienne Harris and Ynestra King (eds) *Rocking the Ship of State: Towards a Feminist Peace Politics* (Boulder: Westview Press, 1989) chs. 6 & 14; Ann Snitow, 'Holding the Line at Greenham', *Mother Jones,* February/March 1985; Leslie Webster and Ginna D. Rose, 'The Uncommon Women of Greenham', *On The Issues,* Summer 1991.

35. See, for example, Lolita McDonough (ed) *United States Bases in the Philippines: Issues and Scenarios* (Quezon City: International Studies Institute of the Philippines, 1986); Gabriela Staff North America, 'Women and the U.S. Bases in the Philippines: Generations Without Future', *Peace and Freedom,* March/April 1989, pp. 18–21 (from Women's International League for Peace and Freedom, 1213 Race St, Philadelphia, PA 19107); *Listen Real Loud* special issue, 'Voices of Hope and Anger: Women Speak Out for Sovereignty and Self Determination', vol. 10, no. 1–2, 1990 (Nationwide Women's Program AFSC); Cynthia Enloe, *Bananas, Beaches, and Bases: Making Feminist Sense of International Politics* (London: Pandora Press, 1989; Berkeley: University of California Press, 1990).

36. From a talk given by Edna Zaretsky and Mariam Mar'i as part of the Women in Dialogue tour sponsored by New Jewish Agenda, New York City, 19 January 1989. Partnership can be contacted at PO Box 9577, Haifa, Israel 31095.

37. See, for example, Valerie Amos and Pratisha Parmer, 'Challenging Imperial Feminism', *Feminist Review,* no. 17, 1984, pp. 3–19; Anne Braden, 'Racism and the Peace Movement', *The Nonviolent Activist,* January 1988, available from War Resisters' League, 339 Lafayette St, New York, NY 10012; Wilmette Brown, *Black Women and the Peace Movement* (London: International Women's Day Convention, 1983); Barbara Omolade, 'We Speak for the Planet', in Adrienne Harris and Ynestra King (eds) *Rocking the Ship of State: Towards a Feminist Peace Politics;* Barbara Smith, '"Fractious, Kicking, Messy, Free": Feminist Writers Confront the Nuclear Abyss', *New England Review/Breadloaf Quarterly,* Summer 1983, pp. 581–92; Alice Walker, 'Only Justice Can Stop a Curse', *Home Girls: A Black Feminist Anthology* (New York: Kitchen Table/Women of Color Press, 1983) pp. 352–5.

38. See, for example, Edward Goldsmith and Nicholas Hildyard (eds) *The Earth Report: The Essential Guide to Global Ecological Issues* (London: Mitchell Beazley, 1988); H. Patricia Hynes, *Earth Right* (Rocklin, CA: Institute on Women and Technology, 1990); John McCormick, *Reclaiming Paradise: The Global Environmental Movement* (Bloomington: Indiana University Press, 1991); John Seymour and Herbert Giradet, *Blueprint for a Green Planet: Your Practical Guide to Restoring the World's Environment* (New York: Prentice Hall, 1987); *Fifty Simple Things You Can Do to Save the Earth* (Berkeley: Earthworks Press, 1990).

39. See, for example, Ynestra King, 'Coming of Age with the Greens', *Z Magazine* February 1988, pp. 16–19.

40. See, for example, Bill Devall and George Sessions, *Deep Ecology: Living As If Nature Mattered* (Salt Lake City: Peregrine Smith Books, 1985); *Earth First!* PO Box 5871, Tucson, AZ 85703; George Bradford, *How Deep is Deep Ecology?* (Novato, CA: Times Change Press, 1989); Michael Parfit, 'Earth First!ers wield a mean monkeywrench', *Smithsonian*, April 1990, pp. 184–204. Debates around deep ecology and environmentalism can be found in *The Ecologist*, *Environmental Ethics*, *Z Magazine* in recent years.

41. See, for example, Paul Ehrlich and Anne Ehrlich, *The Population Explosion* (New York: Simon and Schuster, 1990). For feminist views of this issue see, for example, Eleanor J. Bader, 'Population Control: A Substitute for Social Justice', *Environmental Magazine*, vol. 1, no. 6, November/December 1990; Betsy Hartmann, *Reproductive Rights and Wrongs: The Global Politics of Population Control and Contraceptive Choice* (New York: Harper and Row, 1987); Frances Moore Lappe and Joseph Collins, *World Hunger: Twelve Myths* (New York: Grove Press, 1986); Frances Moore Lappe and Rachel Schurman, *Taking Population Seriously* (San Francisco: Institute for Food and Development Policy, 1988).

42. See, for example, Murray Bookchin, *The Ecology of Freedom: The Emergence and Dissolution of Hierarchy* (Toronto: Black Rose Books, 1990); *Remaking Society: Pathways to a Green Future* (Boston: South End Press, 1990); Brian Tokar, *The Green Alternative: Creating an Ecological Future* (R. & E Miles, 1987).

43. See, for example, Irene Diamond and Gloria Orenstein (eds) *Reweaving the World: The Emergence of Ecofeminism* (San Francisco: Sierra Club Books, 1990); Ynestra King, *Ecofeminism and the Reenchantment of Nature* (Boston: Beacon Press, 1992); Carolyn Merchant, *The Death of Nature: Women, Ecology and the Scientific Revolution* (San Francisco: Harper and Row, 1980); Judith Plant (ed) *Healing the Wounds: The Promise of Ecofeminism* (Philadelphia and Santa Cruz: New Society Publishers, 1989); Karen Warren (ed) 'Ecological Feminism', special issue of *Hypatia*, vol. 6, no. 1, Spring 1991.

44. Mary Daly, *Gyn/Ecology: The Metaethics of Radical Feminism* (Boston: Beacon Press, 1979); Elizabeth Dodson Gray, *Green Paradise Lost* (Wellesley, MA: Roundtable Press, 1979); Susan Griffin, *Women and Nature: The Roaring Inside Her* (San Francisco: Harper and Row, 1978).

45. See, for example, critiques of ecofeminism: Bina Agarwal, *Engendering the Environment Debate: Lessons from the Indian Subcontinent*, (East Lansing: Center for Advanced Study of International Development, Michigan State University, 1991); Janet Biehl, *Rethinking Ecofeminist Politics* (Boston: South End Press, 1991); Joni Seager, 'Making Feminist Sense of Environmental Issues', *Sojourner*, January 1991.

46. See, for example, Lester Brown and Jodi L. Jacobson, *The Future of Urbanization: Facing the Ecological and Economic Constraints* (Washington DC: Worldwatch Institute, 1987); Tim Elkin, Duncan McLaren, Mayer Hillman, *Reviving the City: Towards Sustainable Urban Development* (London: Friends of theEarth, 1991); The Environmental

Magazine, special issue on 'The Greening of Downtown USA', September/October 1991; David Gordon (ed), *Green Cities: Ecologically Sound Approaches to Urban Space* (Montreal and NY: Black Rose Books, 1990); David Nicholson-Lord, *The Greening of the Cities* (London and NY: Routledge, 1987); Richard Register, *Ecocity Berkeley: Building Cities for a Healthy Future* (Berkeley: North Atlantic Books, 1987); Anne Whiston Spirn, *The Granite Garden: Urban Nature and Human Design* (New York: Basic Books, 1984); *The Urban Ecologist*, PO Box 10144, Berkeley, CA 94709; Colin Ward, *Welcome, Thinner City: Urban Survival in the 1990s* (London: Bedford Square Press, 1989).

47. Myrna Breitbart and Gwyn Kirk, *Ecological Urbanism: Women Charting a Course for Change*, presented to the Eighteenth Annual Scholar and Feminist Conference, 'Women, the Environment, and Grassroots Movements', Barnard College, 13 April 1991.

48. Asoka Bandarage, 'Towards International Feminism', *Brandeis Review*, vol. 3, no. 3, Summer 1983.

6

Free Trade Zones: Issues and Strategies

Leith L. Dunn

Introduction

This chapter examines the phenomenon of Free Trade Zones (FTZ) as the cornerstone of the export-oriented industrialisation (EOI) strategy, and the experience of women working in them. The model is essentially that of capitalist accumulation, in which surplus labour is used to create wealth which will in turn, in theory, 'trickle down' to benefit the wider population. Over time, economic development has become synonymous with industrialisation. Many developing countries have used EOI as a means of transforming their economy from an agricultural to an industrial base.

The chapter concentrates on the experience of the Caribbean, but the strategy is used globally (including China), and may surface in the new 'free markets' of Eastern Europe. The incentives offered to foreign companies, many of them transnational, to encourage investment usually include cheap female labour, an absence of foreign exchange controls, unlimited repatriation of profits, subsidised utilities and infrastructure, and a climate of non-unionisation. Most developing countries pursue the EOI strategy with the support of institutions like the World Bank and International Monetary Fund. As the workforce of most Free Zones is female, the impact of the strategy on women is significant.[1] Whereas the FTZs provide employment, there are many problems associated with this method of involving women in the international division of labour. The issues and some strategies are examined, and ideas for policy changes at the national and global level to create balanced development are suggested for the agenda of the international women's movement.

During the 1990s, many developing countries have been adversely affected by lower prices for their primary agricultural exports on the world market. Increased interest rates on loans borrowed in the 1970s and 1980s and higher prices for essential imports such as fuel, medicines and other equipment for production have increased the demand for foreign exchange. Increased life expectancy and high population growth rates have resulted in larger numbers of people to feed, educate and keep healthy. Pursuit of agricultural and other practices that are not environmentally sustainable have in some countries resulted in a reduced natural resource-base and created environmental degradation.

Against this background, the standard of living in many developing countries has been reduced, and significant numbers of people live below the poverty line. Structural adjustment policies of the World Bank and International Monetary Fund, while aiming to create economic stability and reduce inflation, have often had the undesirable effect of further reducing the standard of living for the majority of people, and particularly adding to the burdens of women.[2] Currency devaluation, wage freezes, privatisation of state enterprises, slashing of state bureaucracies, import liberalisation policies and export promotion have often impacted negatively on the poorest and most powerless members of society. Many of these policies have resulted in increased costs for imports, and raised the cost of living. Unemployment has driven people into informal-sector occupations in many countries, and with this trend, workers' rights to defend their interests have also been affected. In many developing countries, employment has been reduced from a right to a privilege, and so international labour standards tend to be sacrificed on the altar of economic survival.

The new international division of labour

Export-oriented industrialisation is guided by the concept of the 'new international division of labour' coined by German scholars (Froebel et al, 1980). They argued that industrial capital from the core was moving to the periphery as world-market factories were set up to produce manufactured goods for export, replacing earlier import-substitution development strategies. It enabled capitalism to expand as it became more difficult to secure high profits in the North, owing to rising industrial conflict, equal opportunities policies, demands for higher wages and an increased level of organisation among migrant workers, who comprised the bulk of the labour force in factories. Developing countries with large supplies of cheap, because usually female, unorganised labour became a viable option for the improvement of the level of profits. Additionally, advances in technology and management were better able to facilitate the use of peripheral labour. The minute segmentation of production enabled unskilled and semi-skilled workers to complete tasks which would contribute to a whole product. Manufacturing, therefore, was moved overseas by multinational capital to the 'periphery', where governments provided increasingly attractive incentives to entice them. With few exceptions, the experience of many developing countries using the EOI strategy is that jobs requiring minimal industrial skills and offering low remuneration are transferred to the South. Technologically advanced and higher-paying jobs are generally kept in the industrialised North.

A common characteristic of world market factories and the new international division of labour is the use of young female labour. Young women are easily exploited because of patterns of patriarchy in the family and the wider society across different cultures. While the employment creation is welcome, women's wages are kept low to justify the dominant attitude that their income to the family budget is secondary rather than primary.[3]

Gender and the international division of labour

Although both men and women are employed in the global assembly of consumer goods, the new international division of labour is characterised by the sexual division of labour across industries. Women tend to be employed in industries that require low levels of skill and pay low wages. In selected industries such as garments, textiles and electronics, women comprise over 80 per cent of the workforce. Developing countries embarking on the EOI strategy and establishing FTZs tend initially to produce garments and textiles, and later introduce industries requiring more skills, such as electronics. In these industries, women play a central role and bear a disproportionate share of the responsibility in creating economic miracles for their country. Despite this, they are not given the support required to realise their full potential as workers, and their wage levels are often too low to support their families adequately.

Women's social role as care givers to the very young and the elderly presents a problem in many countries. The absence of child care facilities linked to FTZ employment creates major problems for women workers with children. Free Zone women workers therefore face a major dilemma. They desperately need the jobs for the income but many find it difficult to balance this with their social and domestic responsibilities, thereby increasing their level of stress.

The limited scope for occupational mobility in the majority of Free Zone jobs, and the marked sexual division of labour that places women in jobs that require low levels of skill and pay low wages have been sources of criticism from women, trade union activists, academics and others about the feminisation of labour, occupational segregation, and the gender division of labour. These issues have been addressed extensively by Diane Elson and Ruth Pearson, among others.

Economic miracles

This model of economic development has been encouraged by the economic success of the Newly Industrialised Countries (NICs) in South-east Asia, including Singapore, Taiwan, Hong Kong and South Korea. These countries, by using cheap female labour, have been able to transform their economies with some success, increase their official rate of economic growth and their level of industrialisation. Some have even established their own transnational companies. Large sections of their workforce have acquired industrial skills which have enabled them to produce a wide range of consumer goods for the international market, including clothing, footwear, toys, electrical and electronic goods, luggage and jewellery. Over the years, use of the export-oriented industrialisation strategy has enabled these South-east Asian countries to produce large volumes of high quality products and compete with the more developed economies of Western Europe and the United States.

Against this background, developing countries in other parts of Asia, Africa, Latin America and the Caribbean, as well as Eastern and Central Europe have pursued a similar strategy, or variations of it, and invested heavily in the infrastructure, in the hope of repeating the NICs' 'industrial miracle'. Whether this experience can be reproduced in the current global economic climate, plagued by recession and debt, is debatable. The cultural characteristics of the NICs have also largely been ignored in the process of introducing these policies. These countries are very disciplined, highly controlled and include some repressive regimes.

As the NICs have moved into manufacturing goods which require higher levels of skill, they too have moved some of the low-skilled jobs to the Caribbean, Latin America and South Pacific. In the Caribbean for example the governments of both Jamaica and the Dominican Republic have provided a wide range of incentives to attract foreign investors. These multinational companies, including some from South-east Asia, are part of a highly sophisticated and vertically integrated network of international financial and trading systems that mass-produce a wide range of consumer goods and services.[4] Both countries lead the Caribbean as investment havens, the Dominican Republic being the more successful in terms of the expansion of Export Processing Zones (currently 19, of which 13 EPZs are operational) and earning foreign exchange. According to the Central Bank of the Dominican Republic, an estimated US$129 million came from the Zones in 1988.[5] They also provided employment for an estimated 130,000 people in 1990. Though impressive in itself, this figure is not very significant when compared to employment needs, and there has been a lot of controversy over wages and working conditions. The proximity of the Caribbean to the large US market also influences the types of investment set up. US trade policy for the region, outlined in the Caribbean Basin Initiative (CBI), also has an impact. The original 12-year trade, aid and military assistance package to countries considered friendly to the US was supposed to boost US investment in the region. The results have been disappointing, however, as there are severe restrictions on the source of materials used in the production of goods that can enter the US market duty free, so many products from Caribbean countries are prohibited. A number of Asian countries have invested in the Caribbean region to take advantage of the CBI legislation and increase their access to the US market. Under the CBI provisions, investors pay duty only on the value added to the product, which in many cases is only the cost of labour, relatively low in relation to the total cost of production.

Free Trade Zones: characteristics and objectives

Free Trade Zones (FTZs) are essentially production enclaves manufacturing goods for export, although some countries allow limited sale of some goods on the domestic market. They provide short-term solutions to macro socio-economic and political problems such as high unemployment and underemployment. They are useful for countries with large populations with low levels of industrial skills, and limited local technology and capital resources. Countries with large foreign debts are particularly attracted to the model of FTZs, as they offer a means of generating foreign exchange.

The employment potential for women in FTZs is unmatched, except in the agricultural sector, and as such it is important. Jobs in agriculture are notoriously badly paid in most countries, although agriculture is usually a major contributor to the domestic economy. FTZs are regarded as having a lower status than industrial work, so many workers opt for the latter.

Host governments introduce incentive legislation to enhance their country's attractiveness as an investment haven for foreign companies. Factory space is provided at competitive rates, as well as a wide range of services, infrastructure and conditions that will generally enhance the economic viability of the investor's company. The range of incentives offered to investors increases the country's competitiveness in comparison to other developing countries, so some governments will compromise national standards and labour protection in laws in order to attract foreign investors. The most common incentives offered include an abundant supply of cheap young female labour, absence of foreign exchange controls, unlimited repatriation of profits, long tax holidays, subsidised utilities and infrastructure located within easy access of international air and sea ports, cheap air cargo, containerised shipping facilities, international communications networks (fax, telephone, satellite links), a climate of anti-unionisation and political stability, which sometimes means using military repression. In some countries incentives are also offered in the form of freedom from planning and environmental controls. This can mean compromising on health and safety standards.

These wide-ranging incentives represent production subsidies provided by host governments, usually financed by resources borrowed from multilateral and bilateral lending agencies at high interest rates. Nationals therefore have to repay these debts over a long period. In this symbiotic relationship, to produce for export, foreign companies complement these incentives by providing capital, equipment, raw materials and technical expertise.

Technology transfer

In addition to creating employment and earning foreign exchange, it is also hoped that Free Trade Zones will help to accelerate the process of industrialisation through the transfer of technology. Governments often try to attract foreign investment with the potential to enhance the managerial and technical skills of their nationals, so that over time, national entrepreneurs will acquire the necessary skills to establish similar industries locally. In addition there is the expectation that the local workforce will acquire an industrial work ethic, which will increase the country's attractiveness as a haven for future foreign investment. This increased competitiveness is expected to enhance the country's chances of becoming more 'developed'.

FTZs, it is also hoped, will create backward and forward linkages with the rest of the domestic economy. The governments hope that, over time, some of the raw materials required will be provided from local sources in the necessary quantity, quality and variety. This implies the establishment of supply industries such as textiles for the garment industry, or electronic components for computers. Local companies would eventually also improve their capacity to market goods internationally and develop their own international distribution networks.

Through sub-contracting arrangements, some local companies are already involved in exports linked to the Free Zones. In the case of Jamaica, for example, local garment companies produce for export under US tariffs which allow cut components of garments to be imported, sewn in Jamaica and re-exported (formerly known as the 806 and 807 programme). Under other tariff arrangements, the material is imported then cut, assembled, and exported to the USA (cut, make and trim). Earnings are higher under this arrangement as more local skill is involved in the process.

Free Zone industries undoubtedly provide thousands of jobs for workers, but most involve assembly-line production using skills that are learned within a few weeks. High levels of unemployment and the lack of alternatives nevertheless create great demand for this type of employment, however unstable and dependent on market demand for specific products and the state of the global economy. Employment at the lower end of the scale is therefore often characterised by job instability and high labour turnover. Industries such as textiles and garments, which sell most of their products in developed countries, are particularly vulnerable, as market demand is linked to the conditions of the economies of North America and Europe, and to the Multi-Fibre Agreement. Free Zone garment workers around the world therefore experience seasonal and cyclical fluctuations in employment.

Assembly-line production is highly segmented. Workers complete very specific components of the overall product and as such, they develop skill, speed and expertise in very distinct areas. Retrenchment and rehiring therefore lead to job instability, and occupational mobility is restricted as there are no guarantees of workers finding similar jobs. Retraining for another job means loss of income, as earnings are linked to high skill and productivity. Expertise is not always transferable, with the result that many Free Zone workers literally do the same job for many years.

A review of many studies done in different parts of the world indicates that most women find Free Zone employment challenging. Given the 'choice' of working in the Zones or facing unemployment, the majority would want to continue working in the Zones. For many, however, international assembly-line production requires a greatly increased pace of work, as the product fits into other components and deadlines. The problems most commonly cited include: low wages and varying levels of income that make domestic budgeting very difficult; shift work (including night shifts); demands to do overtime work, often at very short notice; long hours; the rigid routine which is production-oriented; the monotonous, repetitive and fragmented nature of the work, which many women workers find alienating; and the lack of a union to represent their interests.

Labour codes and unionisation

Under the conventions of the International Labour Organisation, workers are guaranteed freedom of association, the right to organise and have collective agreements, freedom from forced labour, and acceptable conditions of work in respect of minimum wages, hours of work, health and social security. The laws of many countries which are signatories to these ILO conventions prohibit the employment of women on night shifts, or the exposure of pregnant women to dangerous chemicals and materials. Reports on working conditions in many Free Zones show a tendency to violate national and international labour standards, including health and safety regulations.

A climate of non- or anti-unionisation is often offered as an incentive to foreign investors and, as such, even the basic right of association or organising to defend their interests is frequently denied to workers. Intimidation and even violence are used in some countries to break up any form of union activity. Divide and rule tactics are also used by some manufacturers to discourage union activity. In most countries, women generally find it difficult to become union members because of the excessive demands on their time of their domestic and economic roles. They work long hours, often spend considerable time moving between their place of work and home, and still have primary responsibility for managing their homes, caring for children and elderly members of their family; many are also active in their community and church. In some countries, membership in or association with a union is a recipe for immediate dismissal. With few alternatives for employment and major responsibility for supporting their family, the majority of women workers in Zones around the world are non-unionised. In some factories, however, managers have formed in-house unions that attempt to address worker–management problems so as to keep the work situation conducive to high productivity.

Women workers who join unions also encounter other problems. Interviewers of Free Zone workers in the Dominican Republic, for example, reported that there were some difficulties in relating to the confrontational style of traditional, male-dominated trade unions, and had found this experience alienating. They also reported that although male trade unionists were supportive of their struggle, their priorities did not always coincide with those of women workers. Child care or transportation after the late shift, for example, were not seen as priorities. Decision-making structures and leadership style in traditional trade unions tend to be autocratic, and, as newcomers, women were often at a disadvantage. There is need for a new type of union, not necessarily operating within the confines of the Zone or taking the formal structure of traditional trade unions, but one which has new norms that facilitate full participation of rank and file union members, and has a broader remit in representing workers' interests.

One model of a representative group is the St Peter Claver Women's Housing Co-operative in Kingston, Jamaica. It operates within the community, with no organic links to the Free Zone. It represents the interests of its members and addresses issues affecting Free Zone workers, but operates quite differently from a traditional trade union. Another is the Women's Trade Union in the Philippines.

Wages, production incentives and support services

Free Zone wages are also an important issue for women workers. Production incentives are built into wage schemes, so that workers are paid a basic minimum wage, and their earnings increase in relation to their productivity. Assembly-line production wages are based on piece-rates. In the garment industry, for example, production quotas and standards are established for each segment of the process. Workers are then given a particular segment of the production chain to complete. An optimum number of units, adjusted according to the style and complexity of garments, is targeted for completion in a given time, as the basis for earning wages. Strict deadlines are applied and quality control is stringent to ensure delivery to customer requirements.

Production targets and incentive rates are increased proportionally to raise production, but unless workers achieve the new targets, the company gets the benefit of the increased output without having to pay the worker anything extra. Free Zone workers in various parts of the world regard this system as being unfair and it is often a major source of conflict.

Assembly-line production places rigorous demands on the workforce. Time and motion studies calculate the best positions for workers to maximise production using the minimum resources. In Caribbean Free Zones, the garment industry dominates, and garment engineers calculate optimum production targets based on garment style, the type of material, the number of operations required and the time each will take. As production is streamlined, and the work of one section flows into another, there is very tight control over the movement of the workforce to maximise efficiency and profits. This is a common area of tension in the EPZs, as any movement from the work station – to go to the bathroom, for lunch break or for illness – is severely restricted. New approaches to management that are less regimented and allow workers to set their own production targets need to be explored more fully.[6]

Support services for Free Zone workers are a problem in many countries. These relate primarily to health facilities, canteens and bathrooms. The latter two are often inadequate for the large number of workers who use them. It is a common sight to see workers standing, or sitting on the ground, to eat their lunch, instead of being seated in clean canteens, which workers avoid for cheaper and often more tasty alternatives available on credit instead of for cash. Interviewees in both Jamaica and the Dominican Republic reported that in some factories written permission is required to use the toilets; and in the DR workers also reported the removal of toilet doors in some factories to prevent theft of toiletries. Managers rationalise this as a way of reducing theft.

Workers entering or leaving most Zones are subjected to body searches. In the DR there were reports of women being sexually harassed by male guards responsible for searching them.[7]

Working conditions in some export assembly industries are hazardous to workers' health. In Jamaica, findings from research on working conditions in the EPZs indicate that major health problems include back pains, respiratory defects from overexposure to steam irons, stress from working at an intense pace for long periods, headaches, kidney and bladder infections from retaining urine for long periods, sinus problems and allergies from dust and materials used.[8] Research from the electronics industries indicates that soldering microchips over prolonged periods leads to intense eye-strain because of the close work involved. Although some countries provide health clinics within their Free Zones to improve workers' access to health treatment, this is often inadequate. Improved facilities would, however, reduce time lost through illness and could enhance productivity.

Employment and economic independence

At an individual level, Free Zone employment has undoubtedly been a blessing for thousands of young women. It has enabled them to have some level of economic independence and given them the means to support their families. Interviews with Free Zone workers in the Caribbean show that involvement in fairly regular employment has helped to raise their self-esteem, their self-confidence and their social and economic aspirations. Some have acquired household items that they might otherwise have found impossible, and have been able to care for their children almost singlehandedly .

The discipline of attending work regularly and working in a rigid environment has helped to instil an industrial work ethic as well as improve time management skills that help women to juggle their economic and domestic roles. Women who have joined work-related committees indicate that they are now more confident in speaking up in meetings and in voicing their opinions.

The experience of two groups of Free Zone workers in Jamaica and the Dominican Republic provide some interesting insights into the impact of the Free Zone on women workers. Operating in an anti-union climate in both countries did not stop the women from organising groups to represent their interests. Refusing to be intimidated by this climate, the depressing environment of their surroundings or the daily grind for survival in the living nightmare of structural adjustment, both groups of women have soldiered on. Community surveys among Free Zone workers have helped to identify priority needs as being basic education, skills training and, in the case of the Jamaican women, housing.

The St Peter Claver group was formed out of the survey, and it developed programmes to address some of the problems. With the support of the church as well as local and international development agencies, the St Peter Claver Women's Housing Co-operative was established. Funds raised overseas were used to purchase some of Jamaica's foreign debt on the secondary market, and this debt-swap provided them with a significant amount of money in Jamaican currency. This was used to purchase and renovate a number of houses in the community for co-op members. This group, together with other women's groups in Jamaica, has continued to lobby for improvements in wages and working conditions in the Zones. Many of the women interviewed reported that the experience of being involved in the co-operative has helped to develop their social and organisational skills.

Export-oriented industrialisation as a development strategy

Several other issues emerge in relation to FTZs in the Caribbean. At the macro level there is the question of whether export-oriented industrialisation is a development strategy that benefits women. Although the NICs of South-east Asia managed to establish viable economies, their export strategy was combined with an agricultural programme to improve food self-sufficiency. The experience of Caribbean countries is quite different. Whereas agriculture is important in countries like Jamaica and the Dominican Republic, the majority of small farmers, who are very often women and produce most of the food, do not have access to affordable credit, and therefore their production costs are high. This, combined with their limited volume of production, reduces their viability, which is worsened by competition from cheaper imports from countries which produce more and have lower production costs.

A separate, but related, factor is that there are few agro-processing Free Zone industries, which could provide an outlet for agricultural surpluses or add value to agricultural products. With a twelve-month growing season, agro-processing could absorb some of the large volume of products wasted each year.

The global economic climate is not as buoyant as it was during the period of growth of the NICs. It is therefore unlikely that countries in other regions will be able to pursue the same industrialisation strategy with equal success. There is also need to assess whether the benefits of technology transfer that host countries plan to derive from foreign investment can be achieved, and justifies the high cost of infrastructure for the Zones. Similarly, although foreign exchange is generated, it is limited to payment for low-waged local jobs and services. Ways of ensuring that a high proportion of skilled jobs are located in the host country are essential, and that these jobs be allocated to competent nationals, many of whom migrate to the North because they are unable to utilise their skills for adequate remuneration.

Although the FTZs are supposed to stimulate local production of goods that are linked to selected export production industries, the Caribbean experience is quite the contrary. Most investors are laterally and vertically integrated transnational companies. Most of their raw materials and other inputs come from different countries, to maximise profit and reduce production costs. Most countries in the Caribbean, however, lack the capacity to provide sufficient volume and quality of raw materials. There is very little investment to boost the textile sector, for example, which could develop local capacity for the garment industry.

Another knotty issue is the range of investment choices offered for long-term development. Government incentives to attract foreign investment are usually quite generous, and borrowings to finance them require approximately half of what is earned in foreign exchange, which leaves very little for essentials and real development programmes. Governments should therefore take a more critical look at the industries and investments they prioritise for long-term national development. The legislative framework also needs to be reassessed. The incentives mentioned are overwhelmingly more generous to the investor than to the host country. New legislation should help to redress the imbalance in the distribution of benefits and increase revenue from investment. The benefits could be greatly enhanced if they were more directly linked to a country's natural resource base and long-term development goals. This could include developing backward and forward linkages to agriculture, in a way that is environmentally sustainable.

Some strategies

Women now get most of the Free Zone jobs. Imagine how much more they could earn, and the benefits it would create, if highly skilled jobs were more available. Abolishing the sexual division of labour and providing training for women in non-traditional and more highly skilled jobs could boost production and enhance the multiplier benefits from the Zones. Affirmative action in employment policies could increase women's access to previously male-dominated jobs, such as plumbing and machine repairs, that are more highly paid. Work attitudes and productivity could change dramatically if employers changed their sexist perception of Free Zone workers as an easily dispensable commodity, and saw them as a long-term investment. Similarly, job security and scope for occupational mobility can be effective motivators for increasing productivity. Massive human potential is now lost because most workers remain at the same level for long periods.

Working conditions in many factories alienate and demotivate workers. The common practice of employing garment workers on extended probationary periods and dispatching them without compensation is such an example. Their statutory rights for maternity and other leave are affected by job tenure. Active monitoring and enforcing legislation would reduce the number of abuses and boost workers' morale. Regulations related to employment and dismissal also need to be monitored, to overcome the common practice in some factories of firing people in a seemingly arbitrary way, without regard to established practices. Ensuring that workers know their rights and responsibilities can help to ensure compliance and fair treatment across the board. A human relations training programme for supervisors, managers, personnel officers and other staff working in the Zones is essential for reducing conflict, improving job satisfaction, and boosting productivity.

The experience of Jamaica has shown that managers and supervisors from other cultures need adequate language and human relations training as well as cultural orientation, while workers also need training to understand cross-cultural differences related to the work environment. Asian supervisors in some factories in the Kingston Free Zone have created some problems in the past. Complaints about racism, and verbal and physical abuse, were alleged in newspaper reports. Similarly, in the Dominican Republic, there was a well documented case of a pregnant Free Zone worker who was kicked by an Asian supervisor and lost her baby. Some of these tensions are no doubt related to the rigid production norms, and exacerbated by differences in language and culture, which can be a recipe for disaster.

Respect for health and safety, and the provision of basic amenities of a reasonable standard, should also enhance workers' well-being. Health and canteen facilities are still grossly inadequate in many Free Trade Zones. In a 1987 survey of Jamaican Free Zone workers, many complained of back, shoulder, abdominal and joint pains, as well as headaches.[9] These were related to the positions in which they worked, the materials they handled or the rigid work discipline that did not allow them to visit the lavatories. Workers also need to be more aware of the dangerous materials to which they are exposed and their likely effects.

Safety also applies to office workers, again usually women, who may be exposed to visual display units for long periods. In Jamaica, there was evidence that fire safety regulations were not observed in some factories,[10] making it inevitable that there would be a high casualty rate in the event of a serious fire. Fire exits were blocked by stocks that would be difficult to move quickly, and other exits were locked for fear of theft of materials. Staff and workers were not clear on fire drill procedures. These conditions obtained in the case of the fire that killed garment workers in New York in 1910, the event that led to the establishment and observation of International Women's Day.

Where it does not exist, legislation and adequate monitoring are needed to ensure minimum standards for eating facilities and bathrooms.[11]

FTZs are usually located in isolated areas of towns or cities because of the space required for industrial estates. Security for workers (particularly women) arriving early or leaving very late is also a common problem. Although the laws of some countries prohibit women working on late or night shifts, violations occur because of the need to produce to deadlines to fill orders. Without proper monitoring, the exceptions become the rule, and in the process women can be abused.

The same applies to child labour. In the DR, there are reports of 14-year-old girls in full-time employment in the Zones. Interviews indicated that some had started to work at a very early age and that this was a common practice in some factories.[12] Given the state of the economy and the lack of employment alternatives, many of them are desperate for jobs at almost any cost, as this is the main source of their family income.

Conclusion

Several of these problems would be addressed if women workers' basic right to have adequate representation were respected; but it is often sacrificed to attract foreign investment. This would enable them to lobby for improvements in their conditions and wages. There is also much that women activists in developed countries can do, in addition to supporting women workers in their demands for labour representation, by lobbying for legislation in their respective countries that would encourage transnational companies to invest only in countries that observe international labour standards. Ethical investment may seem moralistic, but it could have a positive impact on workers – and on the environment – in many developing countries.

The inherent assumptions of the trickle-down theory must be questioned against the background of the actual experience of countries that have tried the export-oriented gendered industrialisation strategy. The inflationary nature of structural adjustment policies has contributed to reducing the standard of living of poor people, who seem never to be able to 'catch up' and become increasingly marginalised. Wages and working conditions within the Free Zones, which are so clearly based on gender, must be addressed and ways found to ensure a more equitable balance between the needs of nationals and transnationals, while working for long-term development that is environmentally sustainable.

Notes

1. Some authors, notably Peggy Antrobus, Clair Shaffer and 'Mabel Umfreville' (pseudonymous author of $£XONOMYC$, published by CHANGE) see that gender inequalities are used as the strategy itself, rather than merely impacting upon women.

2. See for example, *The Invisible Adjustment*, UNICEF/Caribbean, and Afshar and Dennis (eds), *Women and Adjustment in the Third World*, Macmillan, 1992.

3. See Froebel et al, 1980; Elson and Pearson, 1981.

4. L. Sklair, *Sociology of the Global System*, Harvester Wheatsheaf, London, 1990.

5. A. Abreu, M. Coco, C. Despradel, E. G. Michel and A. Peguero, 'Las Zonas Francas Industriales: el exito de una politica economica', Centro Interamericano para el Desarrollo Economico, Santo Domingo, 1989: 137.

6. F.A. Lorens, et al. 'Revolucion Tecnologica y Reestructuracion Productiva: Impactos y Desafios Territoriales', Coleccion Estudios Politicos y Sociales, Argentina, 1990.

7. Interviews with Free Zone workers, San Pedro de Macoris, February 1991.

8. L. Dunn, 'Women in Industry: a Participatory Research Project on Garment Workers in Jamaica', Joint Trades Union Research and Development Centre/CUSO, Kingston, 1987 (unpublished).

9. L. Dunn, 'Women in Industry', JTURDC-CUSO, Kingston, 1987 (mimeo).

10. Report by Women's Action Committee, Jamaica, 1991.

11. Interview with Free Zone manager in the Dominican Republic, February 1991.

12. Interview with Myra Jiminez, trade union leader in San Pedro de Macoris, February 1991.

7

Political Consumerism:
Concern and Action for Non-Sexist Advertising in some Latin American Countries

Ursula Paredes

Introduction

This chapter analyses the approach and strategies followed in some Latin American countries in the period 1989–91 to obtain legislation to control sexist expression in advertising. Some of the activities described were directly by the Women's Programme at the Regional Office for Latin America and the Caribbean of the International Organisation of Consumer Unions (IOCU), in Montevideo, Uruguay.[1] Others were carried out independently, or in co-ordination with that programme.

The experiment tried to synthesise the advances, and limits, of consumers' and feminist organisations in their endeavours to influence developments in advertising. The aim was to secure legal instruments to guarantee non-sexist advertising on television. From the outset, the challenge was recognised to be great. The proposal to regulate advertising was made amidst the strengthening of neo-liberal ideological thinking and economic policy proposals. To propose interventionist legislation was to go against the tide. It was even more daring to propose it for what mainstream thought considers a trivial issue, namely sexist advertising.

The advertising industry had been rather immune to women's protests in Latin American and European countries. The feminist movement had developed very profound analyses and arguments against sexism in advertising, but had not achieved a permanent and effective instrument to deter its use. This was probably due to the fact that the solutions were left in the hands of advertisers and mass media producers.

For example, in 1986 some women in the feminist movement asked advertising agencies and mass communication representatives to regulate advertising.[2] Feminist work to deter violence against women also pointed out the fact that mass media continually present images of violence against women. While there were no economic resources to develop research to confirm this intuition, it has been a permanent working hypothesis among feminists in Latin America. It is true that violence against women is multi-causal, but one cannot avoid the suspicion that one of the important factors is the manner of representation of women in the mass media.

How should we deal with sexist advertising when sexism permeates the whole of society? The disappearance of sexism has to do with material as well as ideological changes. Advertising is, of course, only a symptom of this phenomenon. Nobody imagined that sexism in society could be totally eliminated through the promotion of non-sexist advertising. Nevertheless, it was assumed that in industrial society, mass media are fundamental to the orientation, legitimation and consolidation of determined cultural patterns (culture being understood in its ideological as well as its material dimensions). Advertising being of such importance for the mass media, as the source of finance, the need to address it was obvious when considering consumers' or women's needs. The advertising industry, represented by advertisers' associations, recognises that advertising has a 'social function' alongside its main objective, which is to sell. In our perspective, this social function is the need to promote the ideology of consumption, and the concept that everything in modern society must enter the economic transactions through money exchange.[3]

A parallel phenomenon to the transnationalisation of production and consumption is the internationalisation of images. In advertising this means either that foreign advertising is transmitted in other countries with the same images, or that advertising for goods of foreign origin is locally produced. Legislation varies in relation to the kind of images permitted, and the forces of liberalisation are inclined to resist controls upon them.

The legal context: regulation v self-regulation

National chambers of commerce and advertisers in Latin America, be they affiliated or not to international organisations, are active and vocal in defence of the removal of existing legal constraints on marketing procedures, including advertising, and claim that their self-regulatory measures are enough to order commerce–consumer relations. To reinforce the arguments for regulation in the Latin American region, it was necessary to compare the contexts in which advertising works. It was argued that in most European countries the discussion as to self-regulation of advertising takes place in a context of practically all television channels being in public hands (this debate started in 1989). Conversely, in Latin America, broadcasting is generally privately owned.[4]

Self-regulation is a constant theme for advertisers. The International Code on Advertising, published by the International Chamber of Commerce, asserts that this mechanism is geared 'to promoting high ethical standards in marketing, through self-regulation' and claims that such regulation shows that industry and commerce, including all the parties involved in advertising, recognise their social responsibilities vis-à-vis the consumer and the community .... The International Chamber of Commerce, with this new Code edition, will facilitate the circulation of goods and services through frontiers for the benefit of consumers worldwide.[5]

The principles of this Code require conformity 'to the principles of fair concurrence, as normally accepted in business' and state that advertisements 'should not harm the public trust with respect to advertising'. In addition to functioning as an instrument for self-discipline that guarantees fair competition among producer–advertisers, as well as to preserve its credibility, the Code is designed to be used in courts as a reference document within the structure of appropriate national laws. In practice, it is used by national advertisers' associations as a pattern to establish self-regulatory measures in different Latin American countries, often without additions or reformulation.[6]

Certain groups of advertisers in Latin America, as in other parts of the world, oppose state regulation, arguing that there is no need for more regulatory measures. Latin Americans add that the state has already developed an excessive number of laws, and that the standards authority is in crisis, most of the regulations being obsolete or inapplicable. This is, as a diagnosis, not incorrect.[7] Nevertheless, the discrepancy is in relation to the solution: non-regulation or new applicable laws. In some countries the argument is also that there is no need to regulate advertising, as it plays a secondary role, owing to the small size and poverty of the market. This is not true, as the majority of products advertised on TV are for mass consumption: they are products for personal cleanliness and personal beauty, as well as domestic cleaning and industrialised food products, and beverages. There are also those which have reached wide sectors of populations, as they are linked to special financing for private consumption, for example of television sets and refrigerators, and to the widening of markets.

Advertisers argue that advertising control is synonymous with control of the mass media and of freedom of the press, and that it reflects a totalitarian mentality. Critics of self-regulation counter-argue that regulation is not totalitarianism but is more democratic as it includes consumers' voices, and thus overcomes the limitations of advertisers alone drawing up standards and regulating themselves.

Definitions used to identify sexism in advertising

Sexism is a social phenomenon. In daily life males and females are perceived and treated in a different manner, and this difference is used to the detriment of women in society. Furthermore, women are subordinated to men, as the differences are located in a hierarchical system, with superordinate individuals being male. In this system women, given the social relations of gender, are subject to oppression. Sexism permeates all institutions and activities; logically, advertising is also permeated by it. Feminists strive to eliminate discrimination and subordination of women, and to establish new forms of relations among people and their environment.

When analysing advertising, it was necessary to look at the different ways in which this discrimination and subordination appears. The first aspect to be addressed was discrimination. Discrimination against either sex (or in relation to national or ethnic origin, health and age) was a target for our arguments for legislation to deter sexism in advertising. A second aspect referred to women's subordination to men, and the third was a specific expression of this subordination: violence against women. This aspect was selected due to the fact that it is so blatant in advertising that it is easily recognised. The distinction was made for practical reasons, so as to be able to transmit the central points to the people we met, and to convince them of the importance of eliminating each expression of sexism in advertising.

A complementary perspective was developed through the years. Namely, the distinction between a sexist advertisement and sexism in advertising. That is, if one believes that the evaluation of individual advertisements as sexist is personal, each one can be a matter of interminable debate. Nevertheless, sexism in advertising is not a matter of controversy, as it can be demonstrated in the sum of sexist advertisements. The fact that advertising could be synthesised into a woman as logo corroborates this sexism.

The first definition used to identify 'sexist advertising' was originally adopted from Ekman and Stigbrand:[8]

> By 'offensive advertisements' we mean presentations which can be discriminating against one sex. That is, they relate a message which is in some way intended to degrade the sex in question.
>
> By 'stereotypical advertisements' (or sex-role preserving) we mean presentations which do not actually contain a blatantly offensive message, but which mirror thinking in terms of traditional sex roles, and thereby counteract efforts to achieve equality between males and females.

Discussion of these definitions posed difficulties in 'drawing the line' between the two. They were used as working definitions. For practical reasons a more embracing definition was adopted: 'discriminatory against either sex'.[9] The standard for evaluation was to be compliance with UN agreements and the Convention on the Elimination of All Forms of Discrimination Against Women, as well as national constitutions declaring equal rights for men and women.

New criteria to distinguish sexist ads were also developed, again based on the Swedish criteria, enriched by the most frequent ones used in Latin America and the Caribbean:

1. Discriminatory advertisements

- Images of women (and men) used with the purpose of attracting attention. The presence of women has no relation or relevance to the product.[10]
- Women depicted in an 'unnatural' or abnormal situation: they are out of context.
- Women represented in 'real-life' situations: eg, Carnival costumes, dancing as starlets, in swimming costumes at the beach. These 'real-life' situations are out of context and chosen as an excuse to expose women's partially naked bodies.
- Women's bodies presented in unnatural positions.
- Women making sexual insinuations, promises irrelevant to the product.
- Women and men represented in the same way, with presentation of 'erotic' body parts at the centre of attention. Women's bodies are fragmented, certain body parts are selected as erotic – lips, breasts, hips, legs. This resource is discriminatory even though the product may be related to the images.
- Women represented as decorative objects.

2. Stereotypical advertisements

Advertising that strengthens stereotypes about genders in society. Reinforcement of sex-stereotyping. Skills and ambitions presented in a manner that can be expected to work against efforts to achieve equality. For characteristics and personality traits of either sex:

- Women are young, skinny or medium-weight, with fair skin and primarily blonde and rich.
- Representation of women as getting their self-esteem through others. Women's objective is to satisfy others, either in nurturing roles, or in sexual ones.
- Women's prime interest being to 'catch a man' and get married.
- Women as rich, careless, and full of buying-power thanks to a man.

- Women as narcissistic, caring only about their physical appearance.
- Males caring fundamentally for prestige and money.
- Women represented as unable to decide for themselves.
- Women as infantilised, represented as scared, incompetent, fearful.
- Women as easily impressed and awe-struck by young, handsome men in a high socio-economic position.

For each sex's working life:

- False images of male–female contribution to working life.
- Women frequently represented in maternal roles, men scarcely represented in paternal roles.
- Discrimination of sex combined with social discrimination (for example, housemaids/virginity).
- Women represented as predestined to do housework, sometimes as obsessive and neurotic, trapped by a cleanliness mania.
- Males mostly presented as exclusively involved in labour market situations.

For sexual relations among people; sexuality linked to age, beauty and money; the way sexuality and sexual relations between the sexes are treated:

- Women are passive creatures, decorative items, to be touched by men or touch themselves for males' pleasure.
- Women at the disposal of men.

3. **Violent advertisements: advertising that shows or suggests violence against women**
- Language contributing directly and indirectly to the physical or verbal violation of women.
- Use of children and youngsters in sexist advertising.
- Youngsters and children act sexually in ways that they would not imagine or act out on their own.
- Advertisements suggesting the willingness and disposition of children for sexual intercourse. Suggestions of incestuous relations.
- 'Machismo' praised.
- Violence in society exalted.

There are certain key concepts for the International Advertising Association when discussing sexism in advertising. Namely, 'decency', 'sexism', 'sexuality' and 'sexual objectification'.[11] However, their evaluation of 'products and categories of services that generate the largest number of complaints on particular issues' reflects the industry's self-regulatory standards. This includes the following concepts: 'decency and good taste', 'sex-role stereotypes', 'exaggerated use of sexuality', 'women used as lure or attention-getters', 'sexual violence'.[12] Their definition combines the articles of the standards for self-regulation as well as the study published in 1987 in Sweden by the National Swedish Board for Consumer Policies (NSBCP). The first concept they use has a reference to upper-class taste and to traditional morality. The second refers to discrimination against either sex and to the use of stereotypes. The third has to do with the distinction between erotism and pornography. The last ones refer to discrimination. Dialogue with producers, creative directors and legal representatives followed the same lines, summarised as follows:

- If society is 'machista' (sexist), advertising will also be, to be in tune with this kind of society. Otherwise, there would be a rejection of the messages. Advertising reflects reality.
- Advertising respects culture, and cannot contradict traditional values about women's and men's position in society. This suggests that cultural values are traditionally sexist and immutable.
- Advertisers produce what consumers want. The best test is the market. If they did not produce what the consumer asked for, they would go bankrupt.
- Advertisers produce what industrialists and business people want. They themselves have little say in the requirements of those who contract them .
- Advertisers respect consumers, who form a critical mass. Efforts legally to control advertisements are based on disrespect for consumers.
- They know what consumers want because they do surveys and market research, asking men and women for their opinions.
- They also ridicule women working for legal action against sexism.
- They insult women working for legal action against sexism in advertising.
- They argue that women models would be without jobs if it were not for their use in advertising campaigns.
- They are producing beauty.
- They are producing technical quality.
- They are for freedom of expression.
- They do not mistreat or demean women.
- They are a source of beauty, sensuality and eroticism.
- They classify feminist demands as moralistic.
- Sexist advertising exists, but they consider that they are not to blame for it. They personally do not produce it; it's a problem for other producers.

- Sexist advertisement is bad advertisement, low quality.
- Advertisers mirror society and discrimination exists; they do not create it but simply present what there is and what people like.

The methodology

The strategy was to try to obtain consensus about the existence of sexist advertisments on TV, which reaches more people than the written media and is the most dynamic medium, reflecting the latest developments in the advertising industry. Together with this, the discussion about the importance of legislation for advertising was fostered, pointing out the limitations of the industry's self-regulatory mechanisms. 'Sexism in advertising, a woman consumers' concern' was taken as the model to demonstrate the limitations of self-regulation.

The opportunity to work with government bodies as well as with non-governmental consumers' organisations was very important to the work. The possibilities of developing international actions were also very valuable, so as to analyse information from different countries and to contrast views from different disciplines. Three international meetings were organised, one in Chile in May 1989; another in Lima in November 1990; the last one in Ecuador in June 1991.

It was deemed important that action should be directed simultaneously towards sensitising governments, reaching advertisement producers and mobilising public opinion.

Different actions and results

Mexico: advertising demystification and contests: Mexico has a consumer law that includes government supervision of advertising. The National Consumers' Institute works regularly on content analysis, and publishes articles comparing advertisements with the consumers' regulations. In September 1989, the Director General of the National Consumers' Institute in Mexico wrote:

> Among the consumer guidance and education functions entrusted to the National Consumers' Institute by the Federal Consumer Protection Law, an important place is held by those related to the use and understanding of advertising as a source of information on which to base consumer decisions and as an element affecting the creation and development of consumer habits.[13]

As part of a consciousness-raising programme directed at consumers, they developed a series of micro-programmes for TV in which they showed how advertising is produced. The public was informed how the different mechanisms and techniques used in advertising appeal psychologically to the viewer. After the presentation of the series, they announced a contest for consumers to judge the best and the worst TV commercial.

Argentina: In Argentina, two different strategies can be identified. On the one hand, that developed by certain groups in communications; on the other, that developed by a consumers' organisation made up of housewives, and controlled by upper-class women. The first strategy was not concurrent with the work described here. It refers to the production of alternative advertising by a group of sensitive women and motivated by the feminist movement. These ads presented the different attitudes of males and females towards the social division of labour, and were more educational than commercial. More recently, certain feminists in the media consider that advertising in Argentina is changing in its presentation of images of women and men. Men are presented doing other kinds of work, and with naked bodies exposed.

The second strategy refers to consumers' action on the truthfulness of advertising, as well as on the quality of information it gives about the product offered. This being the priority, they consider that the problems of sexism are covered by the 'decency and morality' provisions of the industry's self-regulatory codes of conduct. The Argentinian House-wives' League is a case in point. Stimulated by the women's programme, they decided to work against advertising that degrades or humiliates women. They exhorted certain producers and advertising 'creators' to desist from the elaboration of messages 'that degrade women, and that, finally, are deficient from the point of view of the information that they need to give to the consumers about the characteristics of the products that they want to sell'.[14] Their approach was to eliminate certain ads from TV. They sought to obtain the endorsement of powerful groups, such as the Church hierarchy, for dialogue with producers, and used the public threat of a boycott against products that use images of women in 'degrading' ways. This campaign was for consciousness-raising, as these issues were discussed on TV programmes, on radio and in national meetings. They claim that they obtained the withdrawal of certain specific ads for jeans. The action, nevertheless, was left in the hands of those producing advertising.

The campaign for legal action

Peru: A non-governmental organisation, DEMUS (Legal Study for the Defence of Women's Rights) decided to start a campaign to obtain legal sanctions to control sexist advertising. Working mainly in cases of violence against women, they are convinced that the images and messages exhibited in the mass media contribute to the construction and legitimation of violence against women.

They started legal actions, linking these activities to the women's movement in Lima, by lodging a series of complaints related to sexist advertising with the Social Communication Office of the National Institute of Social Communication (INACOSO). In November 1989, they lodged five complaints: three referring to television advertisements and two concerning advertisements published in a daily newspaper; they were against a financial institution (a bank), two jeans advertisers (Wrangler and Levi's) and two coffee theatres. Their objective was to 'reassess the image of women in advertising'. At the same time, they discussed the issue within the organised women's movement in Lima, requesting support and adherence to their claims. The result was a well publicised campaign accompanying their legal claims, which were based on a legal decree, and supported

> in the provisions of the Convention on the Elimination of All Forms of Discrimination Against Women ... which stipulates that the countries who are parties to the Convention shall take the appropriate measures to eliminate discrimination against women on the part of any person, organization or company, applying the respective sanctions ... and that it should be the responsibility of the State to take measures to eliminate discrimination against women in this area [advertising].[15]

They also based the demand on a conception that 'advertising, beyond its merely commercial role, fulfils an educational function in that it modifies behaviour through the use of images', given the 'decisive role that the media play in the perception of our surroundings'. Later, they also started legal action against a beer company, 'Cristal Beer', from Backus and Johnston brewery, whose ad shows a group of young people at the beach, looking at three women in bathing suits, in order to choose one – 'the blonde everyone likes' – which is the beer in question. DEMUS claimed that the advertisement violates national regulations and that it 'exploits the physical aspect of women, identifying them with a consumer product'.

The brewery strongly opposed the complaint and kept the advertisement on the air throughout the scheduled period. They appealed to 'the right to freedom of speech and dissemination of ideas through words, in writing or through images, by any social communication media, without prior authorisation, censorship or any impediment whatsoever'. DEMUS's counter-argument was that commercial advertising falls within the freedom of commerce laws, 'since the objective of advertising is to induce the sale of products'. Freedom of speech, they argued, refers to the transmission of ideas or values. 'In this sense, advertising does not enjoy the licence proper to freedom of speech and instead is subject to restrictions inherent to the freedom of trade.' The company was penalised with the immediate banning of the commercial. This was important in terms of setting a precedent, but the time the case took, with the company's appeal and the legal process, coincided with the period the brewery had scheduled in any case.

The resolution was of such importance that part of the media immediately reacted against the resolution, attacking both the director of the National Social Communication Institute (a woman) and Dr Rossana Favero, one of the two women who signed the demand for DEMUS.[16]

In DEMUS, the linkage of image with violence was shown as follows:

> Daily we have before us images and messages that attempt to show reality, subtly or flagrantly slipping in a whole battery of oppression and discriminations, that attack common mortals from all sides, forcing them to admit as examples of behaviour those that the predominant social milieu sets as desirable. Turning women into objects as a consumer product and their use to strengthen traditional roles allocated to their persons, is one of the axes of this oppressive range that impregnates the routines of our country's advertisers.

They further argue that the Special Senate Commission on the Cause of Violence and Peace Alternatives in Peru recommended that: 'programmes containing violence, morbid eroticism and conflicting social relations should be avoided ... the same applies to promotional advertisements in commercial spots'. With respect to advertising, DEMUS states that 'its main objective is the sale of goods and services. Furthermore, its contents reflect forms of behaviour, of relationship and of social appraisal of one sex by another and, finally, of transmission of models of behaviour that show diverse forms of violence against women.'

DEMUS went on to file complaints against another brewery, for the 'Danker Beer' advertising, arguing that it is discriminatory against women in so far as it degrades the dignity of the person and works to the detriment of her condition as a human being. The ad shows a group of young men 'feeding' a computer with information, saying 'she has to have a good body', 'she must be golden', introducing pictures of women into the machine. In this way 'they make express association of the object that is being sold with the woman's figure'. They also argued against an ad from Casio calculators which says: 'Casio, beautiful silhouette' together with a woman's picture. The text says, 'The new calculators-printers ... are so beautiful to see, as easy to use ... ' This suggests the possibility of 'using' women. 'Advertising comprises what it says and the form in which it presents things. In recent developments we observe a tendency to associate women with products of daily use. We believe this helps to interiorise the idea that a woman is an object for consumption and manipulation ... '

DEMUS women also tried to make an impact on the mass media. They slowly gained access to spaces traditionally closed to such discussion, first on the public television channels, with low audiences. Feminists in Peru took up the issue and published articles about it in all their magazines. The debate was resumed after some years of silence with new arguments linked to possible legal sanctions. Rossana Favero, a lawyer, was later invited to discuss the issue in high-status television programmes on private channels. The debate had an impact and interested public opinion.

Round-tables within feminist circles, as well as at the university, were organised. The Peruvian feminist movement mobilised on the issue, and it was debated on International Women's Day, 8 March, linked to violence against women. It also attracted the attention of international feminist organisations.

At the beginning of 1991 DEMUS held a contest for non-sexist advertising scripts. The response from advertising producers, and others, was very large, with hundreds of scripts received, according to Dr Favero. Two prizes were allocated, one to the best and one to the worst, in consultation with the public. The first contest was held for Alternative Advertisments. DEMUS called together feminist non-governmental organisations, NGOs producing video and movies, and an international network working on women's legal rights, for the contest.[17]

After the international meeting, and using the agreements reached in November 1990, DEMUS sent a package with all the information on the seminar to President Fujimori and to Genaro Delgado Parker, president of the Radio and Television Association. In August 1990, the government de-activated INACOSO, leaving advertising control in the hands of the National Advertising Council. DEMUS demanded the creation of a Control Body that brings together the state, advertisers, consumers, social movements and mass media representatives. Another of DEMUS's actions has been to ask the judiciary to guarantee that its offices are not decorated with posters of nude women or with women used as 'attention-getters'. They argue that women should not be obliged to denounce a violation to any officer who has such a picture hanging on the wall. Their anxiety was heard.

Brazil: In 1990, the Brazilian people obtained a new Consumer Defence Code. Its need as a special body of legislation had been argued for because, until then, consumer rights had been subsumed under the civil code. This meant that consumers had been seen as individuals in relation to consumption. The new code implied that purveyors of mass production and mass consumption assumed responsibilities towards individuals. Advertising was regulated, on the grounds that it was impossible to accept self-regulation, as such a system would imply the acceptance of the principle that one body alone defines the law, judges, executes and penalises. Legislators also took the position that the advertiser does not necessarily reflect the views of all the media, and that the law should allow consumers to take their demands to the courts.

The Director of the Consumers' Protection Office in São Paulo considered that the law guarantees 'supply' and its necessary complement, 'advertisement'.[18] Brazilian legislation prohibits 'misleading' as well as 'abusive' advertising. The first refers to 'any method of information or communication as advertisement, wholly or partially false, or that in any other way, including omission, is able to mislead consumers about the nature, characteristics, qualities, quantities, origin, price or any other information on products and services'. On the other hand,

> abusive implies ... discriminating advertisement of any kind, encouraging violence, exploiting fear or superstition, taking advantage of lack of judgement or experience of children, unrespectful of environmental values, or able to induce consumers to behave in any way that is damaging or dangerous to their health or security ... if this type of advertisement were not prohibited, it would be possible to use the mass media to disseminate sexual or racial discrimination among others. The prohibition of abusive advertising on its own, will make it possible for advertising to be serious and responsible, avoiding turning people, and especially women, into objects, discouraging acts of violence, or the use of children to sell products, etc.[19]

This is embedded in a consumers' law perspective that assumes the need for vigilance over the general, collective and individual rights of the people.

Conclusions

The feminist movement has developed very strong arguments against sexism in advertising, and has been able to influence some government policy formulation. Government officials, as well as executives and workers in the advertising industry, have in-built sensitivity to the issue, as well as strong defence mechanisms based on prejudice. Nevertheless, government officials as well as advertisers are sensitive to women's issues wherever there has been women's pressure. This has several explanations. One, referring to advertisers, is that women are a sector of the population considered important for certain advertising campaigns. Identified as a special market, women in general and certain sectors of women in particular are treated with some deference. The International Advertising Association is aware of this fact, when it states:

> The activism of religious and feminist groups clearly impacts on the relaxation or stiffening of standards ... a vocal minority of women are increasingly objecting to the depreciation of their sex (e.g. in the Netherlands, Norway, Portugal and Sweden) and to commercials about personal-hygiene products (e.g. in Canada and the United States). They oppose ads that belittle women, insult their intelligence, or depict them in an offensive manner, imply sex inequalities, or display violence against them.[20]

Advertisers tend to be much more careful with images of women in the production of ads directed to women than in those produced for a male audience. Their strategies are different. Women's sensitivity is not important when the sale-targets are men. Most advertising violent to women is directed to men and pursues their interest. This is the case for the kind of ads that suggest that women will be reachable through or together with the product promoted. Women are 'offered' to the male audience as a side benefit when buying certain products.

The description of one ad in the Uruguayan advertisers' magazine is illustrative. On a full page, a woman occupies the left one-third of the page. Her picture, largely in black and white, depicts her from head to groin, without arms, cut out from the picture. She has bikini pants on, a bare stomach, while a piece of red cloth covers part of her breast. The upper part of her breasts up to her shoulders are also naked. The picture is accompanied by a text that says, 'Look at her, touch her, feel her, blow her, wash her, wrinkle her, dry her, wring her.'[21] The advertisement is for cloth used in the manufacture of banners. It is for industrial consumption, and, given the prevalent division of labour, the most probable buyers of this cloth will be men. Violence is present in the imperative way the prospective buyers are addressed. The same magazine also says elsewhere, 'Young and Rubicam believe in free love. Our secretaries do not ... '

Women do not automatically reject violence in TV advertisements but, in general, it irritates them. Most violence is linked to authoritarian advertising, which seems to be directed at women with less problem than is the overtly violent. Violence against women therefore legitimises authoritarianism in TV ads and these, in turn, probably legitimise violence against women.

When addressing changes in sexism within advertising, it should be understood that change must be permanent. The strategy against particular advertisements, as well as the presentation of different images of women, are both important steps, but in themselves do not imply real changes in the culture of sexist advertising, as demonstrated in the Argentinian case, for example. Legislation to control advertising is important to deter sexist advertising, as the Mexican experience demonstrates. Nevertheless the fact that this strategy started as a state initiative, with no participation of an independent and identifiable group of feminists putting their demands across, restricts the influence on government. This might be the situation in Brazil, depending on the participation of the women's movement in the application of Brazil's law.

Effective action takes a long time, with advances and steps backwards, as demonstrated by the Peruvian experience. It requires the ability to generate a common perspective for a series of actions, and not only for a content analysis, or for mounting an isolated contest, or obtaining the withdrawal of one or more television advertisements. The benefits of obtaining legislative measures demanded by a movement, and properly monitored by its participants, is a guarantee of more permanent change.

Notes

1. My thanks to Rossana Favero in Peru, Patricia Garce in Uruguay and Maicen Ekman in Sweden. Part of the work described was financed for the IOCU, Regional Office for Latin America and the Caribbean, by the International Non-Governmental Organisation Division of the Canadian International Development Agency. The Swedish Embassy in Uruguay contributed to the Swedish presence. My special thanks also to Nea Filgueira, of GRECMU – Grupo de Estudios de la Condicion de la Mujer de Uruguay.

2. (MUJER-FEMPRESS No. 62) 'the elimination of women's treatment as sexual object and vice seductress as it occurs in the advertising for cigarettes and alcohol'. The Ecuadorian CECIM had asked the industry to sign an 'Honour Treaty' with them so that it 'self-regulates the limitation of programmes and advertising that make an apology for violence, promiscuity, devaluing of the human being in general and of women in particular'.

3. An argument that proved to be very effective within the consumers' organisations is that advertisers are vendors. In the same way as door-to-door selling techniques need to be regulated, other vendors who 'enter the house without knocking on the door' need regulation of their activities. Advertising, as part of the marketing process, needs to guarantee that the demand be equal to the volume of production. The interpretation made by many of them about their 'social responsibility' is that they should take care when transmitting messages through the mass media. There is a recognition that the images they transmit are powerful, and have a recognised impact on people. Even in the case that one of their objectives – to sell – is not satisfied, the other is always functioning.

4. In Europe, only in France was broadcasting 99.43 per cent publicly owned and 0.53 per cent commercial. In Latin America and the Caribbean, there are cases where it was wholly commercial, such as in Argentina, Ecuador, Paraguay and the Dominican Republic; where there is a government-public-commercial mix, such as in Mexico – the proportions are 53-6-41 per cent – Brazil, with 1-9-90 per cent; or Venezuela, with 44-2-54 per cent, respectively. Or with a public–commercial mix, such as in Costa Rica, with 8 and 92 per cent, or Panama, with 7 per cent and 93 per cent respectively; in Cuba it is totally governmental. The information we were working with was from 1987. See 'Latest Statistics on Radio and Television Broadcasting'. In: *UNESCO Statistical Reports and Studies*, Paris 1987, No. 29, Table 10.3. This proportion is changing, especially in the European countries where there is strong pressure to take television broadcasting into private hands. In Latin America the reverse, of course, is not occurring.

5. Spanish version reproduced in *La Voz de Consumidor*, Vol. VI, No. 2, April–June 1988, p. 7. My retranslation into English.

6. An exception is found in Brazil, where the advertisers' association developed, within the pattern, new and modern measures, adding clauses such as the one referring to environmental protection, for example.

7. For example, in Peru in 1989 an advertiser might spend US$5,000–6,000 in producing a TV spot, and has to pay the equivalent of a maximum of US$6 as penalty for any violation of the few existing norms. This, of course, results in very little interest in the laws on the part of producers.

8. Maicen Ekman and Karin Stigbrand. The National Swedish Board for Consumer Policies. *Sexist Advertising – What is That? Basis for a discussion.* 1987.

9. The concept of discrimination against women in advertising was the argument we started to use. That is, women are not represented in the same way as men, nor in the same position. Studies done with the 'content analysis' methodology are very clear at pointing this out. Nevertheless, this argument was insufficient, as we were not pointing out advertisements where men are shown as 'sexual objects', if that were possible. We maintain this is not possible as the representation of women is discriminatory as women are subordinated in society. It happens the same with racial/ethnic representations which are discriminatory. It was not uncommon, during the different discussions, to find people who would say, 'men are also discriminated against'. Even though the discussants could bring a couple of examples, they were the exception. Nevertheless, we found that it was strategically important to stress that we wanted to eliminate discrimination towards men or women in TV commercial spots.

10. Circular Letter. Consumer Issues Related to Women, No. 4, July–September 1989, p. 10.

11. 'Decency refers to conformity to recognised standards of propriety, good taste and modesty. In advertising, such standards typically concern: 1) sensitive issues (for example contraception); 2) the use of tasteless images, vulgar language and offensive appeals; 3) the promotion of 'very personal' goods and services such as undergarments, feminine-hygiene products, contraceptives and massages, and 4) the advertising of tobacco products, alcoholic beverages, pornographic materials, violence-ridden films and comic books, as well as other items whose consumption is considered as undesirable by some people. Sexism concerns distinctions which diminish or demean one sex in comparison with the other, particularly through the use of sex-role stereotypes. It partakes of the broader contemporary concern with derogatory references to sex, race, age, social status, handicaps and the like. Sexuality is about the use of sexual imagery or suggestion ('sexiness') as the primary attention-getter for consumers. It is based on the assumption that 'sex sells', although its use is sometimes combined with the depiction of violence against women in advertising. Sexual objectification (or reification) refers to the use of women (mostly) as decorative or attention-getting objects, with little or no relevance to the goods or services advertised. (Boddewyn, 1989: p. 2, underlined in the original). International Advertising Association-IAA. *Sexism and Decency in Advertising. Government Regulation and Industry Self-Regulation in 47 Countries.* Report prepared by J. J. Boddewyn, Ph.D. Professor of International Business. Baruch College. City University of New York. 1989.

12. Circular Letter, *Consumer Issues Related to Women,* No. 6: 10, January–March 1990.

13. Circular letter, *Mujeres y Consumo* No. 15, IOCU, 1988: p. 9.

14. Ibid.

15. *Circularletter, Consumer Issues Related to Women,* No.5: 10, October–December 1989 for this and following quotations.

16. She had also sent a letter to a magazine protesting at the comparison of 'women's bodies to mermaids … who, while they don't run the risk of being raped, do run the risk of being eaten', as read the original text. Dr Favero wrote, 'In an

environment like ours, in which there is specific violence against women, texts like this contribute to promoting that we continue to be treated as items for consumption, and that the issue of rape – which affects a great number of women – be treated in such a humiliating way.' The magazine responded, among other things, 'We ask Dr. Favero ... if she is a good-looking lawyer, we offer her a full page to publish her photo in the nude.' For the further story of DEMUS see Rossana Favero Gomez, *De imagen a Protagonista. Circular Letter. Consumer Issues Related to Women*, No. 9: 10, January–March 1991.

17. The call to participate was made by Centro de la Mujer Peruana Flora Tristan, the Latin American Committee for Women's Rights (CLADEM), Manuela Ramos Movement, Chaski (a TV and movie producer), SEM-IPS (Inter Press Service), Warmi video and movie collective, Women and Society, Women Documentation Center (CENDOC-Mujer).

18. Jose Geraldo Brito Filomeno, legal attorney, at that time Co-ordinator of the Promoters of Consumer Protection at São Paulo (Brazil)'s Public Ministry. In Circular Letter No. 9: 3, January–March 1991.

19. Marcelo Gomez Sodre. Director of São Paulo's Consumers Secretariat (PROCON). Circular Letter. Consumer Issues Related to Women, No. 9: 4, January–March 1991.

20. Boddewyn, for International Advertising Association-IAA, op. cit.

21. In Spanish, things as well as persons can be feminine or masculine, and in syntax the article is annexed to the verb.

8

Tradition Against Health: The Struggle for Change

Olayinka Koso-Thomas

Introduction

In many communities of the world, beliefs and practices have been handed down from generation to generation without their usefulness or, in some cases, their harmful effects, being questioned. In some of these communities, awareness of the evils of blind belief and adherence to tradition has led to the elimination of those customs which adversely affected their lives. Unfortunately, this enlightenment is not shared throughout the world. In regions where tradition has a strong hold over the lives of ordinary people, the will to examine these beliefs and customs is suppressed, or at least frowned upon, by community leaders and others whose interests may be jeopardised by any shift of allegiance or change in belief patterns.

Beliefs and customs are in themselves necessary social elements. Their values are recognised and accepted in the framework of human development. However, in most African countries, as well as in many other parts of the world, certain traditions which have been kept intact for generations have had serious effects on the health of the population. The continuation of one of these traditions remains baffling to those who understand its consequences, feel its impact on their lives, and suffer from its brutal application. It is the practice of what has been called female circumcision (fc), but owing to the severity of the operation and its objectives, is now commonly called female genital mutilation (fgm). In its most serious form, the operation effectively mutilates the female genitalia, removing healthy parts of the female body (the clitoris, labia minora and labia majora), while the remaining skin is pulled together and, except for a small opening, is stitched together. The three main types of fgm practised are clitoridectomy, excision and infibulation.

Clitoridectomy is the removal of the prepuce or foreskin which protects the clitoris. Excision is the removal of the prepuce, the clitoris itself and all or part of the labia minora, leaving the labia majora and the rest of the vulva intact. Infibulation entails removal of the prepuce and the whole of the labia minora and majora, and the suturing together of the two sides of the vulva, leaving a very small orifice to permit the flow of urine and menstrual blood.[1] This practice is accepted as conferring the status of womanhood. It is believed to enhance fertility, remove ugly protrusions, keep the female clean, prevent promiscuity and stillbirths in primigravida, promote social and political cohesion and increase matrimonial opportunities. It is also believed to improve male sexual performance and pleasure.

There is no logical or scientific basis for these beliefs. In most cases, the opposite of the advantages claimed is true. Where there are 'benefits' resulting from the practice, such as the increase of matrimonial opportunities and the promotion of social and political cohesion, held to be important in some communities, it would be senseless to assume that such benefits could compensate for the permanent damage done to an individual's health. The mutilated female is exposed to a wide range of health problems, a number of which develop immediately or shortly after undergoing the operation; other problems develop later in life. The most serious of the immediate problems are: acute urinary retention, septicaemia, tetanus, pelvic infection, and dysmenorrhoea (pain experienced during menstruation). Later complications may include: infertility, prolonged and obstructed labour, fistulae, prolapse and mental and sexual problems.

Women living in societies where fgm is accepted as normal feel obliged to make whatever sacrifice is necessary to satisfy the dictates of tradition. For the ordinary woman in Africa, and some other parts of the developing world, this sacrifice means submission not only to continual child-bearing and domesticity but also to the pain and suffering from the compulsory mutilation of parts of their bodies. In essence, this is part of the package which entrenches male domination in patriarchal societies, and which is responsible for keeping the majority of women outside the mainstream of national life. It is clear that the quiet and suffering majority are in many cases unable to link fgm ailments to their earlier experience. However, there is enough evidence available today to establish this link.

There have been initiatives by concerned individuals, and international organisations, to stop the practice; some African governments have even taken steps to ban it. But progress in eliminating fgm has been insignificant. Opposing the mass of evidence provided in recent years to the world community, both by researchers investigating fgm, and by those who have personal experience of the great suffering which it brings, stand the institutional mechanisms and support structures which keep the practice in place. A full understanding of these is required if we are to formulate effective strategies to eliminate it.

Supporting structures for the practice

It is believed that the practice of fgm originated simultaneously in different parts of the world where, in early times, communities felt it necessary to introduce control over the sexual behaviour of women. The early Romans, the early Europeans, the ancient Arabs and other national groups are known to have introduced certain forms of sex barriers which, in some cases, involved clitoridectomy. It is known also that such a measure was taken to 'cure' certain sexual conditions, such as nymphomania, epilepsy and insanity. Except for its application for curative purposes, it is not certain how communities outside Africa regulated the practice. In more recent times, it has derived support from religious and traditional organisations. In many parts of Africa the religion most often quoted as demanding the practice among its followers is Islam. But this religious linkage does not exist in the cradle and seat of Islam; Saudi Arabia, for example, does not practice it, neither do Algeria, Iran, Iraq, Libya, Morocco or Tunisia. When carried out under the control of religious and traditional organisations, fgm can take place either individually or in groups. It can be done privately, in the home of a family member, or under the sponsorship of special traditional societies in 'spiritually protected' premises. Because of the secrecy observed among members of such societies in some parts of Africa, they are usually called 'secret societies'. Independent operations can be arranged even in families where there is a tradition of 'secret society' membership, particularly when school work and school calendars do not permit joining a society's programme. In cases where children refuse to join the 'secret society' or to undergo the process independently, they are often taken away, and the operation is performed forcibly. Individual adult converts to the practice, or those who for some reason missed it in childhood, may also opt for an independent operation.

These operations can be carried out in the traditional manner, as they are in 'secret societies', or in modern clinics. Citizens of countries which practise fgm who emigrate to places where it is not practised, sometimes make private arrangements to have it carried out on their children, either in private clinics or by operators brought out from their country of origin for the purpose. Some affluent families have taken their daughters to private clinics in Europe to have the operation under general anaesthesia and in hygienic surroundings superior to those available in their home countries.

In a few countries, particularly in Africa, when fgm is performed in groups – often a 'secret society' – it is part of an initiation ceremony. At times, a 'secret society' wishing to increase the number of initiates at particular periods of its activities may go out on a 'recruitment drive' to encourage families to send in their children, and may even kidnap children belonging to families which do not support the practice. These societies are well established and undertake other functions, including highly regulated training for young girls in the performance of their feminine roles in the home and community. At the end of this training there is some social celebration, which can be attractive, and may include the presentation of gifts.

The timing of the operation on young girls is based on custom, depending on the religious and other teachings of the ethnic group to which the family belongs. It can be as early as seven days after birth, or as late as forty years old. When done at a very early age, children grow up believing that the mutilation is a natural thing and may not even remember the trauma associated with it. At ages of greater consciousness, the ordeal is never forgotten and, depending on the victim's community, may be hated.

It must be admitted that there are difficulties in dealing with the complex situations which surround the practice. Most obstacles to the elimination of fgm arise from the nature of the support structures of the practice. Strategies for eliminating the practice will never succeed unless they take account of the variety of situations involved, and direct specific actions to specific target groups.

Three types of circumstance have to be dealt with. Firstly, there is the individual, where the independent believer in the practice is not exposed to any organised religious or traditional institution. Secondly, there is the community faith, where members of a community of believers hold to and observe the faith and are strengthened by the teachings of their religious or spiritual organisations. Thirdly, there is conformity, whereby people follow customary laws and practices because everyone around them does the same, or because they wish to gain some particular advantage by joining the vogue. Each situation presents the strategist with its own peculiar set of problems.

Approaches to the development of strategies for eliminating FGM

The obstacles and associated factors preventing the elimination of fgm can be classified under specific situations arising from the nature of the supporting structures of the system.

The individual

The first factor to consider is the power of blind belief. Where there is no organised pressure on individuals, or where there are no societies in which authority for the practice is vested, individuals who have been brought up in accordance with tradition are likely to hold that the tradition cannot be violated. They may have no reason for maintaining the practice other than the mere fact that it has always been a family tradition, even if they have been forced into it. But even among this group, the development of a feeling of sorority cannot be disregarded; for those women, the practice has made them similar to 'secret society' members in this respect. The bond that may therefore develop may incline them to feel compelled to fight to preserve the integrity of the sorority and to promote its continuity. In such cases, strategies to persuade them to change their beliefs are not enough. It may be necessary to combine persuasion with some legal device to restrain practitioners from continuing the practice.

Ignorance of the consequences of the operation develops from the indifference shown by many women in developing countries towards health and well-being. In the absence of information on the dangers to health arising from the practice, it is difficult for questions regarding the safety of life to be raised even by individuals who are free to do so, and not sworn to secrecy. Strategies to remove ignorance must be directed at target groups within and outside communities which practise fgm.

Fear of persecution makes it difficult to be an outsider in any community where such a practice unifies the majority. In a liberal community there is little risk of persecution for one's belief; individuals can therefore opt out of the system without fear of reprisal. Where tradition dies hard and rigid rules are applied to maintain it, individuals who do not adopt community practices may suffer deprivation of certain privileges, and even hostile attacks on their person. Those who have been victims of enforced fgm may find themselves trapped in the system from which they and their female children can never escape. The removal of fear will be a delicate matter. Individuals to be discouraged from the practice should be convinced that they will have the necessary protection of the law.

Mental servitude, or the feeling of being an inferior member of the community, produces in many women resignation to all of society's dictates, whether they are for or against their interests. In some societies acceptance of inferiority has been enforced by tradition, endorsed by supernatural power, and accepted as good for women by the community and family – a situation that presents serious obstacles to eliminating the practice. Women in such communities must be given support and encouragement through well designed programmes to free themselves from the subservience to which they have been subjected, and so enable them to reject the practice.

In general, people are suspicious of change and in traditional societies many fear it. They fear the instability which they believe follows change, the absence of a point of reference, the loss of identity and the disappearance of those forms of control by which their communities have been guided for centuries. Unless individuals or groups believe that change will be for the better, they will resist it. 'Better' may mean different things to different people. Indeed, it may be impossible to satisfy those who must have definite information about the rewards of change, unless clear strategies are developed which provide answers to questions such as 'change to what?' and 'change for what?' Change is more likely to occur if influential people in a community adopt it. People follow the lead of those they respect in the community, and encourage other individuals to do the same.[2]

Community faith

Besides the factors outlined above, the love of ceremony, with its attendant festivity and showering of gifts, explains the attraction that the practice of fgm holds for some communities. The weight of social pressure compels many not to miss out on the ceremony and celebration that accompany participation. Any strategy should concentrate on minimising the social appeal of a celebration which follows the imposition of physical damage and even death on others. A successful strategy must bring about an awareness of those things about which a community should rejoice and those about which it should grieve.

Social and cultural myths and taboos promote the mystique that excites interest in group proceedings and easily entices certain types of person to join in the experience. Preventing or even reducing recruitment becomes difficult among such people. The objective of a strategy in this case should be to demystify the practice and expose taboos, highlighting the baselessness of their conventional restrictions and compulsions.

Community pride takes the form of arrogance which makes members of a community feel that what they are doing should be beyond the reproach of others outside their community. They would therefore tend to defend community-wide practices against criticism from outsiders, however just, sincere or honest, claiming that such criticism is interference in their internal affairs. Such pride should be countered by well developed campaign programmes which foster objectivity among specific target groups in the community and encourage the acceptance of constructive criticism whilst acknowledging the virtue of pride based on achievement and high human ideals within the community.

Where fgm is carried out in organised groups, a complex association of emotions is involved. The emotions of vital concern will be those related to authority, fraternity and ritual. Authority is a bond between people who are unequal.[3] In such organised groups, and in 'secret societies', the inequality exists between the group's elders and other members. The former are believed to have superior judgement, and the power to discipline and instil fear in the latter. Inherent in that authority, therefore, is a responsibility to engender respect from all concerned and to ensure the perpetual fixity of the group's or society's values and beliefs. A way must be found to deal with this level of power within the community, by limiting or eliminating the influence of this authority.

Fraternity or sorority, as explained earlier, tends to bind all those in similar circumstances. Of course, the circumstances of women and girls who are identified with a 'secret society' will differ from those of women and girls who may be grouped by religion or tradition, or revered as 'independents'. While the spirit of fraternity may extend to all 'circumcised' women in the community, 'society' members may feel a deeper sense of responsibility to maintain the secrecy and sanctity of their order and prevent any dismantling of their ceremonies and practices. The action required to neutralise this obstacle should include building up confidence in women's ability to maintain a sorority without imposing conditions which violate the right to good health and to protection from bodily mutilation. Sorority should be clearly distinguished from the suffering of genital mutilation, and should be encouraged for other more laudable beliefs and develop a clear focus which excludes inhumane and dangerous health practices. The suffering should be clearly and frankly explained and a plan developed to enable health and social workers to stop the practice and mitigate the suffering of those already affected by it.

Authority and fraternity are bonds which do not always extend to fanaticism. Ritual, however, can be exploited to reach those levels. It is a bond built between people who are unified by an act recognised by them as a solemn symbol of their union. Thus bound, members of the union are expected to keep to strict codes of secrecy. This bond exists where a 'secret society' operates the system of fgm, within the confines of its own shrine. In such a case support for the practice can be so strong as to result in attacks against forces threatening its continued survival. Eliminating a practice steeped in ritual will require other behavioural changes which will lead practitioners and supporters of the practice to reject the provisions of their religious laws or traditional cults, and replace those of their rituals which are inimical to health by other activities which are beneficial to womanhood.

The conforming situation

Some groups, who do not normally practise fgm, become attracted to the practice because of long association with other groups among which they have lived for years. This applies to the Kroos of Sierra Leone, some of whom have now adopted the practice after living for many decades in close proximity to other ethnic groups practising fgm. This involvement springs from the desire to be integrated into the larger community and free to circulate comfortably among its members and enjoy the thrills of belonging. In some cases, people get involved because they wish to gain specific advantages – these may include political, social and economic advantages – which they believe involvement brings. The appeal of involvement should be reduced by introducing another interest group activity to counter the appeal of fgm groups. It will also be necessary to strengthen existing women's societies not involved in the practice to put them in a much stronger position than at present to influence political and economic developments. There needs to be an example of political and economic success outside the traditional linkages to convince those not in fgm groups that political, social and economic success can be achieved without involvement in the practice.

Curiosity is a possible motive of some young girls who have no other reasons to conform to the practice, which may be outside their family's experience. In areas where the 'secret society' operates, these curious girls may find the secrecy a challenge for them to unravel. Again, a strategy should be devised to divert such misdirected energies. Youth clubs and youth organisations should be made aware of this tendency and develop action programmes to channel natural inquisitiveness into more creative activities.

Approach to the care of FGM victims

A strategy for elimination of fgm should be accompanied by a strategy for the care of victims of the practice. Two risk groups need to be considered. The first is women and girls who accept fgm culture, whether they have been conditioned independently or in groups. These appear to adjust psychologically to the practice believing that it is a price they have to pay for preserving their tradition. The second risk group are women and girls who have been forced or even kidnapped into the practice. While those in the first group could be treated successfully in normal hospitals and clinics, it will not be appropriate to deal with the second risk group in the routine manner common in most hospitals. For recurrent symptoms, which occur mostly in patients in the second category, it will be necessary to take account of the various mental states which may have developed in such patients, especially those who have serious conditions leading to permanent disability.

Outline of strategy for the eradication of FGM

The general objects of the strategy are to eliminate fgm wherever it occurs, and to cure and rehabilitate those females who have been its victims. The specific objectives, intended to have an impact on those aspects of the problem identified in previous sections of this chapter, can be grouped into educational, behavioural and legal. Programmes of action should be drawn up to achieve the objectives in each group. The proposal for suitable programmes in this section should be useful in most countries but can be modified to suit special cases.

Educational Objectives:
- To persuade those who hold to the belief that there are advantages to be gained from practising fgm, to change their belief in the practice.
- To change the state of ignorance of health and other consequences of fgm.
- To foster positive attitudes towards change, particularly among those influential in society.
- To counteract unreasonable and baseless myths and taboos.

Behavioural Objectives:
- To uplift human values and standards of acceptability for various classes of ceremony.
- To liberalise communities' attitudes towards critical examination of community practices.
- To provide inhibitors to the perpetuation of fraternity bonds that accord respectability to fgm.
- To arouse society's sensitivities, so as to cause revulsion against and rejection of fgm.
- To introduce new and more worthy group interest, stimulating diversity and offering alternatives to traditional group activities supporting fgm.
- To improve the quality and quantity of youth activities which redirect inquisitiveness, develop a culture for independent thinking and creativity.
- To improve women's attitudes to the status of women so as to strengthen confidence in themselves and in their ability to free themselves from the stranglehold of practices detrimental to their health.
- To limit or eliminate the power or the authority of groups controlling or imposing the practice.

Legal Objectives:
- To change laws in order to stimulate a change in attitudes.

• To provide safety within the law for the free exercise of women's rights which should include the right to refuse fgm.

Programme proposals

Programmes should be developed for the following target groups: 1) adults at home, in the work place, in markets, shops, hospitals and in farms, particularly in countries where farm workers are mostly women; 2) children at school; 3) community leaders; and 4) elders of organised fgm groups, officials of 'secret societies' and initiates and similar persons or groups.

Educational programmes

These programmes should be carried out by a nationally approved organisation established for the purpose of carrying out community education, using what may be called a national community education plan. The plan should address the particular concern of fgm, and programmes should focus attention on dispelling the notion that there could be benefits from its practice. These should include audio-visual and other schemes to communicate full understanding of the injuries and diseases resulting from circumcision, to explain the importance of seeking medical attention for the conditions brought about by fgm, and to underscore the futility of continuing the practice. They should expose the shaky basis of local myths and taboos and encourage change in attitude towards women and their problems, especially among leaders of the community. There should be schemes which will give women a stronger belief in themselves than they have at present, raise the level of their appreciation of finer values, enhance their confidence in making decisions and abiding by them, and encourage them to form opinions on the negative aspects of fgm, and to take a stand against its continuation.

For target group 1, pictures and posters should be used extensively. These will be particularly useful for adults visited at home and women on the farms. For other women, moving and still pictures can be exploited using mobile vans equipped with cinematograph projectors and a video machine to get the message of the dangers of fgm conveyed more dramatically and realistically. The programme should also cover studies of successful female life with contrasting studies of women whose expectations of a happy and successful life after the operation have been shattered. When visits are made to women at home they should be encouraged to discuss freely the problems of fgm, the importance of well-being, the unsatisfactory nature of their social conditions as women and the necessity of dropping a harmful practice, so as to achieve better health and happiness. In places such as hospitals and clinics, co-operation should be sought with the governing authorities, so that instructors may be given access to patients and allowed to hold short instruction sessions in out-patient waiting rooms.

In the case of target group 2, the health risks could be further highlighted through debates in and between schools through field projects in which schoolchildren spread information about the health risks of fgm to the wider community. It will be important in some countries to make prior approaches to community leaders before the programmes are implemented among this group. The objective should be to inform community leaders of the community education plan, and give them time to adjust to the idea. As many schools as possible should be included in the plan; school authorities should be made aware of its objectives and be persuaded, where necessary, to permit supplementary school classes, initially to the upper primary and secondary school. Short courses, talks with slides, and wall-posters may be used in the programme, which should be built around the existing science curriculum. In addition, drama should be used to convey the necessary information to stimulate concern, and develop antagonism against the practice. New types of clubs should be set up with the assistance of school teachers, in which emphasis is given to activities which improve the quality of children's behaviour, increase their stature in society and develop in them independent thinking and creativity. With careful programming it may be possible to get gradual acceptance of the education programme against fgm as a regular course in schools. It may also be possible to achieve such a level of understanding among schoolchildren that they may begin to influence their parents and relatives for the better, and become valuable promoters of the campaign against fgm.

For target group 3, which should include religious leaders, politicians, leaders of welfare organisations and other influential persons, the programme should explain the serious health problems of women in their communities and describe the dangers to which women are exposed. Instructors and volunteers operating the programme should work subtly, earnestly and with determination towards gaining support from these leaders for instituting change in those aspects of religious teachings, community laws, customs and tradition which compel women to undergo fgm.

Planning a programme for target group 4 should be delayed until some progress has been made with programmes for target group 3, and experience has been gained in handling situations outside those of the bond created by the ritual element introduced in some societies. The programme for this group should be implemented by specially trained staff. Such staff should have been beneficiaries of one of the three earlier programmes and should be given intensive training in subjects including nutrition, hygiene, first aid and post-circumcision emergency treatment. They should also be trained in persuasive skills; imparting of knowledge relating to the dangers of uncontrolled authority; teaching methods of exposing weakness in authority, of mobilising action against such weaknesses and of raising doubts in bogus systems; training in character building; development of feminine pride and the capacity to defend women's rights, even against the strongest adherents of the principle of feminine subservience. Trainees should be able at the end of their course to identify, define and isolate feminine terror spots in organisations and to mobilise group action as necessary against them. The first set of staff to be selected should be members of the community who are well respected, but young enough to feel excited by the challenges of the task before them. All should be drawn from the membership of 'secret societies'. They should be screened for certain attributes, such as maturity, personal charm and persistence in their points of view.

These specially trained instructors should be posted to join fgm societies or organisations in regions having a language and custom with which they are familiar, to start the process of change within these closed organisations.

Health care programmes

These programmes should be introduced with the help of health ministries. As special attention is recommended for victims of fgm, measures should be adopted to set up special women's care units in hospitals and health centres in areas of a country where fgm is prevalent. In an ideal situation, special women's clinics should be established. The programmes should be directed towards treating and counselling women who have suffered fgm. As required for the execution of the health programme, it should be co-ordinated by a body responsible for issuing guidelines for examination, treatment and referral procedures.

Information on health care programmes should be made public. Instructions in the education programmes should also bring health care arrangements to the attention of target groups in their programmes. In the operation of the health programmes, distinction should be made between the following cases:

Category 1: Women recently circumcised suffering pain, urinary infections, and showing signs and symptoms of anaemia.
Category 2: Women complaining of primary infertility, dyspareunia due to a small introitus, urinary infections, and other local pains.
Category 3: Women complaining of secondary infertility, torn perineum after first delivery, signs and symptoms of vaginal prolapse, habitual

uterine wastage due to urinary infections caused by unsuspected urinary fistulae, and women with recognised vaginal and rectal fistulae.

Category 4: Women suffering mental depression.

Examination treatment and counselling should be carried out so as to avoid imposing unnecessary mental stress on patients. Patients should be screened regularly to monitor progress in their recovery and to enable early detection of cases of deepening depression which may need to be referred to a psychiatrist.

Legal programmes

Programmes should be developed and implemented that will serve as forerunners to the enactment of laws to ban the practice of fgm. These should involve active campaigns organised by groups of concerned citizens. Membership of these groups should be drawn from professions such as gynaecology, psychiatry, religion, social science and economics, as well as experts in labour matters.

The groups should be organised under a national committee for the promotion of women's welfare. They should mount campaigns to influence public opinion, and make representations to their heads of state, cabinet ministers and other national figures. The press, radio and television should be used and opportunity taken at local social functions to make the issue public. Petition forms should be prepared, circulated and filled. This activity should be regularly monitored to obtain maximum support from the community in the final phases of a national appeal for a law to ban the practice. Through their co-ordinated action the group will be able to demand some statement of policy from the government regarding the practice, and finally to press for laws to be passed banning it.

Programmes will be needed after the necessary legislation has been passed to keep a close watch on situations that might need legal attention. These should include the following:

- Legal advice bureaux to help women exercise their rights to refuse fgm.
- Legal aid for victims requiring redress for suffering resulting from fgm performed against their will.
- Watchdog committees to ensure fair application of the law in all cases and to make public any miscarriage of justice.

Setting targets

Outcome objectives should be specified for each programme developed. Experience of the present level of public awareness and concern in many countries practising fgm suggests that setting a plan period for complete elimination of the practice everywhere will be unrealistic. However a target reduction of the practice to below a few per cent in say twenty years is a reasonable goal where programmes are made to work. There should also be targets for the following: four-year figures for progressive reduction in the practice; annual figures for achieving among target groups awareness of health consequences and other defined educational, health and legal objectives in sequences appropriate to respective countries; evaluation of programmes in convenient time phases.

Conclusion

The continuing disregard for the health of women and children in certain countries of the developing world is stifling progress on many fronts. Women make up roughly half of the population of these countries. Despite this it appears that the majority is content to see fellow citizens suffer debilitating ailments inflicted upon them by traditional practices, by far the most terrifying of which is fgm.

With growing pressure on countries to increase productivity, it is imperative that the huge waste of human resources caused by deliberate injury and other actions that limit women's full participation in the development of their homelands should be stopped. There have been elements of financial gain noticed in the system which supports fgm. This element is a by-product of a requirement deeply rooted in socio-cultural life of some women and children. It has therefore not been treated in this presentation. No doubt, once the urge to satisfy local traditional edicts is curbed by education, information and effective legal devices, the financial element will be an irrelevant issue in the debate, and cannot by itself reverse the decline of the practice.

It is hoped that, not too long from now, those who have begun the struggle to eliminate this dreadful practice will be joined by many who are now silent and whose ideas, energies and audaciousness will be harnessed for the triumph so badly needed over this apparently enduring scourge.

Notes

1. Olayinka Koso-Thomas, *The Circumcision of Women: A Strategy for Eradication*, Zed Press, 1987.
2. Richard Sennett, *Authority*, Secker & Warburg, London, 1980.
3. Thomas Coates, *Family Health International Network*, Vol . 12, No. I, June 1991.

9

What Do African Women Want?

Rose Waruhiu

Africa is a vast continent with many diverse countries and cultures. What the different countries have in common are weak productive sectors, reliance on one or two export commodities, poor infrastructure, increasing debt and environmental degradation. At the root of these problems is the lack of adequate resources. Beyond the economic and financial problems, misguided policies or inefficient administrative institutions reveal themselves in piecemeal development programmes. In this context what women need is not fundamentally different from what society at large needs – a sense of being in control and in charge of their own destiny. Yet the main issue for women remains that, even in the best of situations, they are still at the political periphery.

Early images of the African woman south of the Sahara depict her with a heavy load on her back, a baby straddled on top and hands left free to weave a kiondo or shell maize as she walks. Her back is bent over; she is fulfilling three roles at once: worker-provider, manager, mother. Women continue to balance not only the loads but the demands made on their time every day. Women make important management decisions about growing and marketing food crops, about irrigation and transport, house-building, child health, family nutrition, and about the maintenance of the community, but are left out at higher levels of decision-making that determine society's potential. The scope of this commitment and contribution is underestimated when policy and institutions keep women from political integration and fail to take account of their own impact on women's many roles.

Women may have attained some semblance of integration over the past decades, but they encounter systems that increase their work or that fail to understand them. They, in turn, do not understand and are unable to face the challenges of this development, being by-passed for any benefits. Women could do better in all areas – and perhaps better than men – if they had more know-how, or were encouraged to recognise that what they do know – about agriculture or time-management for example – has value. African women need a more proportionate division of labour, and its rewards, between the sexes, and more support mechanisms (infrastructure or services) to alleviate the burdens they carry. They should be consulted, not told.

Women carry a disproportionate load in Africa. They do 95 per cent of domestic work, and, in rural areas, 85 per cent of weeding, 60 per cent of harvesting, 50 per cent of caring for livestock, 50 per cent of planting and 30 per cent of ploughing. Women's economic participation is not matched by supporting mechanisms, for example the access and right to productive assets, credit, technology and other resources. They lack training, form the majority of the illiterate and the poor, and are by-passed, institutionally and socially, when decisions are being made. They need a mechanism that really links them to the benefits of development, especially in agriculture, the environment, income-generation, health and reproduction.

The traditional approach has been to assume that the status and situation of women in each country are reflections of the prevailing economic conditions; it was therefore expected that as the country developed women would also benefit, presuming that 'everything rises with the tide'. Few expected that, despite positive rates of growth, little development or rise in the standards of living for women would be realised. Another strategy has been to give 'special' attention to women as a way of achieving progress, especially at the community level, but without paying attention to men's roles or other external factors. The adoption of this strategy has meant that women are taking on even more than before. Women remain producers, managers and mothers without proportionate reward.

'Development' has traditionally been defined in terms of national income, improved living standards and the capacity to utilise resources efficiently. 'Developed' countries convey images of gigantic buildings, immense wealth, complex institutions and sophistication. Yet the concern for 'women's issues' has focused attention on how people in every country are being reached by 'development'. The most glaring problem to be tackled in Africa is the allocation and utilisation of scarce resources in the long struggle against deepening poverty. The productive resources, especially land, are mainly in the hands of men, a fact that is the outcome of combined traditional, colonial and modern law and policy.

Women want to create alternatives to prevent further decline. Poverty means suffering, hunger, malnourished children whose physical and psychological growth is stunted for life; therefore they can never take their rightful place in the world's economy. Poverty generates an unproductive workforce; low incomes mean poor demand to stimulate production, even of necessities. Poverty is also a manifestation of social inequality, especially where the poor get poorer and the rich wealthier; but it can be reinforced by the deprivation that is specific to being female.

What development should mean

African women belong to societies facing serious economic problems, struggling to improve their standard of living. The outlook is not encouraging, as the annual rate of growth to the year 2000 is expected to be lower than in the past. Food sufficiency has dropped from 98 per cent to 86 per cent. Africa still has the highest fertility rates, the highest mortality rates and the lowest life expectancy in the world. There will be more than 474 million women in Africa by the year 2000. Do women feel equipped to sort out the problems that lie ahead: drought, famine, recession, foreign debt? People's immediate needs have to be met by the income available to the families. If women have no say in economic policies, it means they are not involved in deciding the values and other priorities in the country. They cannot influence the question of what needs should be met first. Women's liberation still depends on the development of water supplies, food production, health and education services, and the active encouragement and involvement of women in all forms and levels of decision-making.

Thirty years of development 'aid' has generated material transfer from the developed countries without sufficient understanding of the roots of underdevelopment. Official replies to simple questions raised by the people are expressed in phrases that do not encourage initiative or creativity. Aid money is accompanied by conditions that the ordinary poor person does not understand, although they will affect her deeply. Aid is not therefore the only critical issue; a change of attitude – flexibility and genuine commitment to the rights of the potential beneficiaries – is required at government level. Women need opportunities to deal with the details of policy at their own level, and direct access to assistance. Instead they merely experience a rapid change of pace in their lives.

The questions of 'women in development' are varied and multi-faceted, including, for example, poor rural women who want to improve their ability to help themselves; illiterate market women who wish to increase their incomes through credit and training programmes; young school leavers who have no vocational training or employment opportunities; young professional women who are seeking equal remuneration for work of equal value. A woman waiting in a hospital queue with her child should not go home without information on proper nutrition, vaccination or primary health care, nor should she feel blame for her poverty. A woman who gathers twigs for firewood should not be held responsible for the degradation of her environment, as there are no other sources of fuel to help her meet her obligations to feed her family. Lack of formal skills among women usually renders them unable to utilise opportunities fully, and condemns them to survival strategies in the informal sector. In addition to this, frequent strife and man-made wars across Africa have created stress, fear and destitution for women and children. In times of war and strife, it is women who tend mal-nourished and dying babies, while military men control food supplies and remain well fed.

Women face many constraints which are partly the result of their low socio-economic status, and partly institutional. Their needs and priorities arise from a long list of grievances now all too familiar: unequal access to education and training, poor working conditions, arduous repetitive work, and poor entitlement to productive assets such as credit, land and technology, and to health and other welfare services. Many lack safe drinking water or have to walk many miles to get water for the household. At the family level they carry the time-consuming burden of household-related activities in addition to their roles as child-bearers and community workers.

That the roles and participation of women differ from those of men is obvious, but overlooked. Although it has been demonstrated that women are at a disadvantage in every area, there is insufficient positive action to overcome it. The strategies to deal with poverty, ill health and basic needs led to an awareness of women as the key to food production and distribution, to housing and shelter. The move to 'sustainable development' contains the admission that there is no sustainability without the full political participation of women: not only because they constitute half the population, but because they do nine-tenths of the work in the sectors that are being relied upon to take Africa out of crisis, most importantly food production, and are without a voice or means to express their needs. Few African women have the time to explore their own needs; they are preoccupied with the needs of others. They relate their achievements in terms of what they have been able to do for their children, paying school fees or providing food for the family, for example. They have not negotiated for their needs with the bureaucracies, but tend to accept whatever role is defined for them. They are applauded for being hard-working and admired for what they do for the family and community. They accept they must fulfil these roles even where they receive little help from their own family members in sharing the work. If they seek help around the home it will be from the other female members of the household, thereby entrenching the stereotyping in domestic roles.

A proper approach to development must take account of women's needs. This strategy is not born out of militancy, but is based on

practical suggestions to improve the quality of women's economic participation. Projects should focus on increasing African women's access to
productive assets in the key sectors of agriculture, trade and commerce
– as well as the informal sector – and on reducing their time burdens.
Most women want support to get on with what they are doing, but
better; they are usually uncomfortable with high public visibility, power
and conflict. They have been brought up to exhibit the perceived feminine qualities of compliance and harmony. If they shed these attributes,
and step out of prescribed roles, they find themselves undermined and
continually on the defensive. This impairs their ability to communicate
their case. They are diverted from the 'concrete' issues; they cannot act
decisively and forcefully without criticism. While they may deal with
personal and emotional conflict privately, displaying such ability in
public is seen as aggressive.

Organising

A good deal has been written on women in recent years. Research was
initiated by the feminist movement in the United States and other
countries in the West, linked to the perceived inferior status of women.
The UN Decade for Women brought all countries together in a global
effort to address the question of women's status. The issues pursued
during the Decade are well known. Viewed from Africa, it is apparent
that the technical priorities of women in the Third World are different
from those of women in the West. Inadequate education, poverty, poor
infrastructure are greater constraints than lack of paternity leave. There
are, of course, gaps in women's opportunities, as African women with
education and employment are finding, when compared to men of
similar background. But more emphasis must be given to the majority,
the poorer women in rural and urban areas, who do not gain from the
privileges of the few. This requires a common philosophy of the equal
value of human beings.

It is frequently argued that women *per se* should not be the priority.
There is misunderstanding, especially amongst men, about women's
role in the family, socialisation and child-rearing. Dislocation in modern
urban families is blamed on the women, who are supposed to be the
custodians of family values. In most cases the women, who need care
and attention, have never spoken out about their problems, and nobody
asks them. Enlightened women, who may involve themselves in mobilising others, are accused of planting wrong ideas into the minds of
'innocent women'. Societies enforce divisions and stereotypes to counter
the women's movement.

Women should, therefore, organise themselves to ensure that governments respond to their needs. Women have made the greatest impact

at the grassroots level, despite the constraints and barriers in family and community. However, those women who occupy higher bureaucratic or business positions have demonstrated that they can carry important responsibilities outside the home. Whether in villages or among women government officials, the underlying concern is the relative position of women and men, based on age-old attitudes and perceptions. Both kinds of women, out of growing awareness of their subordinate role and their marginalisation in the face of change, saw the need to evolve a movement to address these issues.

In Africa, one approach to women's development has concentrated on how to reduce the burden through work-groups. The scope of the women's movement has expanded through more attention and research. It is now accepted that African women are concerned with such issues as equality of benefits and control of development. This shift was accompanied by the recognition that social and cultural systems, and conditions under which women work, frustrate their potential, and that development efforts must overcome these barriers. A popular slogan during Forum 85, held in Nairobi alongside the World Conference ending the Decade for Women, stated that 'All Women are Third World'. Many statements on basic needs confine themselves to food, shelter, housing and other material needs. Among women, poverty should be viewed in relation to income or resources, but also as the restrictions that continue to marginalise them. An African woman may be considered 'poor', or an object of pity, because she is not married or has no children. She has to face preconceptions, obligations or impediments that limit her self-development and self-determination. The non-material needs of justice, dignity and individual rights are important to African women.

As in the past, women must be the major contributors to the process of empowering other women. They must increase their ability to control and influence choices being made about themselves and their society. This empowerment of women is a big challenge in Africa, owing to high levels of illiteracy – though this must not be identified with ignorance – and poor communication networks. Women need to understand policies, existing expenditure plans or programmes, to judge whether they are compatible with their needs. Women with access to information and other opportunities must act as a resource to other women. Links between grassroots women's organisations and women working at national level are viewed with suspicion by established politicians. In order to create divisions, they readily accuse elite women of being out of touch with the needs of their sisters in the villages. Yet male politicians, themselves engaged in seeking support and followers from the same groups of rural women, know this not to be the case.

Women have overcome some of these limitations through their own associations and groups, through which they explore ideas together and become more involved in each other's welfare. It is from these groups that the concept has evolved of empowerment of women, meaning power from within the person and mutual support for one another, rather than particular power for an individual. Women need to learn to accept each other's leadership and improve their management of their organisations, good training grounds for women to deal with external authority. They can achieve the capacity to handle disputes and conflicts, not necessarily by limiting other women but by empowering each other. This may give the impression that women seek to be empowered by those who already possess political, social and economic power, by sharing or transferring some of that power. This is not necessarily the case for African women; there, the focus is more on women's struggle for control of their own development and a broadening of vision. They require assistance in defining their needs and their capabilities. They need strategies developed especially for women to address the main barriers around the family and household, and methods, services and mechanisms that can provide support. Women need to continue thinking and talking together to formulate what action to take at different stages. Women in a single village may each have a different vision about their future. In the continent, there are millions of visions, but the relative inequality of women as a group is perpetuated by the lack of opportunities and machinery for influencing governments.

The whole approach to development must take women into account, and this is possible only through listening to them. Women's organisations must carry the responsibility for lobbying. To lobby effectively they must inform themselves of the processes of government, so that they intervene appropriately and meaningfully. Women must therefore get a place at the negotiating table. 'Women's issues' should be seen as a society's issues, and be tackled in the same way that governments tackle other issues, by making resources and qualified staff available to implement the mandate. Current trends have diffused the women's agenda by creating too many agencies with limited (and often external) funds, narrow and specific objectives. Women's projects are expected to compete with other projects, instead of being allocated half the resources. Women need a machinery that is responsible, sensitive and flexible.

The political context

Meeting the challenges facing women in Africa will rely heavily on the political will of governments, and the institutional framework within which 'women's issues' are incorporated or received. Governments in Africa play a broad leadership role, which has developed from the tendency for people to look to all levels of government to provide unopposed community or collective consensus, in a way that is not feasible in developed countries where literacy is greater. There is more individualism and more free enterprise in Western countries; in Africa, leaders and leadership tend to be synonymous with government. This is sometimes attributed to the colonial heritage and sometimes to the 'conditioning of the African mind'. It is assumed that decision-makers understand society's priorities best, and have a grasp of all national and global matters. The system expects the people to trust those in power rather than encouraging active participation in decision-making.

This trust can also be attributed to the independence movements, spearheaded by the groups that assumed power after independence and first asserted national sovereignty. Ordinary citizens place their faith in their leader and come forth, if invited to do so, only during elections. In many countries, even elections ceased during the 1980s, and successive groups took the helm of the state through military *coups d'état*. Very few countries in Africa south of the Sahara have elected governments or parliaments. Free debate in the parliaments that do exist is not widespread, or the parliaments are called only rarely. The most powerful organ in most of these countries is the ruling party, which is supposedly more akin to the African culture of consensus. The era of single-party states was entrenched with arguments about fostering national unity and a single-minded approach to basic development. More women have been incorporated in the party machines than in the parliaments, and few feature in military states. Women have kept away from discussing politics, and there is little public indication of what they feel about the continent's political affairs.

The one area in which women have been vocal is the promotion of women's projects, but without women in strategic positions this agenda has not penetrated policy and programme formulation significantly. Women talk among themselves and present their cases, which may or may not be picked up by their party organisations. They benefit from some projects designed for them, but not in proportion to their contribution. Since so much development is financed by donors, the women join in the hunt for outside help, rather than mobilising national resources. They follow not so much their own perceived priorities but what is available in pre-existing programmes prescribed by the donor agencies. They also lose the use of their existing traditional knowledge, which they should be consolidating to validate their own project proposals. African women need an approach that creates collaboration rather than dependency. Development workers at the grassroots level must seek to enhance self-reliance and dignity among women. Women have made many mistakes through poor project choice, poor management and incapacity to monitor and evaluate their input (to other people's standards). These problems occur where the national administrative framework fails to respond to concerns raised by women. Although policy makers are generally aware of women's potential, they do not see women as partners in the management of resources. Women should challenge the customary image of their worth and importance. They have not demanded sensitivity to their needs when nominating representatives for election for public office, or sought equal political participation as candidates. At present, powerful women's organisations toe the line with the rest of the population, and even fail to speak up on issues of concern to women. In many Christian prayer meetings, which have taken root in religious revivals, women are perpetuating their own oppression by accepting that they must suffer and toil, as was 'destined' in the Bible. Women are, for example, unwilling to act against their husbands who barter them or mistreat the family.

There is hope that democratisation of political institutions in Africa will make women's voices heard, but the record of other democracies shows otherwise. African women can be criticised for adding credibility to repressive regimes on their continent; it is difficult to imagine how differently they would perform if they had power. It is possible, however, that larger numbers of women would bring more humane and less corrupt administrations. If there is any element left of what is specifically African in our institutions, it is the concern for personal relations and for traditional cultural obligations. It should be possible, therefore, to build more emphasis on the human person and mutual social responsibility into perspectives on development. If a choice has to be made between rapid industrialisation, new technology, export-orientation or improving the capacity of the people, women would choose the last by focusing more on services such as education and health, thus promoting and improving human resources.

Governments that focus on sectors that support economic development (such as agriculture and food security, health and education) and improve human resources find that they cannot ignore women. In many cases, the women's issue has been institutionalised as a concern for women alone, rather than for the health of the nation, thereby failing to make any reforms or statements in policy documents. Women's economic participation has not always been accompanied by recognition of their contribution or potential, which is why the systems that have evolved, failing to acknowledge or support women, can be said to be exploitative. The same system fails itself by not addressing and enhancing the quality of this participation.

Women's concerns are usually designated to ministries that deal with social welfare and children, because most of the activities in traditional societies emphasise woman's roles as child-bearer, child-rearer, homekeeper and custodian of the family unit. A breakthrough in understanding woman's varied roles came with a wider interpretation of 'development'.

The World Bank was among the first to refer to women as the 'invisible' factor in development, highlighting the work women do that has not been acknowledged in statistics and data. This shift in definition and approach to development, from the basic needs approach to human-centred development, has improved the case for women, at least in theory. Reality, however, contains persistent problems of how to reach women and how to remove the anomalies within society that enforce discrimination against women or their low social and economic status.

Only modest advances have been made in addressing the barriers and in evolving practicable strategies to improve women's position. African women became involved in preparations for the conference that culminated in the Nairobi Forward-Looking Strategies 1986–2000 (FLS). Various machineries and frameworks for implementation and monitoring the progress of the FLS have been set up in different countries. Governments that were quick to respond set up ministries for women, often with the effect of further marginalising them from the hard issues. Women's bureaux and commissions have not been placed in strategic positions, where they can ensure effectiveness and capacity to work across different sectors or at senior policy levels.

Some blame is laid on the complacency of African leaders and peoples, in accepting too readily from other countries and cultures prescriptions for our development. To achieve partnership and sustainability, we need to address the legal and economic capacity of women, and the supportive mechanisms available to them. People must be lifted from bare survival and the struggle to obtain basic needs to a better position, where they can articulate their needs and define their vision.

The woman question is integral to the overall problems and solutions of African countries in deciding their own destiny. So long as major issues are decided from outside, as is often the case, development will not be sustainable. Women want to feel they are part of their own governance, but they have limited opportunities to make an input. In many cases, they are asking for integration into a consultative machinery without a clear vision of their own. Traditionally, no one listens to women, and they have been made to think that they are powerless because they are poorer, and low on the list of priorities prepared by men. Analysis of what women do shows that they are, and have, intricate means of their communities' survival; but with the breakdown of traditional social protection systems – without any replacement – they are made very vulnerable.

Conclusion

If women could state what they want, they would not hesitate. They would want to explore the economic, social and political cultural issues from a woman's perspective. They would want to be involved as partners in development choices. African women face many problems arising directly from socio-cultural changes; they are caught in the conflict of balancing traditional values and knowledge with the new, to which they do not have full access. It is not possible to revert to old systems of social security and recognition, even if they were as satisfactory as is often made out. It is necessary to accept change, and to empower women to manage the change.

Women are seeking total development, in a sense that will give them control of their own lives. Some success has been achieved through women's organisations and women-specific development projects. Women are learning to save and support each other through revolving funds and small enterprises, such as sale of handicrafts through co-operatives. In so doing, they address practical needs. In many cases, women have had limited opportunities to do very much about what they want. They always say they need help. They need help to reduce the burden of the work they do. They want jobs for their children; they are tired of long journeys to fetch water; they need viable projects. They want better representation in the decision-making organs of government, and they want more women in parliaments.

Women-specific institutions must be supported to teach women modern techniques and how to design, use and adapt technology. Women must increase their self-confidence and competence in negotiations at family, community and national levels. At the family level, women require support in child care, health, service delivery, agricultural extension services and sources of income. Women want to work more productively through training in business skills and better access to productive assets. Women need guaranteed equal opportunities in education and vocational training. Differences in women's legal status abound in practice, if not in law. Women take official or unofficial institutional barriers as given, and in many cases are not aware of their rights, or fail to exercise their right of redress out of fear or cultural inhibition. The environment does not create incentives for women to see themselves as part of the overall development of their community. Most women's needs have been identified, but the will to act has failed. African women have been resilient and committed to their societies. Their vision of the future is a better chance for their children.

Japanese Power in Asia:
A Feminist Critical Analysis

Yayori Matsui

It is important for Japanese women, especially feminists, to criticise and check Japan's economic development strategy, which is the root cause of human rights violations of Asian women. The Japanese economy has grown rapidly by discriminating against women at home and exploiting women in the Third World, especially in other Asian countries. Japanese women's situation is thereby closely linked to that of other Asian women. In Japan, people tend not to be interested in aid or foreign investment issues, because they consider it the government's job. For Japanese women in particular, the issue of development is unfamiliar; few women's groups are interested, although it was one of three objectives – Equality, Development and Peace – of the UN Decade for Women (1975–85).

The Asian Women's Association (AWA) is one of the few women's groups that has begun to question the development strategy and aid policy promoted as being in the interests of Japan and other developed countries. This is because AWA members have seen all kinds of human rights violations, especially the economic and sexual exploitation of Asian women, and have undertaken solidarity actions since the 1970s, trying to find out why such injustices occur every day and to propose remedies. Therefore, they began to speak up on the subject of women and development aid, and other development issues, from a feminist perspective, believing strongly that the issue should not be left to men.

It is important that women also challenge Japanese militarisation, and the exercise of power in Asia and elsewhere. Linked to these questions are others, such as the Korean war prostitutes and the present-day sex industry, often considered too shameful to be discussed in public and made into a real political issue.

Asia fears Japan as an economic superpower

Japan has become an economic superpower in less than half a century since the surrender ending the Second World War, rebuilding the country from its ruins and bandaging its wounds. Now, Japan is one of the biggest overseas investors and creditors, with the largest trade surplus and the largest per capita GNP in the world. In the field of economic aid, Japan became the largest 'donor' country of Overseas Development Assistance (ODA) in 1989. It provides nearly Yen 9 billion, of which more than 75 per cent is supplied to Third World countries as bilateral aid. Japan is the largest 'donor' to Myanmar (Burma), Thailand, Brunei and the Maldives, and to some 26 other countries it is the second largest. More than 60 per cent of Japan's bilateral aid is provided to Asia (1989), although aid to Africa has recently been steadily increasing.

The increase in Japan's direct investment, and also in trade, form the basis of Japan's economic power in the Asian region, making an immeasurable impact on the lives of women and men in the region. Renate Constantino, a Filipino nationalist, made this severe comment in *The Second Invasion:*

> Japan has succeeded in building up the Great East Asia Co-Prosperity Sphere by the power of the Yen, which she failed to achieve by military power. Asia is now invaded by Japan again.

Access to information on Japan is still extremely limited internationally. This indifference is due partly to Japan's geographical isolation, but also to the many centuries of European dominance in Asia. Japanese women, for example, rarely participate in international women's conferences on development, the environment, debt, or aid, and reports about Japan are rarely submitted or solicited. Even for Asian women, who are in the position of direct influence, Japan is invisible and hard to understand.

It is in the interests of Japanese companies for so little attention to be paid to their activities, because they can more easily operate globally, across borders, free from the grassroots pressure of peoples in the Third World, even if they have to face conflict with economic rivals, such as the US and European Union countries.

Japan's Overseas Development Assistance

What are the serious problems of Japan's ODA? In 1986, when the Marcos regime in the Philippines was ousted by 'people power', criticism of ODA exploded in Japan. It was revealed that Japan had been providing huge amounts of ODA (Yen 900 billion) to the corrupt dictatorial government that the Filipino people had rejected. This money poured into the pockets of the Marcos family; some of it may have been spent on the 3,000 pairs of shoes that Imelda Marcos bought while 'her' people were starving. It was also revealed that Marubeni and other big Japanese corporations were linked to the regime and had made huge profits out of the aid business.

In spite of investigation by the Diet, the Marcos aid scandal was never fully disclosed, partly because of the Japanese government's secretiveness, and partly because of the pressure it brought to bear on the Aquino government of the Philippines. Through this scandal, however, Japanese people realised how vitally important are information and transparency in the allocation of ODA. Further, it was made clear that 'the request basis' principle, whereby ODA is provided on request from governments of recipient countries, is a major cause of such transactions taking place without reflecting local people's interests.

Japan's ODA is used in the interests of Japanese companies, not for the poorest people in the poorest countries, and especially not poor women. Bilateral aid to the least developed countries (LLDCs) accounts for only 15 per cent of the total, and the proportion of grant aid is smaller than that of other countries related to the Organisation for Economic Co-operation and Development-Development Action Committee (OECD-DAC). The high proportion of loans means that recipient countries have more debts to repay, even if the interest rate is low. The Philippines, for example, with a huge debt of US$30 billion, has to allocate 40 per cent of the national budget to payment of the debt. It received ODA worth Yen 123.3 billion from Japan, 84 per cent of which is in the form of loans. This increased the debt and brought about the imposition of a structural adjustment programme. As a result, the budget for health, education and other welfare, of vital importance to women and poor people, had to be cut.

In the case of India, Japan is the biggest ODA donor country, and 95 per cent of Japan's ODA (Yen 199.6 billion) is in the form of loans. As a result, more than 10 per cent of India's ODA is now used for payment of debt. The Japanese government maintains that 'the fact that loans are subject to repayment promotes self-help', but only four countries – Thailand, Malaysia, South Korea and Paraguay – continue to repay loans; all other countries are rescheduling their debt or taking similar measures. In other words, Japan's ODA adds to the burden of debt and makes people's life harder. Japan's ODA also tends to be used for large-scale projects, such as the construction of dams, roads, bridges, ports, airports and industrial estates, which benefit Japanese private companies' investment. Nearly half of ODA funds is provided for economic infrastructure, manufacturing, mining and other production sectors, but only 10 per cent allocated to agriculture, the most important economic activity for many Third World countries, and only 10 per cent to social infrastructure to meet basic human needs, such as education, primary health care or water supplies.

Besides the problem of priority being given to private companies' commercial interests, ODA has the problem of 'strategic aid', which is used as a tool to promote interests of the state. During the East–West cold war, Japan intentionally favoured such anti-communist countries as Thailand, confronting its neighbouring Indochinese countries, and Pakistan, confronting the USSR and Afghanistan.

Japan's ODA widens the gap between rich and poor, perpetuates the economic dependency of recipient countries, supports dictatorial governments which violate human rights, destroy the environment, take away natural resources and impose the consumer culture of multinational companies. Japan's ODA serves Japanese companies and the government; it hardly serves women and poor people in the Third World.

Some Japanese projects in Asia

In the early 1980s, based in Singapore as Asia correspondent for a Japanese newspaper, I visited the areas of Japan's overseas projects and began to question ODA. In 1982 I saw the luxurious hotel (Shenargaon) in Dhaka, Bangladesh, financed by Japan's loan. The entrance to the hotel was guarded by armed soldiers, while the nightly cost of a room was equivalent to several months' income for the inhabitants of the unspeakably poor squatter areas seen from the hotel windows. It was constructed at the request of President Rahman, who wanted to have a grandiose hotel with an international convention hall for the purpose of inviting more foreign investment. The aid was only for the president, eager to show off his power to wealthy foreign businessmen, and nothing to do with poor women who lost their children one after another from malnutrition. Ironically, the president was assassinated before the completion of the hotel.

During my visit to Sri Lanka in 1981, I made a trip to Kandy, the ancient capital surrounded by tea plantations, visiting the Piradenia hospital in the suburbs. The hospital, with 500 beds, was given by the Japanese, filled with modern medical technology and equipment, and the beds covered with clean sheets. To my surprise, young doctors told me resentfully, 'In this region, more children die of diarrhoea, communicable diseases and malnutrition. Therefore, a network of primary health care in villages to save children is more urgently needed. As the "brain drain" of doctors to foreign countries is a serious issue in this country, it is another problem when so many doctors are employed only in this hospital.' The running costs of such a hospital are high, and considerable funds are needed from the limited government budget. I saw an epitaph at the entrance: 'This hospital was built by President

Jayawardena in co-operation with the Japanese government' – a typical example of a monumental project to glorify a person in power, and one from which Japanese construction and medical equipment companies could profit. In spite of the criticism that this hospital was built not for the benefit of poor mothers who badly needed medical facilities nearby, but in the interests of the Sri Lankan elite and Japanese business, a similar huge hospital was constructed near Colombo.

When I visited Sarawak in Malaysia in 1987 to report on how the tropical forests were being destroyed, I learned that Japan's ODA fund was spent on constructing a road for a Japanese logging company. Japan is the biggest importer of tropical timber, and 90 per cent of that timber comes from Sarawak. Indigenous people, deprived of their livelihood of forest products, started struggling against logging by blockading the roads, early in 1987. Indigenous women are playing an important role in this struggle for survival. It was they who were discussing how to blockade logging-roads, and when they started it was in defiance of harassment, arrest and intimidation. The struggle was spreading all over Sarawak by 1991. This time, I visited the Bastan Ai Dam area in the southern part of Sarawak, because the dam was partly funded by Japan's ODA loans, and I had heard that 3,000 Iban people were being forced to leave their longhouses and move to a resettlement area near the dam. I asked myself, 'Aid for whom?'

A huge amount of ODA funding is also poured into industrialisation, and promotes Japanese business investment. For example, Bataan Export Processing Zone in Luzon in the Philippines was constructed in the early 1980s with Japan's ODA fund, and has many Japanese factories. More than 80 per cent of workers are young women who were courageous enough to go on strike for the purpose of improving their working conditions, in spite of a 'no strike' policy being in force.

In 1990, I visited the East Seaboard Industrial Development area in Thailand, a huge development project consisting of a petrochemical zone, a light industrial zone, and a big commercial port with capacity for six million-ton container ships. This is the Thai government's key industrialisation project, but some call it 'Japan's Project', because JICA (Japanese International Co-operation Agency) made the feasibility and planning studies, while the OECF (Overseas Economic Co-operation Fund) provided more than Yen 150 billion in loans. In the light industrial zone near Pattaya Beach, the famous international tourist area, Japanese companies have already built plants.

The purpose of my visit to the area was to talk to the people of Lemchabang fishing village, which 300 families had been told by the port authority in 1986 to evacuate on the grounds that 100 small fishing-boats might disturb big ships moving in and out of the new Lemchabang port. The villagers had lived for many generations by fishing in this beautiful seaside village, which is why all, young and old, men and women, gathered at the Buddhist temple, expressing their strong resentment: 'Why does our peaceful village have to be victimised by that industrial project?'

Tourism is another sector given priority for Japanese ODA. This, too, entails inhabitants in the project area being forced to move out. One example is Borobudur tourist park in Indonesia, which I visited in 1990. Borobudur is a world-famous, historic, stone-built Buddhist temple, maintained by UNESCO since the 1970s. JICA suggested building a tourist park around the monument; some 400 farming families were ordered to evacuate in the early 1980s, with negligible compensation (two cents per one m^2 of land). The farmers told me: 'The whole village resisted by all means possible, but finally we were expelled from our own village. Life here is so hard and miserable as you see.' Women who used to sell souvenirs and food from stalls are now struggling for survival, carrying out their small businesses outside the park because they cannot afford to pay the entrance fee.

Japan was the last country among the OECD-DAC members to start a Women in Development policy. Of the three chief objectives of the UN Decade for Women, the Japanese paid least attention to 'development', which is the most serious concern for three-quarters of the earth's population. Why? Firstly, reflecting the male-oriented characteristics of society, the number of women on the staff of aid agencies such as JICA and OECF is still small, especially in decision-making positions. Secondly, the women's movement did not put pressure on government about aid policy, owing to indifference to broader social and political issues, such as economic aid or development. In fact, the impact on women of Japan's economic development was not necessarily a topic of interest for Japanese women.

As a result of pressure from women in Scandinavian and other countries, Western governments and the OECD began to revise policy. The OECD worked out Women in Development (WID) guidelines in 1983, and recommended that all DAC countries put the WID dimension into aid policy. Japan, however, one of the biggest donor countries, did not respond until 1990. JICA formed an experts' panel to draw up WID guidelines by February 1991. Responding to the report, JICA appointed a WID co-ordinator in May 1991, and a WID 'contact person' in each section. AWA was the only women's group to submit proposals on WID to JICA, and held three symposia to make WID issues more widely known to the public, especially women.

It is difficult to evaluate how WID policy is being implemented, as long as access to information on ODA is lacking, and policy is formulated without consultation. It should be added that some women's organisations have recently become interested in WID issues, supporting

UNIFEM, or organising development education from women's point of view. AWA, which pioneered the issue by putting pressure on government and public opinion, is strengthening its campaign to direct Japan's ODA projects to serve the independence of Third World women. AWA, in solidarity with Asian and other Third World women, will increase its efforts to establish a more just and fair international economic system that has no need for ODA.

Overseas investment – the effects of Japanese multinationals on women in Asia

In 1989, Japan became the top overseas direct investor nation in the world, and has been expanding economic activities in most countries in both the First and the Third worlds. The sharp increase in overseas investment began in 1986 as a result of the sudden rise in the Yen caused by the 1985 Plaza Agreement. It was inevitable that Japanese corporations relocate their production facilities into foreign countries, in order to retain a competitive position for their export drive. Japanese corporations felt forced to take up a globalisation policy as a result of Japan's high technology and gigantic production power, which comprises 13 per cent of world GNP. North America has received the largest amount of direct investment from Japanese companies, and Asia the second largest. It is mainly small and medium-sized enterprises that have actively invested in Asia. Their primary motivation is to cut production costs by using cheap local labour, mainly female.

In Asia, Thailand became the target country, where direct investment increased so sharply that it was called the 'Thai Boom', with 10 per cent annual growth in GNP. Japan is involved firstly through direct investment by Japanese companies, and secondly through ODA. More than 70 per cent of the ODA that Thailand receives comes from Japan, and it is used to build the infrastructure for Japanese private investment. There are now nearly 1,000 member-companies of the Japanese Chamber of Commerce in Bangkok. The Japanese presence is visible in all sectors of the Thai economy, and is responsible for the problems caused by fast, but uneven and unequal, economic development. Striking prosperity in the capital, Bangkok – with so many skyscrapers, shopping centres and new cars – is impressive, but a visit to rural areas reveals shocking poverty and misery amongst farmers, who sell their young daughters to brothels in cities and tourist zones, and even to the sex industry in Japan. The farmers also send vegetables to Japan, and large areas of farm land have been converted to the cultivation of corn, tapioca, tobacco and cotton, to be exported to Japan and Western countries. In fishing villages, young women work at dry fish processing, also for export.

The number of Japanese travelling abroad reached 10 million for the first time in 1990. Thailand, whose government's policy it is to promote international tourism, is a favourite destination, and receiving nearly 700,000 Japanese tourists annually. It is well known that Japanese men buy sex from Thai women, and Japanese companies engage in developing resorts and golf-courses. The popular Thai rock band, Gatoon, has a hit song satirising Japan's presence, saying 'Japan eats up Thailand'.

Malaysia has also become a favourite country for Japanese investment. The accumulated amount had, by 1989, reached US$2.5 billion, 41 per cent of total foreign investment in the country. The second largest investor was Britain at 21 per cent. Japan is not only the top investor, but also the top trade partner and creditor country. Some Malaysians are concerned about Japan's dominant presence. Since the 1970s, Malaysia has promoted an industrialisation policy with foreign capital, and a number of export processing zones were established to accommodate foreign companies. Giants such as National, Sony, Hitachi, Toray and others have built factories one after another, and most of their employees are young women.

The Japanese management system and women workers

What problems do women face? Repetitious, boring work; low wages; night-work; occupational health problems, such as deteriorating eyesight; and prohibitions on organising unions are problems common to workers in all multinational companies. Outbreaks of mass hysteria, unique to Malay communities, took place often in most modern factories in the 1970s. However, it should be noted that conditions for women workers in Japanese transnational factories are no different from those for women in Western multinational and transnational factories, and very similar to those for women workers in Japan itself. They are given the most menial jobs, and never have an opportunity to develop a career. Because they supply cheap labour, they are expendable, and there is a high turnover as they themselves choose to quit. Wendy Smith, an Australian anthropologist living in Malaysia, has researched the impact of Japanese management on Malaysian women workers, and her findings attracted much attention in Malaysia, whose government had adopted a 'look east' policy.

Malaysia is not alone in tending to glorify Japanese management; a number of Western economists also consider it the secret of Japan's miraculous economic growth. It consists of three elements: lifelong employment, the seniority system, and co-operative labour-management relations through a company house union. In addition, teamwork and discipline are the main principles. The system is based on family ideology: a company is considered as one family; employees are treated paternalistically by their management 'fathers', and in return are expected to be loyal to management.

Under such a system, young women workers coming from rural communities, where they are brought up to be docile and submissive, are never given a chance to be independent and outspoken persons; on the contrary, they become disciplined and quiet members of their company 'family'. Lifelong employment or the seniority system, which may be beneficial to workers, are usually applied only to *male permanent employees* in Japan, and thus women are treated as temporary and short-term employees, easily laid off or sacked.

Japan is also the world's largest importer of prawns and shrimps and, as well as being responsible for wiping out vast areas of precious mangrove forests for prawn cultivation, it also employs women in prawn processing and packing plants at very low wages. These women suffer from health problems, especially damage to their reproductive organs due to working in the extreme cold of the refrigerator.

The impact of the sharp increase of Japanese multinational factories in Asian countries should be carefully monitored from the point of view of the women workers they employ. The export of the Japanese employment system, and its sex discrimination, should be critically watched.

Korean women workers fight back

Japanese multinationals are also accused of shifting their plants to countries with lower labour costs, abandoning erstwhile workers, most of whom are women. Commonly, women workers are simply informed that their factory is going to be closed down, and they are thrown out offering no resistance. Exceptionally, Korean women workers in three Japanese multinational companies, Korea Sumida Electric, TND and Asia Swany, took courageous action. Women in these companies were told, by a fax from the parent company in Japan announcing the closure of the factory, to quit. They had already organised themselves into a labour union. They could not accept such abrupt notice. They therefore decided to struggle to protect their rights.

After a year, four or five union leaders from each of the three companies came to Japan one after another to negotiate with the parent companies in Tokyo and the Shikoku region. They were young women in their early twenties, and it was their first trip abroad. They were worried about what would happen to them in Japan, the country which colonised Korea for 36 years until 1945, and caused so much suffering to its people. To their surprise, many Japanese workers, male and female, supported their struggle by joining their sit-down hunger-strike in front of the parent company's gates in the freezing cold and rain.

Actually, Japanese workers were deeply moved by the brave action of such young women, and solidarity was soon established. The Sumida Union waged the longest struggle, which continued for more than 200 days until June 1990. Those union members who stayed in Korea, already struggling to survive, also fought to support their leaders in Japan by earning a little money.

All three unions succeeded in getting a large amount of compensation, in a retirement allowance, and Yen 88 million for union employment funds. They would never have received such a large amount of money if they had not fought publicly. Even if they could not reverse the companies' policy to relocate factories to other countries, they won some benefits. This case was successful owing to the determination of Korean women workers, and the warm solidarity between Korean and Japanese workers.

Polluting the environment

Another outcome of expanding investment by Japanese corporations is the export of pollution, which affects women and children in the community. One typical case is Asian Rare Earth (ARE) in Malaysia. A joint company of Mitsubishi Chemical and a local partner started processing monazite, a chemical substance taken from tin ore, in a suburb of Ipoh, the mining area. Radioactive waste (trium oxide) is produced in the process, and the factory disposed of it into the surrounding environment without any treatment. I visited in 1984, and was shocked to see the dumping site. The inhabitants were protesting with rallies, demonstrations and sit-ins. Mothers took the lead in the campaign, determined, they said, because the issue endangered not only their own health but also the lives of unborn generations.

After the government banned their protest actions, they filed a suit in the court demanding that ARE move out. Towards the end of the 1980s, health problems were being reported. An increase in miscarriages, leukaemia and physical handicap amongst children, as well as other symptoms, was noticeable. ARE denied that there was any relationship between such health problems and radioactive waste.

Japan itself has a dreadful history of pollution-related diseases, including such cases as the mercury poisoning of *Minamata*, or cadmium poisoning called *Itai-Itai* disease in Toyama, the victims of which were mostly women. Consequently, in the early 1970s, an anti-pollution campaign spread all over the country, in which women were the most actively involved. In response to the nationwide environmental movement, the companies relocated their polluting plants in other Asian countries. This was severely criticised throughout Asia as 'pollution export'.

Japan's growing military power and vested economic interest

The Gulf war had a serious consequence in Japan: the Japanese government, under the (conservative) Liberal Democratic Party, and influenced by the right wing, deliberately tried to break the post-war peace principle and send the 'Self Defence' Forces abroad. The Japanese Constitution, in Article 9, renounces the right to wage war. People call it the 'peace constitution'.

In 1990, while the US and other Western countries were discussing how to force Iraq to withdraw from Kuwait, the Japanese government repeatedly advocated an 'international contribution' and submitted the United Nations Peace Co-operation Bill to the Diet, to enable the Self Defence Forces (SDF) to join non-combat operations of a multinational army in the Middle East. But there was strong opposition from the public, because the bill was seen as being for war co-operation rather than peace co-operation. Women's groups especially reacted promptly, and organised a nationwide campaign against the bill in order to stop the overseas deployment of Japanese forces under any circumstances. The government shelved the bill, owing to strong pressure from the US government, but contributed as much as US$13 billion to the multinational army in spite of nationwide protests from those who did not want to support military intervention at all. The government went one step further in 1991, by sending SDF vessels to the Gulf to remove mines put in the sea during the war. More recently, the government has proposed a Peace-Keeping Operation Co-operation (PKO) Bill, which allows the SDF to join UN Peace-Keeping Forces.

The women's movement, peace groups and other NGOs are campaigning against the Bill, but the government issues incessant propaganda to the effect that Japan, as a world power, must make an 'international contribution' – and not confine itself to 'one state pacifism' – by sending the SDF to Indo-China, probably first to Cambodia. The Chinese government clearly expressed its concern over the PKO Bill, and people from other nearby countries followed suit, even if their governments refrained from openly criticising their powerful neighbour, in the interests of economic co-operation.

Why do these defence policies of the Japanese government invite such strong protests from China, Korea and South-east Asian countries? Because as many as 20 million Asians perished in the 15 years of war following Japan's invasion of China in 1931, and Asian people still remember the war. They fear the growth of Japanese military power accompanying the economic superpower for, in the eyes of many Asians, Japan has already succeeded in building up the 'Great East Asia Co-prosperity Sphere'. It was Japanese militarists who originally advocated that strategy, to liberate Asia from Western colonial rule by military power, which eventually failed. Any attempt or move by Japan to send its army outside the country naturally causes resentment and concern among Asian nations, who interpret it as a step to revive Japanese militarism.

War responsibility and Japanese women's role in the peace movement

It was women who took the lead in organising the peace movement in Japan after the Second World War. Women felt strongly that there should never be another war, nor any involvement in any other war, because more than three million Japanese had been killed, including more than 300,000 victims of the Hiroshima and Nagasaki atom bombs. A mass peace movement persisting over four decades prevented the government from revising the peace constitution and from having nuclear weapons. However, the government violated the constitution by building up the army, under the name of the Self Defence Forces, and increasing defence spending.

The government, together with the country's right wing, has always been reluctant to admit responsibility for the Second World War. For example, the Minister of Education ordered the use of the word 'advancement' instead of 'invasion' in Japanese school history textbooks, and the government attempted to renationalise the Yasukuni Shinto Shrine, a symbol of militarisation, where 2.5 million Japanese war dead, including 'Class A' war criminals, are enshrined as 'heroes' or 'gods'. They had been sent to other Asian countries to kill. It is unconstitutional to renationalise the Yasukuni Shrine, on the grounds that the post-war constitution strictly separates the state from any religion.

Another war-related issue important to women is the question of Korean war prostitutes. During the Second World War, a number of young Korean women were forcibly recruited, as so-called 'women volunteer corps', as prostitutes for Japanese military men. They were called the 'special gift from the Emperor for soldiers of the Imperial Army'. The number of Korean war prostitutes is not known, but some estimate as many as 200,000. They were sent to the battlefields of Manchuria (north-east China), to South-east Asia and to the South Pacific Islands, and forced into providing sexual services for soldiers, sometimes for more than 50 men a day. When Japanese troops began to retreat, many of the women were abandoned in the jungle or shot. However, an official at Diet committee level stated in 1990 that those Korean 'comfort women' had been recruited by civilian agents and that the Japanese government had nothing to do with them.

Such an official comment shocked women in Korea. Women's organisations took up this issue for the first time. The tragic history of the

Korean war prostitutes had never been openly discussed in Korea before because it was considered too shameful. On the occasion of the Korean President's visit to Japan in 1990, women's groups in Korea formed a coalition and sent an open letter to the Japanese Prime Minister, making five demands: a thorough investigation of the issue; a public apology; compensation; the building of a monument for these victims; and non-biased education in schools. Japanese women's groups supported these demands with a petition, rallies and by publishing books and pamphlets. It should be pointed out, however, that the peace movement in which Japanese women were actively involved was severely criticised by other Asian women, for promoting a victim psychology, and for not acknowledging the fact that Japanese women supported the militarist war against other Asian peoples.

The Asian Women's Association noticed this problem early on, and in 1977 declared:

> Japanese women have been collaborators in Japan's aggression in other Asian countries for more than a hundred years. In the past, it was our male relatives and friends who spearheaded the invasions of Korea, China and other Asian countries. It was they who burned, killed, robbed, and violated women. But now we must refuse to allow our men to be sent to these countries, whether as economic invaders or as sexual exploiters. Without this determination, we ourselves will never become liberated.

It is only during the last few years that more and more demands started to be made of the Japanese government and big corporations to take the responsibility for war. In August 1990, the International Forum on Postwar Compensation for Victims in the Asia–Pacific Region started work in Tokyo, and representatives from war victims' groups in thirteen countries gave testimony. The government still insisted that the war compensation issue had already been fully and finally settled by the San Francisco Peace Treaty, or by bilateral agreements with other governments. It has therefore refused further response to demands from war victims, despite accelerated campaigns prior to the 50th anniversary of Pearl Harbor in December 1991.

As far as the US–Japan military alliance is concerned, the US economic difficulties are a factor forcing Japan to play a bigger military role. The Americans pressurised Japan to contribute more during the Gulf war.

How do Japanese women confront Japan's growing power?

One of the most important factors that has made Japan so powerful economically in only a few decades is the economic system based on sex discrimination. The Confucianist tradition is alive and well, and perpetuates rigid sex roles. Men are expected to devote their whole lives to the companies or any other organisations in which they work. They are forced to work as much as possible, despite the fact that this entails sacrificing family life. The yearly average of hours worked by those in full-time employment is approximately 2,100, compared with 1,600–1,700 hours in Western European countries. Since such long working hours are a particular target of anti-Japanese sentiment in the US and the EC, the Japanese ministry of labour is campaigning to reduce them, but without much success.

Despite the fact that married women with jobs now outnumber those without, women's chief role is to support their husbands at home. Wives handle all family matters, from children's education to housing. For employers, this division of labour based on gender is most efficient, productive and profitable, because they do not have to employ women during pregnancy and child-bearing. Japanese women are often thought to have more power than Western women, because Japanese husbands hand their entire salary to their wives. What this illustrates, however, is the prevailing idea that a woman's place is at home, and that she can rule only within the small world of the family.

Family life with an absent father and a dominating mother causes various social problems. Mothers' characteristic chief concern is how to get their children into better schools, leading them to force children to study harder and harder. Under such a competitive school system, children suffer. A sense of failure is fostered, breeding resentment, and leading some to become violent at home or at school, committing serious crimes or even suicide.

The basic problem is that it is still difficult for a woman to become economically independent, with a well-paid, responsible job. It is true that the number of paid working women has been increasing steadily, and now stands at 17.5 million, or 40 per cent of all employed workers, one of the highest levels in industrialised countries. But this does not ensure progress towards equality. Female workers are paid just over 50 per cent of male workers' wages. There are several reasons for this: having lower education levels, women can enter only low-paid jobs, in smaller companies, with shorter working periods, and no opportunity for managerial posts. They are discriminated against at the levels of job entry, training, promotion and retirement. The Equal Employment Opportunity Law, passed in 1988, was supposed to improve this situation, but the majority of women workers are still low-paid or part-time.

Besides being a housewife or an expendable worker, a third choice for women is to get into the leisure and sex industry. Once a middle-aged woman faces a family problem, such as a husband's death, or divorce, it is not easy for her to get a job with sufficient income to support her family. The so-called 'night industry' – snack-bars and nightclubs – attracts such women. Many Japanese 'hostesses' are married with children.

The shortage of young girls in the expanding sex industry has to be filled by migrant women from neighbouring Asian countries. It is estimated that more than 100,000 young women are brought into Japan every year, 70 per cent from the Philippines, 29 per cent from Thailand, the rest from South Korea, Taiwan and other Asian countries. They are exploited and abused at the bottom of the sex industry.

Why does the sex industry flourish? Japan has a long history of prostitution culture deeply rooted in sexist Confucian ideology: Japan's feudal rulers first authorised prostitution areas, called *Kuruwa*, in 1528. In those days, women were divided into two groups. Good women were supposed to follow the Confucian rule of the three obediences: as a daughter obedient to her father; as a wife, to her husband; and as a mother, to her son. Their main role was to give birth to a son, a successor to the head of the feudal family. It was considered unethical for a married couple to enjoy sexual pleasure. The other group of women, who came from poor families, were those who served men sexually. It was accepted that men went to *Kuruwa* to enjoy sexual pleasure, and for artistic and cultural recreation. This division has been carried over to the present day. Japan is filled with all kinds of pornographic magazines, newspapers, novels and videos. TV commercials and other kinds of advertisement still use women's bodies in spite of protests from feminists.

A second factor behind the expanding sex industry is related to Japan's economic system. Japanese men are often called 'business warriors' owing to their intensive work patterns. They frequent entertainment facilities with business colleagues or customers; sometimes sex services are built into business practice. Companies themselves provide 'entertainment' with women for their employees and customers. The sex industry is thus an inseparable part of Japan's economic growth. Even sexuality is used to make profits. The AWA in response launched an anti-sex-tour campaign, aiming at solidarity between Japanese women and Third World women.

Conclusion

The majority of feminists in Japan do not yet fully realise the problems posed by the economic structure, and tend to fight against discrimination on a personal level, while many women active in the peace or environmental movements lack a feminist perspective. It is the vital task of the Japanese feminist movement to challenge and humanise the Japanese economic system, and to make working and family conditions for both men and women more human. Men should have more time for family life, and women should have real opportunities to be active outside the home, in politics, policy-making and society. The development model pursued – for example in Thailand – has brought about extremely high economic growth on the one hand but, on the other, has caused serious problems to women, such as the expansion of prostitution, homelessness, child labour, overseas migration and so on. Women who believe in solidarity will want to be engaged in monitoring, challenging and changing the impact of Japan's economic strategy and ODA as the means to this sort of development.

11

Making the State Serve Women: The Case of Australia

Eva Cox

Of all the Western developed nations, it was in Australia that women seemed for a time to have developed a magic way of making the government listen and act on their behalf. From 1972, when a Tory government of 23 years was replaced for a brief span by a reformist Labour government, the women's movement had access to politics and bureaucracies in ways that others seemed to see as unusual. Some background is necessary. Australia, one of the largest countries in the world, is geographically spread out, but has a population of only 16 million, mostly clustered in the six state capitals. Sydney has a population of over three million; Melbourne is a bit smaller. The federal capital, Canberra, was established between the two world wars, and is essentially a company town, in that most of its 250,000 inhabitants work for the government.

We have a federal system of government, after the six states handed over powers to a Federal Government in 1901. This leads to certain anomalies, in so far as states hold all the residual power, that is, most of the roles of government invented this century. This makes for strange divisions of power. Community groups and organisations of the marginalised can often play the different levels of government off against each other, like children of squabbling parents.

Two other anomalies serve women well. One of these is a centralised wage-fixing system: an industrial court which has set wages on a national basis since early this century. One of its earlier efforts, in 1907, created very unequal pay by establishing a basic wage for a man with a wife and three children, and set women's pay at two-thirds of that level. After 1972, however, it adopted the principle of equal pay for

163

work of equal value, and gave women an hourly rate that was 84.5 per cent of the male rate.

The second unusual phenomenon is a social security system based on general revenue payments rather than on contributions. The advantage of this is that entitlements are worked out on the basis of need, not on what you have paid, so most people are entitled to some form of income support, even if they have not been in paid work. The disadvantages of this system are that eligibility is estimated on the basis of family income, and is strictly targeted to those who are seen as needy. This means that women who are in a relationship are assessed as part of the spouse unit, so that an unemployed wife has no automatic right to payments, nor, if she has separate income, has her husband. It also means that cohabitation is an issue for more than a few parents, with the government able to marry you faster than the church.

The reason I have outlined these peculiarities of the Australian system is that they also explain some of the state bureaucracy. As the population is relatively small, personal networks can be made to include those in power. In a country where there are central agencies for wages and social security, a decision at the political level can achieve fairly widespread and instant change. One basic decision changed the wage structures in 1972 and made for a gender gap smaller than that of other countries. Since then, the process has been much more static, and weekly pay rates for women are still 65 per cent of those for men. I could give personal reminiscences of the lobbying we undertook to get child care up and moving at a national level, to get funding for services such as women's shelters (refuges), and to ensure that we changed rape laws and health services and so on. Each of these victories is a story full of the intricacies of working the political system and the media.

In the 1990s, I am much less sanguine, as I see the processes we established continue to be sidelined, and the new generation of women settle back into a world we made easier. They do not seem to see that they are still unequal, because we removed the obvious barriers, or that the less obvious are still there. So I want to look at the role of the state and what happened to the processes we started.

A feminist view of the state *qua* government

In Australia, the issue of the role of the state has a particular significance because, possibly more than any other country, we have tended to use the state system to meet political ends. My text for this analysis is Carole Pateman's *Sexual Contract*. In this, she develops a critique of the basis of the modern state. Tracing it from its mythical origins in the social contract theories of Hobbes and Rousseau, she points out that this contract between free and equal parties, whereby the individual agrees to cede power to the state, even then took place between men, and excluded women. Her rationale for this argument is that the state itself legitimated the split between the public and the private. Women were left to the private sphere in so far as most of their activities then, and much of what they do now, are seen as being outside the realm of state regulation and, therefore, women are not citizens in the sense of free and equal recipients of the state's protection.

More importantly, because the modern state was the beginning of the legitimation of the division between private and public, with much of what women did being relegated to the private sphere, the compact between men to create the state and make citizenship the return for the protection of the state (by military service) has never applied to women. The state is still a site of contest between competing interests, but in the last decade of the twentieth century, the players and the field have changed. We have moved from the concept of the state as a collective expression of the needs of the people, to a view of the state as a minimum umpire and controller of the worst excesses of greed. As Pateman says, this is the time when all are assumed to be able to contract for their own benefit, with the state acting minimally as a safety net.

These changes to the rhetoric of individual freedom sit uncomfortably in a world where the gross inequalities within and between nations underpin the modern state. In a world asking serious questions as to limits to growth, individualism and eighteenth-century models sit ill with reality. Therefore my approach is to see which form of government is least likely to ignore the needs of the politically disenfranchised. The individual, free and equal, if such exists, is male, and the framework of legitimacy of claims reflects what is valued by men. If women's interests are not represented, we have little stake in the debates of the modern state. The more rationalised – that is, minimised – the role of state, the worse we are likely to fare. We need to consider ways of avoiding agreement and creating debate as, within the contests, there is some chance of fitting into the interstices.

Women have, over the last few decades, consistently increased their claims on the state, but always in a male-defined world. We have translated much of what was private into the public arena, and sought to put it on the political agenda; domestic violence and child care are two examples. Forms and priorities have been male-defined, and we still fight with other 'marginal' groups for some centrality. Therefore, issues of distribution of community services, child care and so on, are still regarded as low-status, and tend to compete with the unpaid work of women at home and in the community.

One of my concerns is that women are making increasing claims on the state when the state itself is coming under attack. The 1970s saw, on the one hand, the rise of the women's movement and, on the other, the start of the diminution of the state, and the move to internationalise economies and cut the size of the public sector.

Muddling through

In this setting it behoves us to look at the possible ways in which we can intervene to make some broad structural changes. On the radio, as I write, is a programme on women's health with commentary on the gendered nature of medical research, and even of no-smoking campaigns. This reminds me that there is an assumption that the norm is male, to which females are the exception. However, the basis of my argument comes from my reading of the literature dealing with the state as not representing the interests of a large proportion of the population. My perspective is that of marginal people: women and other groups whose access to the state is inhibited by their powerlessness. What form of government is most likely to take account of the needs of these groups?

In the present debates, there is an emphasis on efficiency that tends to override effectiveness. An argument put by Robert Lindblom from Yale University sets up 'muddling through' as a better way of managing than efficiency *per se*. This rings some bells, as it is from within the disorder that claims for a reorder can come. Tight controls, which accord with the male view of citizenship, can create a benevolently totalitarian state resembling the dystopia of Margaret Atwood's *Handmaid's Tale*. A male, rational world might have women serve as slaves.

We should follow the tenets espoused in Lindblom's theory of muddling through. A way of changing process and, as part of this, retaining some of the disorders, is the price of democracy as opposed to totalitarianism; out of conflict comes the possibility of change. One of the challenges that face women over the next few years will be to keep a grasp on the concept of the common good, the universality of servicing through government provision. We live in times when there is a move almost entirely to smaller government and deregulation. This is in spite of many signs that deregulation fails to work, that smaller government creates more inequality, and only the rich get richer.

In the guise of reform, governments are corporatising and selling off assets. By questioning the role of public provision of services and replacing them with private sector or corporated entities, we are forgetting the reason some services were removed from reliance upon market provision in the first place. The welfare state is becoming the private charity state, where the welfare sector becomes the defender of the most needy, while colluding in the constant revision of the definition of who those might be. Where once we pushed for expansion of public provision of services, so that those least able to compete could share the benefits of progress, we are now retreating, to protect the fewest possible, using a wide-mesh safety net. We can no longer assume that continued growth will provide resources to distribute. We can see only that those with power are moving to protect their resources from the possibility of redistribution. Calls for a smaller public sector and reduced taxes are calls for the protection of privilege, disguised as growth.

In the now apparently halcyon days of the 1960s, arguments about the state were couched in terms of left liberalism: an end to censorship, withdrawal of the state from the nation's bedrooms, the right of women to decide upon their own fertility. The state was then seen as an unnecessary intruder into personal choice, and an outdated controller of public morality. Certainly, in the dying years of the post-war boom, continued growth and development was not in question; political lobbying was more about the pace of change and some adjustment to directions, not about fundamentals.

The growth of the women's movement, and its relatively brief period of semi-acceptability, coincided with the reformist zeal, which varied in the developed countries but had generally run its course by the end of the 1970s. The alliances and movements to bring into the public sphere issues once seen as private ran somewhat counter to the 1960s moves to eliminate state control of sexuality, in that they tried to involve the state in controlling relationships within the family to reduce the oppression and exploitation that had been publicly identified by feminists.

As a sociologist and a political being, I find it hard to explain why the changes we sought, and sometimes achieved, had relatively little impact. Two decades' experience of policy agendas and attempts to make changes from a feminist perspective have made me aware that whatever we have done is insufficient, even for the ends we sought. In exploring these problems, I constantly become aware of the marginalisation of my interests and concerns. In the early 1980s, I wrote that we had replaced recipes with rape, but that we were still confined to women's issues. In the early 1990s, I am exploring ways to explain this process. I would like to run through some of the areas in which I am working, and trace some parameters of the debates. Through this I hope to illustrate the ways in which basic presumptions are male-oriented, that women are left as the 'other', alien to a world where they do not fit.

In doing this, I am conscious that my theoretical base is not derived from the recent explorations of the politics of difference. While using some of the insights of deconstruction, I find the processes by which we are divided to be part of a theoretical direction which leads to some dangerous political traps. While acknowledging that the simplicity of sisterhood in the 1970s undersold differences of race and class, the paralysis of marginalised group diversity provides no solutions.

I am a self-confessed activist: the object of my understanding is to change things. My daughter's post-modernist acceptance of understanding being sufficient in itself painfully illustrates generational change. But I ask, whose interests does the inability to represent others serve? In an era where the dominant emphasis is on the individual, it serves the powerful, by keeping us separate.

From general to specific oppression

There are two parts to the problem, which appear to be firmly linked: one is the new world economic order and its relationship to the environmental problems that set limits to growth. This means that no longer can redistribution occur from new wealth but must be taken from those that 'have', if the 'have-nots' are to share. This means that those who 'have' are interested in women's oppression, as a matter of self-protection. The other is that women have moved as far as they can with permission. From now on we have to look at redistribution, as male dominance and paradigms need to change. Change, however, seems to be set in the opposite direction. In a world where reform and greed have been tried, we now face the possibility of regression. We must continue to protect what we can, in the hope that the mistakes made become so evident that they cannot continue.

An example of this is drawn from a recent research project, originally designed to identify the skills that women have acquired through unpaid work. The research design was devised on the basis that certain presumptions about language and concepts could be made and applied. The term 'skill' was assumed to be understood and its meaning accepted without significant gender bias. This has proved not to be the case: we discovered, through the use of unstructured focus groups, that the language of skills, abilities and learning was not gender-neutral, but sufficiently gender-biased and variant to affect significantly the whole area of skill definitions and skill development.

The words themselves appear to be relatively unacknowledged and under-recognised aspects of the processes of skill definition and recognition. 'Skill' is seen by most women we have talked to as a word that does not apply to much of what they do. The exceptions are those skills validated by certification, or those involving the use of tools or machinery. On the other hand, there are activities often seen as female: communication; interpersonal relationships; ability to do many things at one time; emotional and physical caring; and even the work of organising and producing materials without machines. These are not seen as 'skills' by women or men. Where women do it well, they call it 'natural'; where they enjoy it, they call it a 'gift'; but as it is not seen as learned, it is therefore not 'skilled'.

The research we have done indicates two major problem areas: that women are likely to under-report their skills substantially because of female non-recognition of the word; that the workforce skill base will be deficient because the defined 'skills' will omit many which derive from female household experiences, and which are crucial to effective workplace functioning. The good secretary or personal assistant has many skills. Advertisements for 'mature' persons often obfuscate what is wanted: an effective office housewife able to deal with complex tasks while doing the emotional housework. But these skills are never defined as such, as they are seen as attributes rather than skills. Their genesis is in the community, family and home, and they pre-date the industrial revolution. Perhaps the post-industrial workplace reproduces many aspects of the household production models lost in mass industrialisation. Women who bring these skills into the workplace are not usually advocates of their own areas of expertise.

It is possible that this, in part, is a consequence of women's need to be accepted in the paid workplace on male terms. In the process of trying to avoid office handmaiden roles, women sell themselves short. They have tried too hard to look at paid workforce roles through male paradigms, and have eschewed anything that smacks of wifely duties. In that process, perhaps they failed to recognise that changing workforce requirements could validate their knowledge.

Management courses are beginning to recognise that people, not machines, are the core, and that people-skills and strategic planning are essential. We realise that the language of planning comes from the military, but there are fewer generals than housewives, and the ability to juggle time and resources is practised more often at home than in battle, as it comes with family responsibilities. As it is not genetic, males and females taking responsibility for multiple roles often find the simplicity of the workplace a relief after the complexities of early-morning family chaos. This does not devalue the role of management; it points out that similar skills can be used in diverse settings.

Fusing the settings

Feminist analysis has identified some of what had been classified in the private sphere as being a part of the public arena. The family was displayed as a collection of individuals often subject to oppressively unequal power relationships.

I do not wish to underrate the efforts of feminist groups in the 1970s. The battles were hard and often bitter, and there was much soul-searching about the use of the state apparatus to solve problems. Many of us came from the left of the political spectrum, and had analysed the state as being the oppressor. It is crucial to recognise the interaction of the state's representing the interests of the powerful, and its protecting male privilege. Many of the changes referred to above are not necessarily economically rational, but can be explained only in terms of the continued subjugation of women. In periods of growth, it is comparatively easy to remove redistribution from the top of the agenda, and women can gain without obvious losses to men.

When it became clear that growth was limited or negative, and that redistribution would necessitate real losses to the privileged, women were badly affected. A return to family provisions can be argued as cost-saving to the public sector, but it can also be argued as imposing unacceptable costs in other areas; for example, the loss of the availability of additional workers in child-rearing households, which would allow for further depression of individual wage rates. However, these changes have not been greeted with howls of rage by the theorists of the women's movement. Nor has there been much protest from the bureaucracies or women's services. This may be an inability to cope with economic issues, combined with a political re-focus on other areas of state activity. It also springs from a lack of alternative frameworks.

In a paper written in 1985,[1] I commented that the UN Decade of Women had allowed us to broaden the women's agenda from recipes and children to a range of new issues, such as rape and incest, but not to a recognition of our right to comment on the whole of human endeavour. Herein lies a dilemma. The feminist movement needs the power of the state to counter the power abuses that can occur within the family. State power should prevent and punish abuse of the less powerful. However, involving state power in these processes carries the danger that the state will co-opt the issues and rework them to suit dominant male values. The ability of women, let alone feminists, to use state power on their own behalf needs a more thorough analysis.

As an independent feminist in the broad state sector, I can see many dangers. In times of reform in an expanding state environment, the state can be a source of change for the better. New programmes, new laws and new policies can be the building blocks of a better society. But in times of recession and contraction of the state, the lack of will to maintain, let alone expand, the public sector, and the more limited definition of public responsibility, make reliance on the state a dangerous strategy.

Gender inequalities are most evident in the relative privacy of the family; this is an area usually out of public scrutiny. But it is public measures, legislative prescriptions, service provisions and income support that mitigate these inequalities. The diminution of the role of the state in any or all of these areas is damaging to feminist objectives.

Some public issues open up political minefields. These include: pornography; foetal protection, which assumes women are incubators;

and unpaid work. Pornography and unpaid work are both areas in which I have a long involvement, so I want to air some initial concerns. The debate on pornography is a passionate one within the women's movement. When I spoke in a radio debate on pornography in 1991, one caller characterised a 'feminist' view as pro-censorship, and a civil liberties view as anti-feminist. As a feminist libertarian with a great suspicion of ceding power to a male-dominated state, I objected that it was not so simple a division.

The battles of the 1950s and 1960s formed my reaction to censorship. I remember censorship as the means by which sex education material, anything about homosexuality, and in fact almost everything about sexuality and sensuality was banned. A combination of moralism and prurience was the basis for this banning, and I cannot imagine a system which would ban violent anti-women material and let us enjoy sexuality, however defined. We got condom ads only when men became vulnerable to AIDS; women becoming infected or pregnant was never a sufficient reason for offending the moral majority. Violent pornography is a reflection of a sick, women-hating society, but for just that reason, I would not trust the men of that society to make laws against it. I am also convinced that pornography is causal in creating attitudes as well as reflecting and reinforcing attitudes created elsewhere. The stance that many younger women take assumes that the state is going to do our bidding; that we will be able to devise and implement laws on pornography that will control what offends us but not what still offends the vocal moralists who disapprove of sex and sexuality. While it may be possible to arrive at satisfactory legal definitions of pornography, it would be difficult to make the laws stick, or have primarily male judges implement them.

We tread dangerous ground once we start being our own moral crusaders in areas relating to sexuality. My worry is that we give comfort to those who see women as a species in need of protection, not as citizens in our own right defining what we need and want. When I ask whether our target should be violence, not sex, even women assume that this is not feasible. Why? Surely a campaign against violence alone would create enough debate, and women are most often its victims rather than its perpetrators. I fear it is because women would have few male allies, and less general moral indignation to tap.

How does this relate to unpaid work and the pressure for its recognition in national accounts? Both issues separate women from men, playing the politics of difference without incorporating an analysis of power. In one, women are in need of protection and the male state will act as protector, in the other, women's special roles need recognition and the state will pay them a pittance for their services. I pulled some material together for the *Melbourne Age* in response to an increasing clamour from traditional women's groups for payment for women at home. These groups were working on the assumption that women's major function was to service the common good by providing unpaid services. By building on debates about double burdens, put in good faith by women's groups, these supporters of traditional families appeared to be making headway.

Why is unpaid work raised as a public issue just at the time that paid work appears to be again diminishing? Women's groups who first raised the issues, in an attempt to raise awareness of women's contributions, now find the ground shifting. We wanted to show that men's escape from housework contributes to their ability to concentrate, in the comparative peace of the workplace, at the cost of women's unpaid labour. However, the material is again fuelling debate on whether women should withdraw from paid work in return for a small tax advantage for their husbands or a social security payment.

The first point to note is that household tasks are not the sole responsibility of women. We all do something for ourselves and most women do something for others. Women in the paid workforce also do housework and nurturing. In fact studies suggest that there is only about an hour's difference a day in time spent on housework and caring, between those working 20–35 hours a week, and those not in paid work. This is hardly enough to merit a stay-at-home wage and, more to the point, it is men who make the difference in time, not children. This is clearly shown in two areas: the first is a near doubling of housework when a husband appears, where there are no children (90 minutes per day to 164 minutes), with children adding a mere 30 minutes per child under five. The second is the situation of single parents, which shows that children make less work than a spouse. The results show that these women spend less time on cooking and housework than any partnered woman, and have more time for community activities and friends. These official figures indicate that those claiming payment for stay-at-home wives are suggesting a taxpayer subsidy to male comforts.

As the major beneficiaries of the unpaid work are husbands, perhaps we need a levy similar to the training guarantee – a certificate of household compliance showing that adults share housework and caring, or else the non-participants pay a tax levy on income. We must make sure that unpaid work is counted. This is necessary because in many areas it underpins and replaces the paid sector. More women in paid work means more eating out, creating more jobs. Fewer public services for the aged mean more women at home and more dependency on pensions and benefits. The unpaid work is a necessary part of the equation. However, again it is being used against us; in the US there is a plethora of articles on the way women are giving up work and going back to mothering because the double burden is too much for them. The cause was a 1.2 per cent drop in the work participation rate of women between 25 and 34. In fact, male participation in the same age group had fallen by an identical percentage, but this was either ignored or correctly assumed to be a result of the recession, clearly the cause of the women's drop.

Our hold on the positions we have gained in the last twenty years is tenuous. It is more tenuous now than it was a decade ago. We need to be vigilant about the political possibilities of certain options, and make sure we are aware of our history. The last decade has seen the dysfunctionality of many of the present paradigms and we need a change. I do not subscribe to the essentialist femininity argument, but to a materialist one which sees women's experiences as being different from men's, and therefore giving rise to alternative views. But what we see in practice is women avoiding what is male and therefore allowing men to define by opposition. This means we are caught in the shadow world as reactive not active.

So we move slowly, still tied to dominant modes of thinking, unable to free ourselves to take a new view, to see the alternative. Feminist theory is critical but does not construct new possibilities, outside the powerful masculine frameworks which limit our ability to change. We need to develop a new set of metaphors. If we cannot develop a clear sense of what we want, the troglodytes of racism and aggressive nationalism – particularly male tribal rituals – are still close to the surface, and capable of defining the near future.

We need to make our utopias, but within a framework of creating the basic building blocks. We need to find what constitutes a decent and caring society, which will not use gender to reinforce privilege. The task is urgent, because the possibility of communities becoming ungovernable and unsafe is very much a present worry. We must weave a new fabric of community, which gives people a vision of a new society. We have seen the possibilities of a better state apparatus; its failures were not ours, but came from the protectors of privilege. Can we find the practical means of creating the feminist dream?

Note

1. E. Cox, 'Decade of Women or Decayed Women's Issues', *Labour Forum*, Adelaide, 1985.

12

Women's Citizenship and Human Rights: The Case of Brazil

Jacqueline Pitanguy

Introduction

In unequal societies the problem of exclusion is inherent in any analysis of social and political participation, and leads immediately to the question: who are the citizens? Or, in other words, who are the groups which are politically disadvantaged and discriminated against? And by what criteria? A prerequisite for such questions is the acknowledgement that this exclusion is part of the structure of most of the so-called equal and democratic societies.

Historically, the way in which so many women have defined and represented their experience of disadvantage and discrimination, widening and redefining the political sphere, has varied. Such variations occur both in the issues raised and in the political methods of raising them. The historical expression of discrimination against women will wear different features according to the interaction of the main protagonists in the political arena, among other factors.

Feminism can be seen as a social movement creating and projecting a new collective identity within social space. Its relationship with the social space has, as a starting point, the perception and experience of sexual hierarchy in both the public and private spheres. These perceptions and experiences direct the survival strategies of women and lead them to assume different forms of political struggle and participation. This participation – either in political institutions or in social movements – and the success of feminist collective action have to do with the structural characteristics and the political conjuncture of each society. These variables, together with the specific capacity of the protagonists to act upon the social structure, are responsible in large measure for their relative weight in the balance of power.

If we agree that the sociological configuration of the political scene is due to the appearance (and visibility) of new historical actors claiming an appropriate role within the dynamics of power, and if we consider feminism as a new historical actor, we have to examine its efficiency in reshaping this space. Has it been successful in extending a political voice to new actors? In other words, are the questions raised by women considered a legitimate part of the political debate of that society? Has feminism been able to introduce new questions, related to the uneven distribution of power between men and women in both public and private space, into the voices of those to whom society gives legitimacy to speak? Has it been successful in taking away the legitimacy of those who do not consider such questions valid political issues?

Has it been successful in lifting the veil with which the dominant political ideologies have obscured the exclusion from and the deprivation of full citizenship of large sections of the population, such as women and racial groups? Has it been successful in influencing the legislature, the executive, or the judiciary, or in articulating women's demands to those institutional powers?

Awareness that the discrimination suffered by women is the result of historical processes and can thus be transformed establishes an immediate logical connection between women's demands and the need to have access to power to respond to them. Although this seems to be a logical and simple connection, the linkage between demands and public policies is very difficult to establish, since it affects the political processes of the country and the reshaping of relations between the state and civil society. To start from this logical relationship to bring about real change in women's condition was the great challenge that women's movements in Brazil faced in the 1970s and 1980s. This chapter deals, basically, with the role of feminism in widening women's citizenship rights in Brazil, and with its role as a new historical actor on that country's political stage.

The general political context

In countries where full citizenship is not so far assured for large sections of the population, social movements can play a fundamental role in the expression and articulation of the claims of disadvantaged groups. It is important to call attention to the fact that while, in certain developed countries, some people consider that feminist debate can be superseded nowadays, because they believe the institutional sphere has already incorporated its demands, this does not prevail in Brazil where, even considering recent important advances, women are still in many respects second-class citizens.

Brazil has a population of 147 million, 72 per cent of which is concentrated in urban areas. Although female workers tripled their presence in the labour market during the period 1970–85, from 6 million to 18.5 million, it is still a supremely male space. Women occupy a limited number of functions, performing inferior tasks and receiving lower salaries. According to 1988 data, the median income of a female worker is 52 per cent of that of a male worker. There is a higher percentage of women without a registered professional card, which means that they do not have access to social benefits and allowances. This situation is more sharply accentuated in the rural areas, where, in certain places, up to 86 per cent of female workers lack this access to social benefits. In urban areas it is rare for women to articulate their survival strategies in the informal market.

Although women's participation in the legislature at state and municipal level has been increasing significantly, they are still a minority in those assemblies. At the Federal level, female deputies constitute only five per cent of Congress, and there is only one female senator. The situation of women in the public sphere is a result of the division of sexual roles still in force in our culture, where women's concrete reality and presence are closely associated with domesticity. They have difficulties, therefore, in establishing relations with the so-called institutional world. The pattern of sexual asymmetry is reinforced by an overall devalued social representation of women's image.

Oppression and discrimination arouse the desire to change and to resist. In Brazil, in the 1970s and 1980s, women have been resisting and trying to transform the patterns of relationships amongst themselves, with others, and with institutions, finding expression as new political actors through social movements. In this process of redefining rights, of denouncing exclusions, and of social change, the crucial relationship between the individual and the state, which defines the boundaries of human rights and citizenship, is being reshaped.

In 1964, a military regime was instituted in Brazil, and the 1960s and 1970s were characterised by the establishment and consolidation of an authoritarian regime, on the basis of militarisation of political power, and the diversification and modernisation of the state apparatus by rigid repression of the formal channels of political expression open to civil society, such as political parties and trade unions. The authoritarian style of the regime was at its strongest between 1969 and 1973, a period which coincides with the so-called 'economic miracle', when growth in GDP reached 13.6 per cent per year.

In 1974, parliamentary elections were allowed because, trusting in the substantial economic growth, the government expected an electoral victory to legitimise the authoritarian political system. The elections (which had a clear referendum character) resulted, however, in a significant electoral defeat for the government party, ARENA. From that year on, the government started to put into practice a transitional strategy which, broadly, proposed the creation of a strong party in power, and coercive methods to maintain control over the process. It is important to note that this political project took place with considerable reinforcement of central government, marked urbanisation and significant industrial development.

Between 1964 and 1974, civil society organised itself to resist the military regime, to struggle against it, and to survive within that struggle. There was no room for the individualisation of political actors in that struggle. On the contrary, the political organisations had the unity of the so-called 'Brazilian people' (regardless of sex or race) against the military government as a principal objective.

From 1977 to 1978, the country experienced an intense political mobilisation, with the resurgence of unions on a new basis and with the appearance of social movements on the political scene, qualifying the opposition and bringing new elements to the concept of democracy. Within the economy, GDP growth rates declined, and even became negative in 1981 and 1983, reflecting the effects of revenue concentration policies on the overall decreasing standard of living. The country's transition to democracy took place, in general terms, against a background of economic difficulties and significant differentiation of the protagonists of political struggles.

In the 1982 elections for state governors, the opposition won in the most important states and, in the legislature, the government party obtained only 36 per cent of the votes. During 1983 and 1984, Brazilian society mobilised its largest mass movement, *Diretas ja* (direct [presidential] elections now). This explosive mass movement brought together various politically organised associations, groups, parties, grassroots movements and traditional politicians who, while keeping their diversity, acted jointly in the contest over the legitimacy of the government to represent civil society. Despite the fact that the parliamentary majority needed to change the electoral law was not obtained, an alliance of parties enabled the election (through the electoral college) of a civilian member of the opposition as president, after 21 years of military presidents.

Feminism in Brazil

Feminism as a social movement in Brazil experienced a historic watershed in 1975, when a group of women organised a seminar in Rio de Janeiro, under UN auspices, which centred on the discussion of the role of women in Brazilian society. Although the organisation of one seminar may seem much too simple to deserve such an appraisal, this was exceptional. The seminar was held in the post-electoral period, in which the defeat of the conservative party brought about the opportunity to realise some of the rhetoric of gradual transition and, at the same time, caused a recurrence of political violence from the repressive structures of the state. During this week-long seminar, hundreds of women met to discuss their situation in the labour market, their image in mass media, their rights to control their bodies, their rights under civil and penal codes, and so on. The seminar permitted the systemic formulation of a number of questions which were already present but hidden.

In fact, civil society had already started to widen the political space, through claims from movements for amnesty for political prisoners, in defence of human rights, from ecclesiastic communities, press associations, and others which expressed resistance. Among the social movements that had built collective action on the basis of their individuality, the women's movement – in which feminism can be seen as the ideological avant-garde of its political theory, but which included a number of other organisations – was one of the most expressive during the 1970s. In 1975, the first feminist organisation in Brazil was created: the Centre for Brazilian Women. Since then, numerous feminist groups have appeared and disappeared throughout the country, acting in different areas and with different methods and organisation, along with other women's organisations like neighbourhood associations, mothers' clubs, women for amnesty, women's sections of political parties and trade unions, and so on.

It is not possible, therefore, to deal with this social movement as a monolithic bloc. Social groups built through solidarity originating in the sharing of a common collective identity incorporate, as part of their dynamic, discussion of the elements defining such an identity, and of the ways to project it in the public space. Taking the interconnection of such social movement with institutional politics in Brazil, it is possible to distinguish some key moments of that dynamic.

1975–79: This phase corresponds to the establishment of feminist controversy in the country. The main protagonists are the left wing (organised in clandestine or legal parties), the progressive sectors of the Church, and the universities. There was a frail dialogue with the legislature, basically through an attempt to present a project to change the civil code. The Church was an important element, but it created divisions within the movement, since some themes, such as sexuality, contraception and abortion, were taboo. There was no contact with the executive. During those years, debates in the university, public demonstrations, academic discussions, denunciations of violence against women and claims for equal rights gave visibility to the question of discrimination against women. Treated at the beginning as exotic and frivolous, little by little they gained respect from large sectors of the press. Although there were marked differences among feminists as to the alliances that should be made (and thus the priorities of the movement), feminism became part of the political debate in this period, raising the following basic issues:

- women's entry into the labour market, and the invisibility of unpaid housework;
- sexual stereotypes in education, the lack of free public day-care centres;
- proposals for amendments to the civil and penal codes;
- reproductive rights, abortion, sexuality;
- violence against women, including symbolic devaluation of their image.

1979–82: In 1978, the government was defeated in the main urban centres, and the process of differentiation of the political actors was accentuated by the appearance of new elements in the political arena, such as black movements, homosexual groups, movements for the demarcation of Indian lands, strong neighbourhood associations and ecological groups. A law abolished the two-party system, and the government lost control of the democratisation process. In this period, the women's movement did not expand the numbers of feminist groups, but grew by broadening the type of its participants. The Church lost influence, as the majority of the movement no longer accepted the exclusion of 'taboo' themes from national debate. In this period, strong links were established with political parties, urged to include women's claims in their programmes. There was also a visible growth of women's studies centres at the universities, and the academic world made sexual hierarchy and women the subject of theses, congresses and seminars.

At the moment the opposition no longer expressed itself as a homogeneous front, linked by the slogan, 'no to the military regime', and gave public visibility to the diversity of their projects, feminism, too, faced its own heterogeneity in discussion about interaction between social movements and institutional politics. A tendency within the movement considered that it was necessary to participate in the process of democratisation, occupying spaces at the executive level, in view of the opposition's victory in the 1982 governmental elections. The movement discussed the possibility of the creation of a state-level organ, to develop public policies to improve women's condition. There were three main positions: those who were for the creation of and participation in such an organ; those who did not want to participate but approved of the project and gave political support to it; and those who were against any kind of interaction with institutional power.

1983–85: In this period, the economic and political deterioration of the military regime that had run the country for two decades was accentuated. The loss to the government of states as important as São Paulo, Rio de Janeiro and Minas Gerais, and defeat in the National Congress were responsible for the elites who supported the party in power losing control of the democratisation process. The opposition, demanding direct elections for the presidency, brought about the renewal of power dynamics in the country.

In 1983, a group of feminists from São Paulo decided to take the momentous step of walking into government after years of opposition to it. The Council of Women's Condition of São Paulo was then created, followed by the Council of Minas Gerais. In 1985, another huge step was taken, this time into the repressive apparatus of the state, the police. Starting from the premise that feminist rescue groups could not deal with the problem of violence against women in all its vast scale, feminists proposed the creation of special police stations to be run entirely by policewomen, who could attend victims of sexual abuse and domestic violence. Councils at state and municipal level were established in many parts of the country, and at least 70 special police stations, all over the country.

Along with the campaign for the election as president of Tancredo Neves, a civilian representative of the opposition to the military, the creation of an organ to advise the President and ministries on public policies for the improvement of women's condition became a major topic of discussion among feminists. The experience in São Paulo was quite positive, but there was always the fear of being co-opted by the state, of the social movement being weakened by occupying institutional space. It was decided to establish this organ as part of the presidential campaign.

Activists did agree, however, that at this crucial moment of political democratisation, it remained necessary to enlarge the concept to encompass the recognition of gender and race discrimination, the existence of which ensures the impoverishment of democracy. A majority of the women's movement also agreed this it was the right moment to establish, through concrete proposals, a link between governmental power, public policies and gender.

Gender and power at federal government level

The project to occupy an institutional space at federal government level mobilised women all over the country. President Jose Sarney was pressured to keep the promises made by the late Tancredo Neves, and strong lobbying was exerted in the National Congress to ensure approval of the law creating this organ. The National Council of Women's Rights (CNDM) was created in 1985.

To keep a clear vision of social change and to build bridges between the state and civil society, divided after so many years of military rule, and to try to work democratically in a state apparatus that had served authoritarian governments for 21 years was a great challenge to those who worked there for four years organising its structure and the implementation of its proposals. We have seen positive results, confirming the belief in the use of institutional power as a passport to full citizenship for politically disadvantaged groups, and we are (with great pain) protesting against the destruction of the experiment.

The National Council worked on three fronts: the women's movements, the legislature and the executive. The dialogue with civil society has been its main political force, based on a view of feminist groups and other women's organisations not only as targets of public policies but, more importantly, as subjects designing those policies. An example of the feasibility of establishing proposals, both for the executive and the legislative assemblies, through democratic discussion, was the strategy adopted by CNDM to present women's proposals for the new Constitution and to exert pressure to ensure that those proposals would be incorporated.

Broadly, this strategy began by launching national campaigns organised by regional women's councils together with the various groups and organisations at state level. At the same time, using the mass media with messages on TV and radio, in newspapers and on outdoor hoardings, the National Council would give national visibility to the issue under discussion. CNDM would also prepare documents with statistical data, current and comparative legislation and so on to support the debates. These campaigns would then culminate in large meetings held at the National Congress in Brasilia (the federal capital), with the representatives from the various groups and organisations that, throughout the country, had participated in the debate. They would arrive in Brasilia as political actors with a legitimate voice to be heard by politicians and other elements of the executive.

The second main protagonist in CNDM's work was the legislature, chiefly the National Congress, where an intense interaction with women members of parliament and detailed work in the private offices of party leaders created clear channels of communication between this governmental organ and the Congress. It is interesting to note that CNDM's legitimacy with opposing parties was very strong; the reason for this, I submit, was that they sensed that the CNDM was representing civil society's claims and not a technocratic governmental position.

The strong interaction between social movements, the CNDM and Congress led to the inclusion in the new Constitution of 80 per cent of women's demands. The final source of support for the CNDM was in the executive itself, where different relationships were established with various different organs in this sphere. It is important to note that the executive is never a monolithic bloc, that different interests are represented there, and that its dominant profile is usually the result of internal tensions and disputes. This characteristic of the executive was accentuated in Brazil at this time. At the moment of CNDM's creation, the country was at the beginning of a process of transition from authoritarianism to democracy. In the first years of Sarney's government, progressive and conservative forces were struggling for hegemony in its composition. New alliances were being made, and the ideological profile of the executive was not clearly defined. There was a wide margin for manoeuvre, and the National Council was able to act without suffering strong conservative pressures.

Between 1985 and 1989 CNDM worked chiefly in the areas of health and reproductive rights, rural and urban labour markets for women, the struggle against violence, and for day-care centres, education, culture, legislation and black women. Up to 1988, when the new constitution was approved, CNDM worked intensively with the National Congress. It also established its Centre of Information and Documentation, CEDIM, and co-ordinated the National Forum of Women's Councils, forging a network, which is fundamental in large countries like Brazil. Throughout those four years, many campaigns in the mass media were developed, in order to give social visibility and political strength to women's denunciations, claims and proposals. CNDM's work, in each of those areas, was political and not charitable. In each of those fields, CNDM also developed its own programme, organising meetings, elaborating studies and information, bringing, for the first time in our history, the discussion of gender issues to the highest level of the executive.

CNDM also played an important role at the international level, especially at the UN, where it participated actively in the Commission on the Status of Women. It is important to remark that international influence was relevant for the creation of the Council, as the UN strongly recommended the establishment of national machineries in the fight for implementation of the Convention on the Elimination of All Forms of Discrimination Against Women.

I began this discussion by pointing out the need to insert the specific analyses of social movements into the larger boundaries of general political processes and power dynamics, since those variables are largely responsible for the definition of the limits and possibilities of any attempt to create social change, either by direct action from the state or by struggles to change the state, or both. The limits and possibilities of the institutional spaces conquered by women, at municipal, state, or federal level, are interrelated with their relative weight within the state apparatus, which will be determined by, among other factors, the political visibility of the groups whose interests they represent and by their stance towards the hegemonic ideological line of the executive.

The first years of Sarney's government were not very clear ideologically, but it acquired more and more conservative features. Each movement by CNDM to strengthen ties with social movements and to enlarge the concept of democracy and the duties of the state was a political conquest that represented a menace to the conservative forces within the executive. The enforcement of the democratisation process in terms of empowerment of the social movements had, in contradiction to it, a tendency for the executive to re-establish its conservative profile. After all, this governmental machinery had for 21 years served the interests of classes and social categories with no links to civil society in general, and still less to the so-called 'sociological minorities' like women. The predominance of conservative forces in the balance of power led to the loss of important positions and institutions within the executive. The Ministry of Land Reform was abolished, more progressive politicians who held high office resigned, and the President reinforced links with conservatives in the Federal National Congress.

The constitutional conquests of CNDM in different fields, and the clear promise of empowerment to social movements, so as to guarantee full citizenship to women, was a menace to the hegemony of conservative forces inside government and in Congress. In February 1989, a new, extremely conservative Minister of Justice was nominated by President Sarney. The pressure on CNDM became stronger. However, the National Council's political legitimacy was very high, and the minister was criticised publicly by women's movements, state and municipal Councils of Women's Rights, and by progressive Representatives in the Chamber of Deputies and the Senate. The minister, however, pursued his persecution of CNDM, and cut 72 per cent of its budget. Resistance continued until he interfered with the political composition of the advisory board, achieving the nomination by the President of a majority of conservative women with no links to social movements .

To remain in government under those conditions would have entailed accepting a complete change of CNDM's original proposals, being co-opted by an executive that no longer recognised changing gender relations and improving women's condition as one of its own goals. Consultations with women's organisations led the councillors and others who held management and co-ordinating positions, including the present writer, to resign. The decision came as a result of collective political reflection and not as an emotional outburst. There was no longer any place for a progressive organ to defend women's rights within the bureaucratic machinery. The state, at federal level, was no longer an instrument for the extension of human rights and the redefinition of citizenship rights for women.

Since then, CNDM has lost its importance in Brazilian politics. I believe that the purpose of this destabilisation was not even to replace its progressive role with a conservative equivalent, but simply to destroy its efficiency and effectiveness. In fact, nothing has been done, and the National Council is today a moribund body, remembered only for its past actions .

General considerations

After 1990: We are still writing this story. Democracy is a permanent process of political participation, of gains and losses, of constant demarcation of the boundaries of citizenship. This is especially so in countries where long- and medium-term projects are frequently aborted owing to conjunctural alliances. Democracy is especially difficult for those who, like women's movements, come to the political arena without the economic force that powerful interest groups have, but only a belief in the legitimacy of its claims as its chief weapon.

The dynamics of power, resulting from the interaction and the relative weight of the various political protagonists, will determine the basic trends of the future relations of feminism and institutional politics in Brazil. The movement has been strong enough to relinquish an institutional space that no longer represented its proposals for the use of power to create social change, and by this refusal it took away the political legitimacy of the Council. This legitimacy was not taken because there was no longer any need for such an organ, but because of the immediate circumstance.

I would like to go back to some of the questions I raised relating to the efficacy of feminism, as a political actor, in reshaping the political space. I do think that, in Brazil, issues like sexual hierarchies, violence against women, unequal legislation, inequality in the labour market, and the right to basic reproductive rights are part of today's political questions for most protagonists in the public sphere, and that the majority of them can no longer pretend that these questions do not exist, nor that women's voices should not be heard. As for abortion, although there is much resistance to its political visibility, feminism has been successful in bringing it into the national debate, and ending its cultural suppression as a cursed and hidden subject.

Feminism was also successful in becoming a protagonist and actor in the political arena. Its importance has risen or fallen according to a number of factors, but since 1975 it has been part of the scene. There are, however, many questions to be answered and many others that cannot yet be formulated, which will arise from future social and political dynamics. Among the first, I would like to ask whether it is possible to relate the democratisation of interpersonal relations and non-institutional political practices to the democratisation of the state? This is certainly a challenging question, for the answer to which, in our country, we shall have to wait.

Note

This text is basically the result of reflections on my experience as a feminist, as a member of Rio de Janeiro's women's movements, and as President, for almost four years, of the National Council of Women's Rights. In this sense, it has a very limited bibliography.

I would like to point out Michel Foucault's large contribution to the study and understanding of the micro-mechanics of power. For a discussion of his methodology, see Michel Foucault, *Microfísica do Poder*, Rio de Janeiro, ed. Grall, 1979.

The analysis of social movements and, particularly, of feminism in Brazil was done, in part, by myself and Branca Moreira Alves, in our book *What is Feminism?* published by Brasiliense, 6th ed, 1981. Annette Goldeberg presented an interesting paper at the International Political Science Association (IPSA) World Congress in Rio de Janeiro in 1982, on the story of the Brazilian Women's Centre, *Feminism under an Authoritarian Regime*. I analysed feminism and social movements in Brazil in a paper presented at the IPSA World Congress in 1985, in Paris, *The Women's Movement and Political Parties in Brazil: A Discussion on Power and Representativity*. Renato Boschi, in *The Art of Associating: Social Movements, The Middle Class and Grass Roots Politics in Brazil*, a post-doctorate report to Stanford University, 1984, has interesting questions on Brazil's new political culture, with the presence of social movements in the country.

13

The Popular Initiative: The Feminist Impact on History[1]

Judith P. Zinsser

The exclusion of women

The modern study of history, as it evolved in the United States, and elsewhere, left few places for women, either in the historical record or in the historical profession. As one male scholar described it: 'The subject matter of history is always men in the midst of other men – men in collectives and men in groups.'[2] Those few women thought worthy of inclusion in the chronicle of 'mankind's' progressive march through the centuries usually appeared tangentially as wives, mothers, and mistresses of famous men. The only active female agents – such as Empress Theodora, Joan of Arc, Anne Hutchinson, Catherine the Great, Florence Nightingale, Carrie Nation – gained a place in the history books because they had assumed roles usually assigned to men. Whatever the reason for their appearance, most fell prey to stereotypes as ancient as Western culture: the selfless helpmate, the manipulative queen, the evil seductress, the martyred virgin, the shrill reformer.

With the professionalisation of colleges and universities in the nineteenth century, only men seemed competent to recover and analyse this history. The few women who acquired the credentials and position of university scholars braved ridicule and subtle humiliations, found themselves marginalised in female institutions and subject to a double standard that required them to perform like 'superstars' if they hoped to achieve recognition, doing more and doing it better than their male contemporaries. In most instances, the attempt to combine marriage, children, and a household with scholarship forced other choices; some gave up their careers, some took leave of absence that called their seriousness of purpose into question, others became the last, best acknowledgement in their husband's work.

Since 1969, feminist historians in the United States have challenged and worked to alter these scholarly and political realities. In that year, the *Journal of American Social History* published Gerda Lerner's article, 'New Approaches to the Study of Women in American History'. That same autumn, Berenice A. Carroll successfully petitioned the American Historical Association (AHA) for a study of women in the profession, and organised a coalition of feminist scholars committed to change. These feminists saw their tasks as two-fold: to broaden the definition of 'history', and to alter the concept of the 'historian'.

By the early 1990s, their victories could be quantified. More women had gained access to training, had completed their degrees and found positions. Professional organisations like the AHA had supported their demands. Women had held offices of every variety, including headships of university departments and the presidency of the two major professional groups, the Organization of American Historians and the American Historical Association. The field of women's history had become a major subspeciality of the discipline, with every trade and university press heralding its newest works by and about women. Journals from a feminist perspective flourished. College catalogues regularly listed courses in the new field. Women's research institutes and women's studies programmes were established on campuses across the country. By 1988, 63 universities offered graduate degrees in women's history.

Amidst the reality and genuine sense of accomplishment, feminists also identified changes that had *not* occurred. As one scholar described: 'From my perspective, women's historians are like unexpected and uninvited guests. We have arrived, but we have been left to fend for ourselves, unfeted and unwelcomed.'[3] Women trained and were hired, but they did not advance as quickly as their male contemporaries; nor did their salaries rise equally. The senior woman professor remained 'a rare creature' even in the 1990s. The highest-paid university chairs still went to men, the overwhelming majority of adjunct and part-time positions to women.[4]

Even more disheartening, despite the vast scholarship about women's past and a range of suggestions for the synthesis of women's and men's experiences, in the early 1990s, few writers of 'mainstream' history had incorporated this new knowledge, these new analytical approaches, into their courses or their research. The majority of academic historians remained traditional in their outlook and failed to understand, or even acknowledge – beyond a few bibliographic references – the significance of alternative histories or of gender as a category of analysis. A pessimist would describe women's history as separate, segregated in women's courses, in the later sections of textbooks, in monographs and collections of articles and documents kept on different shelves in the library. In short, the study of women had not become part of the general scholarly inquiry, had not changed the basic framework of historical study.

All historians agree that the ways in which we perceive our past have significance well beyond the numbers of pages in a textbook or of minutes in a lecture or class discussion. It is a truism of nineteenth- and twentieth-century historiography: the connection between a people's discovery of their history, their coming to national, ethnic, or racial awareness, and their subsequent rejection of second-class status. For women the phenomenon has been the same. Since Europe's first feminist, Christine de Pisan, sat in her study in the early fourteenth century, using the lives of queens and martyrs to counter the vilifying contemporary portrayals of women's nature, learning of the past has given women pride and elicited outrage. The modern feminist Sheila Rowbotham has called this 'historical selfconsciousness', that moment when a woman realises that her experiences, her sense of disadvantage and denigration, are not unique; when she understands that she holds this in common with other women both from her own time and from the past.

Historically, these feelings of identification and connection have brought comfort and the courage to oppose that which had 'always' been accepted. It is for these reasons that knowledge of women's history has been so important not only to feminist scholars, but to all feminists. By reading, writing and teaching about the female past, historians create bonds between women and make possible 'the reproduction of feminists', the training of new generations to strength and autonomy.[5]

Local tactics to national strategies

Women historians have not been alone in this endeavour. While they have worked to transform their discipline and the academy, across the United States feminists in local and state government agencies, in factories and offices, in social and professional clubs, have initiated their own challenges and programmes for change. The leaders of these groups publicise women's history as part of their overall strategy. They ignore theoretical arguments about categories and causes, academic questions of segregation and marginalisation. They simply want people thinking and talking about women's history, valuing women's accomplishments and contributions. The impact of such appreciation they see as two-fold: women will act to bring about change; men will not oppose that change.

Most influential of these 'grassroots' initiatives has been the National Women's History Project (NWHP), which from the late 1970s has devoted its efforts to advancing multicultural women's history in virtually any place, shape, or form that seemed to catch people's attention. The idea of a public celebration of women's history evolved when Molly Murphy MacGregor was taking extension courses at Sonoma State College. She worked with other feminists on plans to make an event out of International Women's Day, 8 March. The establishment in 1975 of the Sonoma County Commission on the Status of Women, 'to eliminate discrimination and prejudice on the basis of sex', created the local institutional framework for taking the event out into the community. In October 1977, MacGregor, Bette Morgan and Evelyn Truman, all volunteers with the Commission's Task Force on Education, proposed that the local schools observe a 'Women's History Week'. In their proposal to the Commission, they admitted that it would be 'impossible to cover women's history in only one week', but they hoped that 'this exposure will inspire students and teachers to question further and discover more of women's heritage'.[6]

Their first 'week', in March 1978, set the pattern for subsequent local commemorations and for the kinds of events that would ultimately be organised throughout the United States. The Task Force enlisted everyone's help. When school administrators seemed reluctant, they went straight to the teachers. They talked to local politicians, to federal and state equity officers, to leaders of women's organisations. They developed the idea of 'Community Resource Women', women with all kinds of jobs and talents willing to go into classrooms and speak about their life: artists, carpenters, dentists, a salmon fisher, needleworkers, all pleased to be asked and able to hold students' attention. MacGregor and other members of the Education Task Force took a slide show on women's history, which had originally been done for a class at the state college, and presented it for women's groups and school assemblies. In February, they ran a one-day conference suggesting resources and activities with the motto 'A woman's place is in the curriculum'. When their week in March had arrived and passed, they could point to success across the county: approval from county officials, 90 elementary and 30 secondary schools participating, and support from the feminist community.[7]

By March 1979, Sonoma County and its rural communities had instituted a wide range of activities in connection with women's history: the teacher workshops sponsored by the Commission on the Status of Women and Sonoma State College, library displays and talks, and a printed guide for a week's worth of classroom activities. They organised their first parade to Santa Rosa's Courthouse Square, giving public officials, store-owners, and women's groups something practical to plan for, something specific to do. More than any of their other ideas, the parade made Women's History Week into a community event that everyone participated in, around which all kinds of activities could be organised. Most important, the parade made the week more than a feminist statement by a few dedicated activists. The County Board of

Supervisors, community leaders, and local educators could imagine it as an apolitical act, and think of their support and participation as simply a way to honour women's experiences and contributions to United States history. One early organiser remembered how significant it seemed 'that women could have a parade all their own'.[8] These political choices and tactics distinguished MacGregor and the Commission from other local feminist initiatives, and explained their early effectiveness and subsequent impact. They had a single mission: to expand and sustain awareness of multicultural women's history. They believed that this new awareness would change attitudes, lives and futures. Boys and men would come to understand that the majority of women for most of their lives have two jobs: their household and their waged work. They argued that historical omissions and distortions had robbed 'our children, and all members of society [of] the richness of women's heritage and often the inspiration to become active participants in society'. They saw this new knowledge as a way to make all women 'more self assured, more responsible for our deeds, and more optimistic about the power we have over our lives'. As MacGregor explained at the press conference just after the California legislature's declaration of the state's first Women's History Week: 'We're trying to make them understand that they are the makers of history, that it's their responsibility and if they sit back and let someone else make those decisions for them, they lose out on life, and we lose out on the kind of culture we want to live in.'[9]

Their goal from the beginning was to find ways to spark this awareness and to inspire this sense of power: clear, simple tasks; symbolic acts and words that turned a concept into something practical and tangible. In their hands, a feminist scholar's commitment to alter the discipline of history became one month out of the year to celebrate women's past. They valued any positive response to their initiative: a banner across a Santa Rosa shopping centre parking lot, a women's history group meeting in a factory cafeteria, a community college art show, a slogan on a beige canvas tote bag, one working women's song in a school assembly, a display of women's writings in a bookstore window. Alice Kessler-Harris once said, 'a token is better than none', and this was how MacGregor and her colleagues thought as well.[10] Everything, as MacGregor explained, became a 'vehicle' for implementing the overall goal. In this way, the NWHP offered what Gerda Lerner suggested the women's movement needed: 'new structures and focus', which gave 'continuity' to feminists' efforts to bring other women and men to 'historical self-consciousness'.[11]

In order to have the broadest possible support and participation, MacGregor and her friends avoided language or pronouncements that might turn away supporters. MacGregor had, in fact, worried about the first parade and the ways in which massed groups of women might alienate the northern California rural community. Mary Ruthsdotter, a volunteer who later became chair of the Commission on the Status of Women, rewrote the original curriculum guide to remove what might have been considered 'leftist' rhetoric. When they stopped working with the Commission and formed their own organisation, this sensitivity intensified. They changed their 1982 Women's History Week poster when they realised that green and white were the colours associated with the National Organization for Women and with the campaign for the Equal Rights Amendment. As Ruthsdotter explained, their ultimate goal was for people to understand 'it's not political, it's just history'.[12]

Their approach, MacGregor proudly announced to workshop participants, 'by just about any standard you can name has been a success'. They have made popular celebrations of women's history a national reality. The 1987 Congressional resolution turning National Women's History Week into a month-long commemoration, justified passage with a series of clauses describing the role of 'women of every race, class, and ethnic background', and the need to value and include their 'critical' and 'unique' contributions to the history of the United States. By 1990, in cities, suburban and rural communities, the month meant multiple activities on many days, some officially initiated by municipal, state or federal authorities, others by voluntary and educational organisations and institutions, some spontaneously generated.[13] State and city departments of education sent display materials and sponsored workshops. The New York City Commission on the Status of Women published a calendar with different events for each day, and distributed voluminous information and curriculum packs. Affirmative action offices and human resource departments encouraged activities. In 1990, the United States Patent Office organised an exhibit on women inventors, and the NASA Space Center in Houston sponsored a month-long programme of events. The Hazelton, Pennsylvania and Booneville, Idaho historical societies used the occasion to initiate oral history projects.

Throughout the 1980s, the range of non-governmental organisations that used and promoted the month expanded exponentially; everything from the Iowa Inter-church Forum to the Girl Scouts of America, the Cherokee Nation of Oklahoma, the Association of Retired Persons, and Kirkland Air Force base in New Mexico. Even industry became involved: there is a women's history club at Bell Labs in New Jersey, and a women's group at AT&T in Lisle, Illinois. The leaders of the AT&T celebration wrote a newsletter and put posters up in the company cafeterias. Cities and organisations thought of innumerable ways to publicise women's accomplishments past and present. They exhibited art works, and sponsored plays. They brought in women speakers much like the original Sonoma County 'Community Resource Women', with every kind of expertise: writers to speak or read their work, such as Molly Ivers of the *Dallas Times Herald*, Sara Paretsky, the mystery writer, the novelist Sandra Cisneros and memoirist Maya Angelou; politicians like Shirley Chisolm, Geraldine Ferraro, Chief Wilma Mankiller (leader of the Cherokee Nation), and Reita Rivers, who had worked with Jeanette Rankin (the first woman to serve in Congress); the folksinger Gerri Gribi; Bonnie Dunbar, the astronaut. Local and national groups sponsored writing contests and award banquets to honour local notables. The National Organization for Women offered US$1,000 prizes to the winners of its essay contest. Other kinds of events encouraged broad participation in more active ways: the women's history fair in Canton, Ohio, and the candlelight march in Moro Bay, California. Although it did not generate as much publicity or involve as many people, Laura Hotchkiss Brown's banner showed the power and excitement generated: a former student at Columbia University, Brown hung a 140-foot banner across the decorative facade at the top of the university library. Where, under the eaves, Socrates, Aristotle, and the male intellectual elite had been named, now everyone on the campus saw proclaimed instead Christine de Pisan, Simone de Beauvoir, Virginia Woolf, and other feminists.[14]

From college to Congress

The local initiative became a national phenomenon, the local tactics part of national feminist strategies, when MacGregor read about a women's history course for community leaders at Sarah Lawrence College. She sent off all the material they had about what they had done in 1978 and planned for 1979, hoping that she would be chosen as a participant. (She was then Deputy Director of the Commission, a paid staff member, no longer a volunteer.) MacGregor thought of this course as a special opportunity, 'the chance to go national', the means to excite women in other parts of the country so that they would 'go back and do it within their own organisations'. They imagined women's history week celebrations all over the United States. The story of the response from the course organisers is now part of the lore of the NWHP: no word, nothing for weeks, until finally a very thin envelope arrived. Sure that it was a rejection, MacGregor opened it to find only a brief message: 'Congratulations – you have won a sistership.'[15]

Gerda Lerner, one of the organisers of the course, had spoken of education in women's history not only for students and scholars, but also for those outside the academy, ever since her 1971 presentation to Sarah Lawrence's Committee on Restructuring the College. A volunteer activist herself in the past (in the civil rights movement of the 1960s), she hoped particularly to attract and involve women community leaders. Between 1972 and 1977 the college sponsored a fellowship programme for such women, offered seminars for them in women's history, and enlisted their participation in a conference on 'The Future of House-work, the Role of the Housewife, and Sharing Arrangements for Child Care'.[16] In the late 1970s Lerner and Barbara Omalade of the Women's Action Alliance applied for a grant from the Lilly Foundation for a 19-day women's history course for community organisers. With the US$55,000 award, Amy Swerdlow, director of Sarah Lawrence's women's history programme, and Omalade enlisted faculty and selected participants. They chose 39 women from varied groups across the United States. In addition to MacGregor from the Sonoma County Commission on the Status of Women, representatives came from the Girl Scouts of America, Comisión Feminil Mexicana Nacional, the Lesbian-Gay Task Force, the National Council of Negro Women, the Leadership Conference of Women Religious, Rural American Women, NARAL, and Carolyn Reed's organisation for domestic houseworkers.[17]

In addition to the lectures and discussions organised by the course leaders, MacGregor wanted time for the participants to learn about each other's organisations. She needed such an opportunity to convince them to become involved in their own women's history week celebra-tions. They were given one evening. MacGregor explained the idea of a women's history week and showed slides of the 1979 parade. Though not all of the participants would have described themselves as feminists, they all supported the goals of the women's movement and believed that knowledge of women's history would not only make their organ-isations work better but would also benefit the cause in general. They saw the potential of the Sonoma County events at once. It seemed natural to use this course as a means to publicise the idea of a national commemoration, a federally recognised national women's history week. Some of the participants, and the graduate student teaching assistant, Pam Elam, reworded and expanded the 1978 Sonoma County Board of Supervisors' resolution. Gerda Lerner read it at the Smithsonian break-fast in Washington DC, which both honoured notable American women and celebrated the end of the institute. The participants' resolution called on Congress to establish a national women's history week. In this way, the idea was included in the press releases for the Smithsonian event, and gained its first national hearing.

Pam Elam, a feminist lawyer and former executive director of the Kentucky American Civil Liberties Union, took on the task of making the institute resolution a reality. She and Peggy Pascoe, the other gradu-ate student teacher, began the campaign: letters to mayors, governors, members of Congress. In the autumn, staff of the women's congressional caucus – from the offices of Barbara Mikulski, Patricia Schroeder, and Elizabeth Holtzman – met Elam and MacGregor and agreed to support a bill. Things happened very quickly. *Ms* magazine published a short piece on the idea. Requests for information and materials came from all over the country, deluged the Sonoma County Commission office, but demonstrated the immediate popularity of the concept. The resolution was introduced on 26 February 1980, but with too little time for passage before March and the week of the 8th, the time around International Women's Day designated for the celebration.

But the lobbying had an effect. On 28 February, MacGregor answered the telephone at the Commission. It was the White House calling to speak with 'Ms MacGregor'. President Carter's special assistant, Sarah Weddington, came on the line to tell her that the President had decided to issue a 'Message' declaring National Women's History Week. This presidential support and Elam's and Pascoe's efforts led governors in 16 states (including California) to make similar proclamations. To get the congressional resolution passed, a network of women politicians, community organisers, feminist activists and women historians worked throughout 1980 and 1981. The Committee on the Status of Women at the American Historical Association enlisted the executive director's support. When Gerda Lerner became a president of the Organisation of American Historians, she brought that group's endorsement as well.[18]

Mary Ruthsdotter later remembered that the 1981 congressional vote gave them 'the legitimacy we'd been hoping for all along'.[19] This success justified decisions already made. They began to experiment with ideas for their own organisation and with ways to raise funds outside the Commission on the Status of Women. By 1981, they had separated in a variety of ways: MacGregor left the Commission in the spring of 1980, and she and Morgan, Ruthsdotter, and two other supporters, Maria R. Cuevas and Paula Hammett (then a student at Sonoma State College) named themselves the National Women's History Project, an independent non-profit organisation.[20] They stopped doing all the work on shared typewriters in someone's kitchen and moved to their own offices, patched-together space donated by Nell Codding, owner of the local regional shopping centre. They acquired their logo from Kathleen Smith (a Pomo/Miwok Indian): a designer for the county group, Women of Color. With MacGregor's profile added to the other four, all of the major racial groups in the United States were represented, with their philosophy, information about Women's History Week, and the beginnings of what they would call the 'Women's History Resource Service'.[21]

Changing lives

Directly and indirectly, each of the founding members of the NWHP came to an appreciation of their history as women and their determination to use it as feminists because of Alice Wexler's course at Sonoma State College. Though a rural area of northern California, by the early 1970s even Sonoma County had been affected by anti-war activism, agitation for migrant workers' rights, and feminism. When students insisted on a course in United States women's history, Wexler, a Latin Americanist and the only woman in the history department, agreed to teach it. Bette Morgan told a classmate, who suggested she take Wexler's course, that she 'didn't really have time for it'. She had four children to raise and support, her work as a Catholic activist for migrant women, and a major to complete in architectural history. An artist friend persuaded her to change her mind; Wexler, and women's history, led her to change the direction of her life.

This was the era when each bit of women's history came as a surprise, each heroine's accomplishment as a personal discovery. Morgan remembered that Wexler always began by asking the students to name five women in history; 'and, of course, no one could do it'. For Morgan, the moment of 'historical self-consciousness' came in Spring 1972, when she helped to create a women's history slide show as part of the campus celebrations for a visit from the French author Anaïs Nin. Morgan was part of the group collecting the pictures. She particularly admired Viola Luizzo, a white volunteer from Detroit, shot by the Ku Klux Klan in Mississippi. 'I couldn't find her, and that made me think.'[22]

Although Nin became ill and never did speak on campus, the slide show (which was shown to her in hospital) almost overnight became part of a continuing effort by the college's feminists to publicise women's history throughout the whole community. When, in Spring 1974, MacGregor came to take courses, she was recruited to help in the presentations. 'We the Women: Advocates for Social Change' – five reels of slides, taped music, and a script to be read by multiple voices portrayed 'the story of the common woman and how she has worked to create a better world for you and for me'. To emphasise this point, the first images were photographs of women from their own families, a particularly moving segment for all who created the sequence. However, for their audiences, for women who had never known about women's activities, never seen the faces of famous women, and never heard their words, it would have been the procession of 'stars' that elicited the biggest response: Anne Hutchinson's heresies, Sojourner Truth, Clara Lemlich, Ida Wells Barnett, Jeanette Rankin voting against war, Alice Paul, Margaret Sanger, Bessie Smith singing, Dolores Huerta speaking, and many more. In its final version, the presentation ended with Helen Reddy's 'I Am Woman', as the evocative background music for pictures of contemporary activists such as Bella Abzug, Angela Davis and Gloria Steinem.

In subsequent years Morgan, MacGregor and Cuevas would speak and write with intensity about the power of feminist history because of their own and other women's experiences.[23] Morgan remembered: 'We'd stand in the back of the room and read the script, do all the different parts, and the lights would go on, and women would be crying.' Often, she and MacGregor recalled, 'the women in those early audiences got angry. They felt they had been deprived.' They wanted to act on this new-found awareness. As Morgan explained, we saw 'that history could do that, that history could have an impact ... could reach out to certain women and really change their lives'.

The academy and the network of professional historians gave encouragement, but the NWHP soon discovered that state and federal agencies and departments would be the more valuable allies in promoting their multicultural vision of women's history. At the 1979 founding conference of the National Coalition for Sex Equity in Education, they met Barbara Landers, who not only supported them through this organisation (US$3-4000-worth of sales at the Coalition's yearly summer conferences),[24] but also in her capacity as Director of the Title IX Assistance Office of the California State Department of Education. Landers saw women's history as a means to sex equity for young people, and the Project as an effective agent to bring women's history into schools. She showed them how to write convincing grant proposals, and financed their first official teaching conference in 1983. In 1981, NWHP was awarded US$104,000 from Women's Educational Equity Act (WEEA) funds to make an in-service teacher-training tape-slide programme.[25] The US Department of Education subsequently funded curriculum units, a workbook, three programme guides, and six videos. State and city departments of education sometimes bought materials on a grand scale; in 1982, Vermont purchased information packs for all of its 400 social studies teachers.[26]

State and national equity and affirmative action programmes supported the project with consultancies and money for training conferences. For example, Equal Employment Opportunity Affirmative action officers were responsible for the Workplace Organizers Conference in 1989. Ruthsdotter discovered that it was the Sex Desegregation Assistance Centers, under Title IV of the Civil Rights Act, that still had budgets for materials in 1991. Companies like Hewlett-Packard used their videos in employee training programmes to satisfy government requirements for the encouragement of multicultural sensitivity and gender equity.

At first, the group tried to maintain the feminist ideal of a women's collective, but the practical realities of their many tasks created a hierarchy despite their egalitarian intentions.[27] As Morgan remembered, 'in order for things to move forward ... there was a distinct need for the buck to stop somewhere'. More and more often, 'the buck' found its way to MacGregor. Over the years, she had become a particularly good spokeswoman.

With MacGregor as executive director, Ruthsdotter and Morgan developing materials, and Cuevas overseeing the business arrangements, they made 1983–84 the pivotal year of the NWHP. They established sources of revenue other than government grants, and stepped into their name.[28] Together they learned successful small business tactics: loans to finance an inventory for the Resource Service's peak sales period in January and February (with their houses as collateral), catalogue design, product development in new areas, such as history videos and spin-offs from previous guides and curriculum units, the creation of new services like the Network, and a newsletter. They wrote professional loan applications, and explained with confidence that 'direct market competition will not develop in the foreseeable future'.[29] With each year, the NWHP became more sophisticated and more efficient in every aspect of its operations: a glossier product delivered, faster and more varied services.[30]

As in many effective enterprises, their enthusiasm, their optimism, and especially their ability to translate their own and others' experiences into general practice have been key reasons for their impact. When Ruthsdotter wrote a summary of their entrepreneurial services in 1990, she used the sub-headings 'successes' and 'problems'. Techniques that proved useful have been passed on requiring little or no change. From the beginning, they included in their planning guides copies of everything that they had used at the Commission in organising their first women's history events. They even printed essay prize award certificates ready for duplication. The 1991 catalogue offered a 'new' item for the novice organiser: a 20-minute keynote speech for US$15.

A good idea would be expanded upon and appear in a different form. Ruthsdotter's visit to a Santa Rosa classroom to talk about quilting turned into a kit with pre-cut construction paper to piece and sew. By 1991, the original slide show had been transformed into five videos; the 1978 elementary and secondary school curriculum packages, with five topics for each of the five days of Women's History Week, had become a variety of individual history units and three separate activities guides: one focused from a curricular point of view, one from a planner's perspective, one emphasising creative arts.

From the first observances of National Women's History Week around the country, the Project solicited participation and disseminated the responses: 'Your Help Is Needed', read the 1983 flyer, accompanied by a questionnaire. The NWHP promised to 'pass on your ideas, experiences and suggestions', and sent thank-you letters when people sent contributions.[31] The 'Real Women' essay-writing contest, now an event in many states, originated in the Sacramento Unified School District. A play by four Minnesota high-school students was included in the 1991 catalogue. The activities of Barbara Tomin, a Santa Rosa second-grade teacher, are now like traditions in some school districts: celebration of Susan B. Anthony's birthday, costumes and banners for parades, and a kids' variant of Judy Chicago's Dinner Party. The '101 Wonderful Ways to Celebrate Women's History', a staple of the NWHP publications, was created because so many good ideas came in from teachers and administrators. When a donor wrote that she had wished she had known of the Project in time for Mother's Day, the staff acted on the suggestion and turned their annual solicitation into a way of honouring someone for mother's day.

In many ways, the NWHP in-service training video, 'History Revisited', illustrates all of the strengths, the intuitive and purposeful techniques, that explain the feminist impact of the organisation in public history classrooms. MacGregor remembered that her own education in women's history had begun when she was teaching 11th-grade United States history. A student asked, 'What is the women's movement?'[32] Her own experiences became part of the video script: a male teacher confronted with a similar question, the interested look on his face, and then MacGregor's voice explaining: 'it's time we opened our classroom doors to all the women in America'. Every aspect of the video emphasises the multicultural nature of the subjects, the revitalising effects in the classroom of women's history, and the ways in which student attitudes will change as a result of its inclusion: a boy learning to appreciate his grandmother's stories, a girl admitting that she 'never thought about my family having anything to do with history', and deciding that she liked the subject now.

True to their ideal that women's history can give a sense of power and purpose, the video declares that it will demonstrate 'what human strength can accomplish'. They make no effort at synthesis, at the formulation of a new history. Rather there is a positive, progressive view of events, and one that focuses on the biographical. From the perspective of the NWHP, history has had its male heroes, now female ones will be lauded as well. The choice of the positive is intentional. In the spirit of Mary Beard, the project, through all of its materials, shows 'women as active participants in the events of our nation's past'.[33] Also, the biographical happens with less conscious purpose for practical reasons: biographies sound more interesting than 'history', and fit easily into slots in a curriculum.

This consistent simple message, the pragmatic, inventive choices, the energy and persistance of the leaders, the ability, as Cuevas phrased it, 'to do what's in front of me', have had an impact on the way history is perceived both inside and outside schools across the United States. In addition, the NWHP has fostered a more positive view among the general public of what otherwise might be labelled, and even dismissed as, 'feminist history'. The NWHP uses the slogan from the first National

Women's Conference in Houston in 1977 to describe its work: 'We're here to move history forward.' The Project's impact exemplifies the ways in which women's history and feminism have come to intersect and interact. The NWHP has affected one, then another, and another classroom generation. As early as 1984, a young supporter wrote: 'I am a 11-year-old girl concerned about women's rights. I am behind you 100%. Most of the girls in my 6th grade class are also fighting for you. But not as much as me.' She described a successful draw, 'your favorite woman contest', that she and a friend had organised: 'Even boys entered!' She concluded, 'Well I just wanted to write this short letter (that could have been 9 pages long!) to tell you there's more people out there fighting! With you forever.'[34]

Feminist historians in the academy also have a connection with this confident little girl. They have their own successes to applaud. They have created the scholarship and professional authority that the NWHP has translated and promoted. They can count professorships and graduate programmes, they can cite publishers' lists and women historians' names in professional journals. They have nominated and voted for feminist colleagues for campus offices and for jobs within professional associations.

In the end, the transformation of the discipline and the profession that feminist historians have worked for may require both kinds of strengths and both kinds of strategies: the intellectual and the intuitive, the rational and the pragmatic. All feminists must come to terms with the political realities of the culture. As Bette Morgan explained, 'We put our lives into changing people second by second ... I know I can't control the change – control how it happens. I just know I can make a difference.'[35]

Finding ways to fund their activities and the most effective structure for their organisation evolved in much the same way.[36] At first, all of the original founders thought in terms of volunteering, sharing expenses and doing as much as possible themselves. All except MacGregor had to have jobs outside of the Commission – adjunct teaching, historic preservation projects for local townships, campaign planning for local politicians, working at the local unemployment office. Cuevas had formed a singing group called 'De Colores' with a friend, and was trying to make a living as an entertainer. Their first fund-raising successes came from cookie sales at peace demonstrations, and requests for donations.[37]

Although an ardent feminist, MacGregor could walk into a room full of social studies teachers, most of them team coaches, and put everyone at ease with anecdotes about her five brothers and growing up in a large Irish Catholic family. Willing to use any teaching technique that proved effective, she intuitively developed an ingenuous, intense way of working with groups, which combined an air of the homespun with the confidence of an expert. Invariably, when the meeting was over, she had convinced the participants that they had always believed in the importance of women's history. In addition, it became obvious that MacGregor had not only become the public image of the Project, but the central figure for each of the other women founders as well. In the next two difficult years of completing their first videos (no one knew how to make one), of trying to keep money coming in, juggling person- alities and tasks, though they referred to MacGregor as 'M3' and had their teasing stories – that 'brown on brown' was her 'favourite colour scheme' for publications and posters, that she wore a heavy wool coat when she first moved north from southern California – each of the original members said that 'Molly' was the reason she stayed on.[38]

The women who conceived the NWHP began promoting women's history in their community – Santa Rosa, California – at the local branch of the state college. They continued their efforts, first as volun- teers and then as paid staff members of the Sonoma County Commis- sion on the Status of Women. Their first activities included presenting their own slide show about notable women, encouraging a group of high-school students to evaluate history textbooks and library resources, and requesting that area teachers celebrate International Women's Day in their classrooms.

By 1990, their week-long Sonoma County celebration had become National Women's History Month, declared by congressional resolution and commemorated throughout the United States. The group of friends had become the National Women's History Project, with a staff of seven, and a budget in the hundreds of thousands of dollars. Over 300,000 catalogues went to classroom teachers, leaders of non-profit organ- isations, public education administrators, state equal employment oppor- tunity commissioners, and corporate affirmative action officers, all of whom acknowledged the group's expertise and their particular vision of history as a means of raising awareness and countering discrimination against women. In the mid-1970s, the slide show went with them to the Education Task Force of the Commission on the Status of Women. By this time, it had been shown all over the county, even, in San Francisco, to a group of secretaries at the Standard Oil corporate headquarters. With the first celebration of Women's History Week in 1978, it was natural that the slide presentation should be the focal point of the Commission's annual dinner. This was the evening that made Mary Ruthsdotter a convert to, and a proselytiser for, women's history. She remembered that MacGregor kept ad libbing because something happened to the projector, then to the tape recorder. 'I was really glad for the equipment failures because I was just sitting there stunned .... All this was up there on the screen ... . Why hadn't I ever heard of any of this? I was amazed.'[39] Later, she realised how much her own

experience mirrored that of other women. As her father was a pilot in
the Marines, she had always lived near airfields; she raced around her
backyard pretending to be a plane, and kept model jets in her room.
She even had a biography of Amelia Earhart, but it never occurred to
her that she could be a pilot.

Morgan, MacGregor, and Ruthsdotter had their own styles and
perspectives, but they shared the same overriding goal – to promote
multicultural women's history – and a willingness to do whatever works.
Morgan later remembered that the shift from a local initiative to a
national project 'just seemed a natural progression'.

After Bonnie Eisenberg joined them, with experience not only at the
Commission on the Status of Women as MacGregor's successor, but
also with newspaper and small press publishing (she founded and edited
the Marin County *Women's News Journal*), they expanded the catalogue
(to 48 pages in 1992), researched and wrote more guides and curriculum
units, and took on new tasks, such as editing an elementary textbook
series for McGraw Hill.

She illustrated this delicate balance between action and impact with
a story from her own childhood. She recalled a walk on the beach with
her father. He stopped in the midst of what he was telling her, took her
hand, opened the fingers and filled her palm with sand. He told her to
close her fingers as tight as she could. The harder she squeezed, the
more the sand pushed through and fell from her hand. Then her father
told her to begin again, but this time to hold her hand open. The sand
stayed still and heavy in her palm.

Notes

1. Much of this material appears as a chapter in a larger work on history and
the historical profession in the United States, *The Feminist Impact on History* (Twayne
Publishers, forthcoming).

2. David Hackett Fischer, *Historians' Fallacies: Toward a Logic of Historical Thought*
(New York: Harper & Row Publishers, 1970), p. 217. See also, for descriptions of
history and historians as male, E . H . Carr, *What Is History?* (New York: Alfred A.
Knopf, 1963), pp. 34–5.

3. Gay Gullickson, 'Comment', *Social Science History* 13 (4) (Winter 1989), p.464.

4. The Committee on Women Historians of the AHA has made periodic studies
of women's status, beginning with the Rose Committee Report in 1970. For the
'cohort' of PhDs of 1982–88: by 1988, 2.9% of the women had risen to the rank of
full professor. The equivalent figure for their male contemporaries was 12.1%. Women
represented 8.9% of those in adjunct and part-time positions, men 0.6%. Over all
ranks, women's salaries in four-year colleges and universities were 80.6% of men's.
See *AHA Perspectives* 29 (2) (February 1991), pp.17–18.

5. Hester Eisenstein, opening remarks, unpublished, Columbia Seminar on
Women and Society, 15 April 1991, New York, NY.

6. Molly Murphy MacGregor, Bette Morgan Patterson, Evelyn Truman, 'Proposal for Women's History Week', 19 October 1977, Molly Murphy MacGregor private papers. The information on the Commission came from Elizabeth Bock's files on the Sonoma County Commission on the Status of Women.

7. Information on the first year's activities came from the Sonoma County Commission on the Status of Women, Annual Report 1977, Bock files.

8. At first the city refused to close Main Street for them, so all the groups marched on the sidewalk. On these first years see, for example, the Board of Supervisor's 'Resolution' proclaiming 6–10 March as women's history week, National Women's History Project Archives and NWHP Celebratory Program, video, Santa Rosa CA, 18 May 1991.

9. Molly Murphy MacGregor, 'Annual Report 1979–1980' to the Sonoma County Commission on the Status of Women, Bock files. Sacramento Press Conference, 4 March 1980, tape, NWHP Archives. This reasoning is a staple of all NWHP publications; see, for example, 'Academic Rationale', 1982, pp. 2–3, and flyer for Women's History Week, 1981. Other feminist historians have written on the debilitating and denigrating effects of the omissions and illusions of traditional histories – see Gerda Lerner, preface, *The Majority Finds Its Past: Placing Women in History* (New York: Oxford University Press, 1979), p. xvii; Lerner, 'The Majority Finds Its Past', *Majority*, pp. 163–4; Dolores Barracano Schmidt and Earl Robert Schmidt, 'The Invisible Woman: The Historian as Professional Magician', *Liberating Women's History: Theoretical and Critical Essays*, ed. Berenice A. Carroll, (Urbana IL: University of Illinois Press, 1976), p. 53.

10. Alice Kessler-Harris, panel discussion, Berkshire Conference of Women Historians, 13 May 1989, New Paltz, NY.

11. Gerda Lerner, 'Report on Summer Institute for High School Teachers', 13 November 1976, p. 3, Amy Swerdlow private files.

12. Mary Ruthsdotter, interview, Santa Rosa CA, 13 May 1991.

13. Molly Murphy MacGregor, 'History Revisited', video, National Women's History Project; 1987 Congressional Resolution, NWHP Archives.

14. Descriptions of events came from NWHP Archives.

15. MacGregor, interview, 18 May 1991. For a description of the 'Send-Off Party' and the plan to make T-shirts like those sold at the parade for all of the Institute participants, see 'Status Quotes: News from the Sonoma County Commission on the Status of Women' (July 1979), p. 1, Bock files.

16. As part of this broader commitment, in 1976, Sarah Lawrence, in co-operation with the American Historical Association, had run the first National Endowment for the Humanities teacher training institute. See Gerda Lerner to Committee on Restructuring the College, 29 April 1971, pp. 1–2; 'Minutes of Feminist Studies Committee', 3 April 1973; 'Call for Planning', March 1977; 'Evaluation Report: Women Studies Program', p. 6; all are from Amy Swerdlow private files.

17. See *New Directions for Women* 8 (4) (Autumn 1979), pp. 12–13, 23.

18. The account of the events came from interviews: MacGregor, 15 May 1991; MacGregor and Pam Elam, interview, New York NY, 7 July 1991. The lobbying continued because the resolution has had to be repassed, first every year and now every two years. Mikulski is the sponsor in the House of Representatives, Orrin Hatch in the Senate. Passage has become more not less difficult over the years, because of general congressional annoyance with this type of commemorative resolution. For 1990, MacGregor remembered that it was harder than ever.

19. NWHP video No. 1, May 1984, NWHP Archives.

20. Initially, the Project had non-profit status as part of the Women's Support Network, which they had founded to deal with these problems.

21. The first flyer for the National Women's History Project offered three guides: one on how to initiate celebrations, one on activities, and one giving elementary and secondary materials (much of it taken from curriculum units developed for Berkeley public schools). To raise money to finance their continuing efforts, they sold T-shirts, badges, a tote bag, and their first commemorative poster. Descriptions of these early years came from interviews with: MacGregor, 15 and 18 May 1991; Cuevas, 15 May 1991; Morgan, 25 June 1991; NWHP Video No. 1, May 1984, NWHP Archives.

22. The stories of Morgan's responses and actions came from her interview.

23. For the leaders of the NWHP, the establishment of their own non-profit organisation meant a kind of professional autonomy they had never experienced. Each exemplified Gerda Lerner's definition of what 'autonomy' means for women: 'moving in a world in which one acts and chooses, aware of a meaningful past and free to shape one's future'. Lerner, 'Majority', *Majority*, p.162.

24. In 1990, they realised net sales of their own and others' books, curriculum materials, and videos of over US$713,000, with 64% from out-of-state orders. They run yearly training conferences in California and six other states. Maria R. Cuevas, speech for International Coeducation Conference, University of Valencia, Spain, 3 November 1989, p. 6, and published in edited form in *Women of Power* No. 16 (Spring 1990); Maria R. Cuevas interview, Santa Rosa CA, 15 May 1991; Net Operating Profit Worksheet, June 1990, Maria R. Cuevas files. Mary Ruthsdotter notes, May 1991.

25. The Project had already been funded under Title IX with a more modest grant of US$25,000 in 1980 to replicate an assignment MacGregor had done with students to evaluate gender bias in their textbooks and classes.

26. Notes on 1982 Celebrations, NWHP Archives. Information also came from MacGregor interview, 15 May 1991; Ruthsdotter notes, May 1991.

27. See, for example, the flyer for 1982: 'The staff is not salaried; decisions and expenses are borne collectively.' 1982 Flyer, p. 3, NWHP Archives.

28. Cuevas interview. In June 1982 they made approximately US$26,000 in sales of materials they had created themselves, and others they had chosen from educational and trade sources; the equivalent figure by June 1984 was US$106,000.

29. NWHP, n.d., information sheet for bank loan, pp. 2–3, Cuevas files.

30. For example, in 1988 they added a mailing for Women's Equality Day, the 26 August celebration of the passage of the Women's Suffrage Amendment. 'It was a marketing thing for us', explained Ruthsdotter, 'we needed another time of year'. Not only did Women's Equality Day add another occasion to commemorate women's history, but also a new category of individual and institutional supporter. Every federal office, even military facilities, had a Women's Program Manager or a committee established to foster affirmative action and broader opportunities for women. When other groups lost their funding in the late 1980s, these organisations could still purchase materials and offer workshops. Ruthsdotter interview.

31. 1983 flyer and form, and postcard for 1986, NWHP Archives.

32. MacGregor interview, 15 May 1991.

33. Cuevas speech, p. 8; 1990 workshop video No. 1, Santa Rosa CA, NWHP Archives.

34. Mary Alice Carter to NWHP, 26 November 1984, NWHP Archives.

35. Morgan interview.

36. Morgan interview.

37. They proved ingenious at finding ways to finance projects for less. The 1978 poster was silk-screened by students funded by CETA (Comprehensive Educational Training Act). The 1979 parade cost almost US$1,000 for banners, fees, and other expenses. As the organisers, MacGregor, Ruthsdotter, and their Commission and Task Force friends went to the Youth Fund in San Francisco for a loan, paid it back with donations collected at the parade, and used the extra money raised to make a new copy of their slide show. This pattern of borrowing, making up not only the loan but enough to move on, became characteristic of the Project. The plans just became more elaborate and more costly.

38. Information about this period came from Cuevas interview; Bonnie Eisenberg interview, 18 May 1991; Ruthsdotter notes, May 1991; Morgan interview.

39. This account came from NWHP Video No. 1, May 1984, NWHP Archives; Ruthsdotter interview, 13 May 1991. Ruthsdotter and her family moved to Santa Rosa from Los Angeles in Summer 1977, primarily to have a better place to raise their daughter. Trained in urban planning at UCLA, Ruthsdotter had also made time to be active in political campaigns, in anti-war and abortion rights groups. She was looking for a group to work with and, having heard of the Commission, she, her husband, and daughter went to one of their evening meetings. She volunteered and eventually became chair of the Commission. On her marriage, she had taken her husband's name, Dawson, but changed it in the early 1980s to a version of 'Ruth's daughter'.

14

Making a Dent: Feminist Writing in Mainstream Media

Anita Anand

The 1970s marked the beginning of three international events and processes that were to become a principal focus of feminist writing in mainstream media. These were the United Nations Decade for Women (1975–85); the New International Information and Communication Order (NIICO), spearheaded by the United Nations Education, Science and Culture Organisation (UNESCO), and, less known, less recognised and often not accredited, the international women's movements.

The UN Decade for Women was announced after the 1975 International Women's Year conference held in Mexico City. Two follow-up conferences were held in 1980 (Copenhagen, Denmark) and 1985 (Nairobi, Kenya). The NIICO's goal was to redress the perceived imbalance of information and communication between North and South, and the lack of it between South and South. Within this project, the need emerged for special attention to be paid to the absence of women's voices from mainstream media.

At the same time, the women's movement, North and South, was gaining momentum. Despite the failure of the mainstream media to report these movements accurately and adequately, women managed to keep each other informed, through newsletters, bulletins and by word of mouth. This form of communication was useful and vital, but could not address a major problem of concern to the two UN projects, which were interested in changing the systemic discrimination against women in mainstream media. It was clear to them that the portrayal of women in those media – negative, inaccurate and stereotyped – had to be revised in the course of any real change in the status of women, both North and South.

The networks created by the women's community in the last two decades are impressive. The exchange of information between these networks has enabled initiatives to be taken that are clearly 'by women, for women'; getting their analyses into the mainstream media was neither the principal goal nor the strategy. It was also very difficult. But these women's organisations decried the negative portrayal of women in the mass media.

Reaching mainstream media, especially print media – more traditional and male-dominated – has been a real challenge for those individuals and organisations wanting to intervene in large-circulation newspapers. Radio and television have been open to women's participation, but most is at a non-decision-making level. The print media, like radio and television, has the capacity to do in-depth reporting on events and processes, but it is less likely to. For the nature of 'hard' news is on-the-spot: a drought, a flood, an assassination, an election, a demonstration; it is the world of politics and economics, which, in newspaper journalism men cover, write about and read. The 'soft' stuff is what women are all about – fashion, the home, children. For journalists, both male and female, the 'hard' is preferred if they are to 'make it'. The soft stuff is scorned as second best, relegated to the women's pages and Sunday editions.

Besides that which has traditionally been perceived to be the world of women, there are also the 'women's issues' – birth control, abortion, prostitution and many others – as if men had no part to play in either reproduction or sexual behaviour. Men and women have fallen prey to this strange and inexplicable dichotomy.

For the 'hard' and the 'soft' worlds impact on each other in real ways, and both are needed for a holistic approach to the perception of problems and initiation of solutions.

Just as men had appropriated the world of politics and economics, women felt the need to stake out their territory and jealously guard the kitchen, the children and their bodies. Feeling less in control, women convinced themselves that they had rights over these issues. This meant that the street, the workplace (other than the home) and parliaments were out of their reach. It was no accident, therefore, that when men were obliged to cover women's marches, manifestos and successes, they did it through the 'hard' lens. The treatment was short, to the point, get-it-over-with. Women, when allowed to look through the hard lens, often saw the same picture as their male counterparts. It was no surprise. Years of conditioning that all that is female is 'soft' and there-fore not that important, and professional training from men with men's perspective crushed most imagination, intuition and the inner voice. Women journalists who have nourished and nurtured this perspective rarely survived in the profession and left for other pastures, the soft stuff, the home and the children.

What intervention is possible under present conditions – a male-dominated profession which is willing to bring in women as long as they conform, put in long hours and become one of the boys? Attempts have been made at various levels in various ways. Women have created press agencies, women's projects have been part of other news agencies, and many women, singly and together, have persisted in mainstream media, determined to effect change.

One specific example of an intervention at the national, regional and international level will be presented and analysed with the purpose of drawing lessons for the topic at large. The labours of UNESCO and the UN Decade for Women brought forth a rather unusual project – creating women's feature services, with the specific purpose of supplying mainstream media. UNESCO initiated a request for US$132,600 for the years 1977–78 to 'promote worldwide action aimed at the advancement of women, with special reference to their right to determine fertility and their fuller involvement in political, social and cultural life, and in the development process'. The funding (from the United Nations Fund for Popular Activities – UNFPA) was to serve as seed money for a five-year period for five women's feature services, to be controlled and operated by women within existing news agencies. The purpose was to disseminate information to mainstream media outlets (newspapers, radio and television). The main targets were opinion leaders and policy-makers in major organisations, who could influence policy related to women and development.

UNESCO contracted five news agencies for this work. Inter Press Service (IPS), a Third World news agency with headquarters in Rome, agreed to experiment in 1978 with a service from Latin America, and this became the Oficina Informativa de la Mujer (OIM). A year later, through their office in Nairobi, they took on the Africa Women's Feature Service (AWFS). In 1978, UNESCO also contracted the Christian Action for Development agency in Barbados to sponsor the Caribbean Women's Feature Service (CWFS), to be distributed by the Caribbean News Agency (CANA). In the same year, UNESCO also approached and reached an agreement with the Press Foundation of Asia's Depth-news Feature Service to create a women's feature service. In 1979, UNESCO entered into a contract with the Regional Arab Centre for Information Studies on Population, Development and Construction (ACISPDC), based in Cairo. The agreement was short-lived, and the Federation of Arab News Agencies (FANA) took on this work. The Arab States Women's Feature Service (ASWFS) was the fifth and last such service to be established by UNESCO.

The services normally operated with a regional co-ordinator, who was responsible for recruiting women to write for the service. UNESCO often underwrote training programmes for co-ordinators and writers.

From 1978 to 1983, UNESCO played a major role in supporting, programmatically and financially (by locating donors), the various feature services. At this point, the UNESCO staff member who had been a major supporter of this work left her position, and the service had to find their own way organisationally and financially.

Today, of the five started, the feature services sponsored by IPS and Depthnews still exist. The former became an independent organisation in January 1991, and the latter continues under the sponsorship of the Press Foundation of Asia. There are reasons why these two services have survived, and at least one has achieved the goal UNESCO set – women's features services controlled and managed by women. The reasons for the survival of the two and the demise of the others are important to examine, as possibly instructive for the future.

The Caribbean service, which struggled for several years, collapsed owing to lack of funds and insufficient interest from the regional media for which it was designed. An evaluation in 1982 revealed very low take-up and use of the service. One of the reasons suspected was that the features focused mostly on the non-traditional role of women in development in the region, which contrasted sharply with the stereotyped vision of women held by local male editors. Lack of funding was another reason, especially after 1983, when UNESCO stopped underwriting the project. Lack of experience and expertise in fund-raising for the work, as well as the challenge of locating journalists to write for the service, proved to be too much for the network, and it folded.

In the Arab states there was, not surprisingly, a lack of women journalists who could write on issues as spelt out by UNESCO. In addition, the overwhelmingly male-dominated Arab media did not have full faith in the project, and the little there was lapsed as time went on. Lack of trained women journalists and meagre resources have also plagued the other services. The AWFS, started by IPS in 1979, dwindled to nothing in 1981, in spite of the agency's attempts to inject life into it. The work was revived in 1986 with the appointment of a full-time co-ordinator based in Harare, Zimbabwe.

What did IPS do right that its WFS survived and was able to come into its own in 1991? After many years of experimenting with low investments and part-time staff, it appointed a woman at its headquarters in Rome, to a full-time job with a half-decent salary, giving her the mandate to rebuild, initiate and expand the network. The first task the co-ordinator set herself was to develop editorial and management guidelines for the project, and then design an infrastructure to implement them.

Between 1986 and 1989, full-time co-ordinators were appointed in anglophone and francophone, Africa, Asia, the Middle East and Maghreb, the Caribbean and Latin America. From a staff of two half-time workers at the beginning of 1986, the WFS had, by 1990, a staff of 12 full-time and about 6 part-time people, 120 freelance contributors (paid by the piece), and consultants as and when required. The work of the staff was facilitated by having access to the IPS telecommunications network, which made it possible to create a work environment that was democratic, firm, accountable and speedy. The WFS also had a ready-made market in the existing clients of IPS. In addition, in countries where IPS did not have a presence or a marketing strategy, the WFS designed and carried out a marketing plan. The IPS monitoring service also enabled timely feedback on the use of material by the media. This information was used annually to evaluate its performance in terms of theme and regional preferences, and for future planning.

The service, up to 1990, had an average pick-up rate of 70 per cent; the highest rate was in Latin America, then Europe, Asia, and the Caribbean. African use is low, and there is no marketing effort in the Arab region, owing mainly to the absence of an Arabic service. A marketing initiative was begun in the USA, by providing the service online through Peacenet. Future targets include the USA and Europe, and selected countries in Asia that have the capacity to pay for the service.

A digest of the service is available as a bulletin for non-media individuals and institutions. Unfortunately, most NGOs and women's organisations prefer to 'exchange' their products or publications for the WFS. This is neither useful nor productive for the WFS in terms of its goals. Firstly, the information in the publications of most NGO and women's newsletters is already known, as most of the WFS staff and freelance contributors have their ears to the ground regarding the issues of women and development. Secondly, the kind of information required – background and statistics, or detailed interviews, with colour, atmosphere etc – cannot be provided by these publications and groups.

The dreams that UNESCO had for the WFSs – independence and self-sufficiency – are hard to realise. The WFS of IPS, in its independent status, does not, on principle, give the service free to anyone. Some payment, however small, is insisted upon. This principle has often made it difficult for the WFS to market its features, as editors routinely get 'free material' from competing feature agencies, who are funded for this work. For aid agencies and donors, clippings are adequate.

While the WFS had not reached self-sufficiency, several points need to be made about money and the effort to reach its goals. Since 1986, the WFS has received, on average, US$300,000 a year for its work. With this, it put out 600 features a year, on the teleprinter wire, in English and Spanish, and these are selectively translated into Dutch, Norwegian, Swahili, Nepali and Finnish. It also puts out a bulletin in Spanish and English for subscribers. Sales rose from 1986 onwards, and in 1990 were US$12,000, not counting revenues that accrued to IPS from use of the WFS by IPS clients. These figures IPS has not been able to provide, arguing that their extraction was more trouble than it was worth. The donor community having argued strongly since 1975 in favour of initiatives such as the WFS, this annual contribution of US$300,000 is, at best, meagre. For the WFS to become self-sufficient, it will have to diversify its product and venture into the non-media market. Selling a WFS feature is more difficult than selling a feature on travel, the stock market, or the latest fashions or beauty-queen contests. Editors have standard responses, the world over: it is too long, too short, it doesn't have photographs, is timeless, there is no interest in these issues, give us something sexy and sensational.

While the WFS is not about sex and sensation, and would prefer not to be dictated to on the content, length and other aspects of its features, it has learnt a thing or two about what sells, what doesn't, and about how to sell. Since newspapers want news, the WFS has attempted to provide a news angle to its features. This enables it to address the serious and more long-term aspects of development, while picking on a recent news event. What do not sell are dull, long, detailed reports of atrocities against women, without a context in which the problem is occurring. For these can only evoke horror and pity, and what beyond that? One of the media's aims is to entertain its audiences and clients, besides informing and educating. If issues can be presented in an entertaining form, chances are that their impact will be more thought-provoking and long-lasting. An example of this is *Salaam Bombay*, a commercial film made by Mira Nair. It depicted many realities of the present-day urban lives of people who must live by their wits. It did this without preaching, and with a sensitivity and skill that should be recognised and aspired to.

Presentation of a problem, no matter how urgent it is, is never its own justification. Skill in treatment, style and timeliness are essential. If editors are not ready for a story, this is a good barometer of the fact that probably neither is the overwhelming majority of readers. However, progress can be made. The WFS has learnt that if not successful at the first attempt, try and try again. Repeated visits to newspaper editors have resulted in some access to the pages, despite protests. For every chauvinist editor, there is a closet feminist who comes forward to champion the material.

Listening to positive feedback and criticism has also helped to increase the pick-up and visibility of the service. Complaints, especially from colleagues in the North regarding quality, lack of background, data and thorough research have resulted in changes in the management of the service. For example, what was once a centralised (1986), then decentralised (1988), system of editing features has, since 1989, become again more centralised. Recognising the shortfalls of having editors independently put on the teleprinter wire features from Costa Rica, Jamaica, Zimbabwe, India, the Philippines, which led to inconsistency in quality, features in English are now all released from Delhi, and in Spanish from San Jose (Costa Rica). In addition, further recognising the need for better quality-control, editors-in-chief have been appointed for the English and Spanish services. Once, country contributors were left to submit features which they considered to be within the WFS guidelines. Repeated experience resulted in almost eight in ten of the features having to be commissioned, and submissions that did not make the grade being rejected.

Recognising the importance of a scientific approach to marketing, the WFS conducted a strategic marketing survey in selected countries in Asia. In some of the countries the WFS already had a presence and in others it did not. A survey of feature services similar to, but not quite the same as, the WFS was also conducted. The survey revealed that all these services offer their features at low or no cost, and that there is no deliberate focus on women (with the exception of Depthnews WFS) as a subject, or the promotion of women journalists as such. Also, most of the services were based in the region, and none had an international network.

The goal of self-sufficiency and independence has raised broader questions among the staff and Board members of the WFS, such as the need to collaborate with the corporate and commercial world not just for financial reasons but for outreach as well. It is clear that the WFS cannot continue with the meagre grants it receives from the various UN agencies, and contributions from development co-operation agencies of the North. At present there is inadequate co-ordination among the donor nations for active support of this work, other than in 'women and development' sections.

Even these sections are facing budget cuts which affect their capacity to work effectively, while reduced staff, increased workload and an ever expanding agenda lead to an inability to keep up with what the world of women and communications is doing, and to maintain an active dialogue. The trend in funding is also to decentralise, and place decision-making in the regional or national centres of the agencies' work. While this is a step in the right direction, it tends to overlook the international planning that needs to be done to avoid the cutting and paring of the picture in too many parts, with no centre to hold it together.

Despite the distrust of corporate and commercial connections amongst many feminists and feminist organisations, this is a link that needs to be pursued. For years, feminists have argued that we cannot sell out to the interests that oppress women, and some level of autonomy will be lost should this alliance be made. However, this lack of confidence is unjustified; it needs more serious study, and more courageous engagement.

Recognising the need for generating income other than solely from the sale of features, the WFS, in an attempt to diversify its product, initiated in 1989 the 'dossier' service. All its features were abstracted and put in an electronic database from which dossiers on any subject, country, region or theme could be retrieved in seconds. This service has been used by many individuals and institutions. At present, the WFS is creating a background database for its internal use, with the idea that this, like the dossier, might be made available to other interested parties.

As the WFS consolidates, grows and changes, solutions to certain problems continue to elude it, and therefore require greater attention by the community at large – for example, the relatively low use of the material in Africa, the complete lack of use in the Arab states and the Pacific, and the potential market in North America. With several years' experience, it has become clear to the WFS that each region, and each country, needs a targeted marketing strategy, for which resources are required.

Perhaps the trickiest problem to tackle is that of human resources. Unless qualified and committed women are available to do this work, the best objectives and strategies will look good only on paper. The WFS requires unusual people to work with it. Journalists, although trained, need retraining, and marketing staff need a knowledge not only of marketing but of mainstream media, especially print media. Over and above this training is the need for formalising the training so that it can be continued by others. While there are no ready-made formulas for good writing from a progressive women's perspective, some elements can be captured on video as well as in training exercises. The WFS staff have developed over the years a curriculum that should be formalised and made available more widely.

The WFS is planning to do this, and continues to expand its training to journalists outside its own staff; it is currently negotiating with several leading dailies in selected countries of the South. How to acquire a progressive women's perspective is not easy to impart. A combination of intuition, insight, understanding of political, social and economic systems, and of development, along with writing skills is a tall order. But it can be done, slowly, and the WFS's advantage is that it has a ready-made market and clientele in which to test the new trainees. Writing from a progressive women's perspective for a local audience is not as demanding as writing for an international audience, where nuances of language, custom and concept have to be kept constantly in mind. Terms have to be explained, and territory clearly defined.

Not only is this difficult to inculcate and draw out, but it has also been a major stumbling block for feminists and feminist organisations wishing to make an impact on mainstream media. Writing about issues about which women feel strongly, and which will be accepted in mainstream media locally, regionally and internationally is difficult. Feminists reject, often rightly, the criteria of 'reality' of these media, and insist that they have a message that they would like to convey as they see it. It is this insistence, plus the reality of the media that are at present incompatible. To reverse this, women will have to write about what they feel is important the way they want to, but with some attention to the 'rules' of the media. And the media will have to change their perception of their 'rules', and make way for new, creative ways of expression. Without this, there can be no visible and lasting impact of feminist writing in mainstream media.

The experience of the WFS has revealed other insights that could be of interest to those creating new networks and investing in new initiatives. While the dream of UNESCO, through its NIICO debate, was that there should be more South–North and South–South communication and information, the reality is otherwise. The market survey conducted by the WFS in Asia, and the evaluation based on monitoring the use of its service in the mainstream media, dictate otherwise.

By and large, newspapers are interested in features that document events and processes from their own countries, their own region, and then from the North. The Latin American pick-up is mostly of Latin American countries, with interest in the Arab world being second highest. In Asia, usually Asian themes are preferred, unless there is an outstanding news-related feature (for example, the trial of Winnie Mandela in South Africa). Where migration has been and is becoming routine, for example Hong Kong, the media are interested in the life of Chinese communities in other parts of the world, especially the North. The same is true of the Caribbean, which has a mixture of ethnic groups, African and Asian; copy from these regions that makes connections to the Caribbean context is better received than others. In Western Europe, it is either the familiar or the exotic that is picked up. Bride-burning in India is a sure pick-up. The protest of people's movements against an environmental threat is also well received. These findings support an age-old theory in social science: people are most comfortable with what is around them and with that with which they can identify.

Newspapers in the North are more comfortable with their own journalists travelling to the South and covering issues from their own perspective. Their correspondents often know exactly what phenomena have to be explained, in what language and in what terms. The WFS has observed (through the writing of its contributors) that there are distinctly different ways not only of looking at the world (perception) but of describing these views. The use of language is shaped by the culture, and writing style and attention to detail, statistics and background are

viewed differently. To a large extent these differences, real and perceived, decide the acceptability or unacceptability in the North of
material written by journalists from the South.

In the South, newspapers routinely subscribe to the expensive news
agencies and syndicated material of the North and use them, no matter
how biased or irrelevant they are. The fact is, such material is well
written, well researched and entertaining. The news media of the South
have not imposed the same high standards of writing on their own
journalists, and are much less demanding. The WFS is routinely told by
contributors that it is far too demanding, that they have to work much
harder to produce features for WFS, compared with the local media.
The endeavour to raise the standard of journalism needs to go hand in
hand with an endeavour to recruit younger writers with a fresh perspective on issues, as well as with an attempt to balance gender, class
and race. Most mainstream media in the South can be described as
male-dominated, upper-class and not representative of wider interests.
Given the reality of mainstream media, North and South, how can
feminists have a lasting impact on them? Their resources are as limited
as their political clout. Unless there is more of a commercial angle to
the few efforts that are being made, feminist news and analyses will
remain marginal. Feminist groups and projects are by and large non-
commercial, and to bring about this change requires a unique blend of
the politically correct and the commercially possible. It requires taking
risks, thinking big and acting smart. While this is not impossible for
feminists, it goes a little against the grain. For too long we have been
fighting from the outside, developing our own ways of working and
thinking; therefore, functioning within a system that we have little
respect for is difficult. The easier path is sought – that of working
outside the system – for this allows us the safety of retaining our values
and not having to compromise.

But change is and should be about more than safety. Feminists inside
and outside the system have shown over the last two decades that they
can make a difference. The feminist movement must take on the mainstream. This is different from being mainstreamed. The mainstream
has the power, through newsprint, radio and television, to transform
people's opinions overnight. The mainstream also has the power to
legitimise the small, the insignificant and the most noteworthy. What
the feminist and women's movements have achieved since the 1960s
can be brought before the public, and there is no reason why it should
not be. Every argument made to keep women out, by friends and foes
alike of the women's movement, brings with it the assumption that
women cannot be brought in and should be kept out.

The strength of the women's movement – that it is small-scale, local,
that it responds to basic needs, makes the connections between the

micro and the macro, takes on power and authority – must be maintained, keeping in mind that we must not become victims of our own thinking. With every effort that starts small, local, basic, there comes a time when it needs to reach out and project itself on to the world; not distant, enemy territory, but around us, reachable and possible. The media and the field of communications are probably the most powerful means of expression of change. The tremendous strides made by women can only realistically and accurately be recorded and interpreted to the media by women who have a progressive perspective. This means women who have the inner strength to know their roots, have a heightened understanding of the environment around them, and wish to see society go forward in a democratic and participatory way. It means women who have that special skill to combine the 'hard' with the 'soft', who understand means and ends, and see the interconnectedness of matter and being.

It is almost two decades since the two UN initiatives and the women's movements gathered tremendous momentum on the issue of women and the media. The time has come to take stock of what has been achieved and how this was done, as supporters of the UN Decade for Women get ready, hopefully, for another international conference in 1995.

15

The NATO Alerts Network

Paula Rose

In 1983, at the height of the discussion on the deployment in Europe of Cruise and Pershing nuclear warheads, the 'Euro Missiles', 3,000 women came to Brussels for a three-day conference called The Star Campaign. The campaign, created by an alliance of traditional women's organisations and peace movements, such as the Women's International League for Peace and Freedom, the Belgian National Council of Women, and the younger feminist movement, brought together women from many different backgrounds and beliefs. The climax of the campaign took place in the Flemish Free University of Brussels, in an atmosphere of joy, gentleness and friendship. One objective was common to all – total and committed opposition to the deployment of more weapons of mass destruction on European soil.

Among the participants in this international campaign was a small group of women from a feminist organisation established in Brussels, Women Overseas for Equality (WOE)[1]. WOE decided that it was an essential part of its feminist beliefs to be there. We needed to understand firstly what was happening politically, and then why there was so much concern over these new missiles. Surely enough people were opposed to their deployment? Surely governments would not dare override the popular will? None of the WOE group could have been called radical, for most of us lived comfortably in suburban areas on the outskirts of Brussels, with our children attending the cosmopolitan European schools. We met weekly to discuss 'feminist issues' (but not missiles). We produced a newsletter and organised monthly public meetings. Meanwhile, women were literally digging in around US air bases in the United Kingdom, the USA and Italy, sleeping in plastic bags, getting arrested, defying the law.

But what did Belgian women know about NATO's new weapons? Were they in mass demonstrations against them? Did the Belgian peace movement try to find out how many women were able to participate in

THE NATO ALERTS NETWORK

demonstrations, how many women were in local organising committees? Or how many women parliamentarians were in the foreign affairs and defence commissions able to vote against Cruise and Pershing deployment in their country?

The first of what was to be several years of Sunday evening meetings was arranged, and Women for Peace Brussels was established. What on earth could a small group of women do? We did not even know what a missile looked like, but we did know that there was massive public opposition to these new missiles. So we wanted to understand how decisions to deploy them were made. We read the week's newspapers together, horrified; we scanned technical books on the impact of a nuclear war; studied civil defence promises in the event of war. And we continued to ask why men would actually want to place the risk of so much devastation before us. It was literally unthinkable!

To increase our numbers – for eight women were not enough – we placed an advertisement in the local newspaper. It read 'Women interested in discussing peace, nuclear war, and who feel angry, alone, and too ill-informed about the subject – please contact etc.' The original eight became twenty. We liked each other, we felt politically together, slightly to the left; we were educated, with frustrations, energy and time to spare. None of us could leave Brussels and move into a tent on Greenham Common, but we could help and be part of the women's anti-nuclear, anti-militarist movement. The group felt connected to the international women's peace movement. It could work towards solidarity, and support those women who were able physically to oppose the imposition of the missiles, and had made the choice to give up their comfortable lives to camp at Greenham Common indefinitely. Some of us travelled to international meetings. Others spent weekends at Greenham. We could put our energies into weekly information stalls at a market, where we could reach women in the street and encourage them to resist, or at least to recognise what was going on. Since the Second World War, there had been no active women's peace movement in French speaking Belgium. The Greenham Women were rekindling the embers of resistance, and we were part of it.

Plunging in

How were the decisions to deploy new missiles for NATO forces taken? In 1986 we met the men who held the office most closely representing our government's decisions: that of Ambassador to NATO. There are sixteen NATO ambassadors, and a Secretary-General. This was at that time Lord Carrington, a long-serving career diplomat, and close friend of Margaret Thatcher, then the British Prime Minister. Our first approach to the ambassadors and Lord Carrington was not successful.

They could not understand what might be beneficial in such a meeting. After all, there was an entire Information Service employed at NATO at our disposal. 'What concerns you? Civil defence? The Soviet threat?' they asked. 'Just ring "Information", and you can spend the day, have lunch, at NATO!'

Many letters and telephone calls left us without an appointment. But women were moving everywhere. The Nairobi World Conference, the end of the UN Decade for Women, had taken place; the *Forward-looking Strategies* had been adopted. Women's right to involvement in arms control and peace negotiations was one of the Articles agreed to by all our governments. And so we used the document to justify our call. A petition was circulated to every woman member of the European Parliament, which most of them sent on to their national parliaments, insisting that the NATO ambassadors take the request for a meeting seriously. It worked. We had our first interview with the NATO Secretary-General and six NATO ambassadors on 6 June 1986. It had taken a year to achieve! We were a curious group: six women from six NATO countries, of whom two were women parliamentarians, and four from the peace movements. Our discussion at that first meeting was almost irrelevant. What was important was that it was the first step in a series of meetings that would include women from both military blocs. Later, the first person from the then Soviet Union to enter NATO was to be a woman: an important point to be recorded.

In another part of Europe, in Athens, Margarita Papandreou, as International President of Women for a Meaningful Summit, played host to its International Assembly in November 1986. One of the workshops was animated by Margot Miller, British vice-president of the Women's International League for Peace and Freedom (WILPF) and a solid member of the Greenham Common Peace Camp. She had visited NATO ambassadors with us earlier that year in Brussels. The discussion in the workshop covered women's role and participation at the grassroots against military build-up and new nuclear weapons. Alongside Margot Miller in this workshop was Scilla Elworthy (McLean), director of a newly established research centre in Oxford concerned with the way in which decisions about nuclear weapons were made, who was particularly interested in talking to decision-makers. The workshop considered the NATO meeting: could women involve themselves more in this direction, and would it be useful? Scilla Elworthy, keen on the idea, suggested that a women's delegation to NATO would be considered far less threatening than a group of men, and that it was time women were seen at NATO.

One Sunday morning, I received a telephone call from Margarita Papandreou. Women for a Meaningful Summit International was considering coming to Brussels to meet NATO ambassadors, and if the money could be found, would it be possible to organise from Brussels, and would I be interested in organising the meeting in co-operation with Margarita and Scilla Elworthy? This was now getting serious. A division of labour was agreed: Margarita Papandreou had compiled names and addresses of individual women, MPs and organisations in the NATO countries; Scilla Elworthy had the skills and knowledge to put together some working papers; I was to secure the meeting at NATO with all 16 ambassadors and the Secretary-General, Lord Carrington.

The women's defence dialogue with NATO

Some 33 women members of parliament, leaders of large women's organisations, and defence analysts from 14 countries gathered together for this dialogue. We met together the day before our scheduled meeting with NATO, producing a cogent list of questions, a statement that we wanted to read, and the background preparations for our press conference to be held at the end of the session. This was no mean task. The 33 came from different political parties, from different areas of Europe, and did not know each other beforehand.

The visitors met in twos with their respective ambassadors, each of whom was asked the same five questions, with notes taken of their replies. The finale took place in a large meeting room, in which all sat waiting for the entrance of Lord Carrington. He was surrounded by advisers, all carrying recorders, and obviously discomfited at having to address such a large group of women. For those who have never been to NATO, it is important to describe the atmosphere. Having been there many times, I am always struck by the fanatical conviction that anybody who does not wear a NATO security clearance badge is automatically a Soviet spy or, worse, a terrorist. Posters suggesting that if you are member of a peace group you are RED were pinned on the walls of the corridors. Women members of parliament, who hold positions of responsibility towards their constituents, have been disallowed from going to the toilet without a security guard to accompany them across the hall. Once inside NATO, particularly the Political Affairs building, into which run corridors from all 16 national delegations, the visitor cannot leave without going once again through a great deal of security. To go from one delegation to another requires massive amounts of administration, heavily armed guards, and miserable secretaries who are obliged to walk kilometres with you in their high-heeled shoes.

In the event of an ambassador, as was often the case, deciding to give a half-hour lecture to the visiting women, who then still had to ask their questions of him, the schedule, drawn up by the ambassadors themselves, would become completely unstuck. In addition, we had to go through a security routine of photos, passports and so on, in order to get from where we met the ambassador to where we would meet the Secretary-General. Not surprisingly, some of the women arrived at that meeting late. Lord Carrington continued regardless: 'You are young women, what do you know about war? ... I stood on the rubble somewhere in Germany at the end of the last World War and know today the guarantees that NATO can provide for us.' And so on. He had not bothered to look around him, nor had anybody bothered to brief him, for he did not know to whom he was talking. One of our number was the wife of a Prime Minister, and others were well known politicians: was he too blinkered by his patrician upbringing to perceive women as significant?

A pleasant reception that evening, organised by the wives of all the non-aligned ambassadors, at the house of the first-ever female mayor of Brussels, made up for the cold, military atmosphere of civil servants and diplomats, who tend to have little joy about themselves, and certainly feel extremely uncomfortable faced with groups of women.

The questions and answers of that first meeting are less relevant today than the evidence that most decisions inside NATO were taken without the agreement of all nations. Worse, most nations were probably not even consulted. There was a clear need for co-ordination between the 16 countries at parliamentary and grassroots levels, in order to compare notes. A network of women seemed to be the ideal formula, working across borders, so that we could share the knowledge put together by researchers in Washington, London, Bonn, and so on, and make sure that each participant knew the response of each member state's defence minister. Responses to a simple list of questions covering the new military programmes of NATO, especially nuclear weapons systems, given by, for example, the Norwegian defence minister, and then compared to those given by the British or German minister might identify contradictions, hesitations and lies. All this could help to stop US financial support for the continued research and development of new NATO weapons.

The European Nuclear Disarmament (END) conference in Coventry in July 1987 formalised the NATO Alerts Network. In a small room during a lunch break, Margot Miller, Margarita Papandreou, Luciana Castellina MEP, Giancarla Codrignani MP, Scilla Elworthy and I agreed to support and look for the financing of a small office in Brussels in which I would start working part-time. A private donation of £1,000 was immediately located, and I contributed another £1,000 in order to purchase a computer, telephone and office equipment. Further funding to maintain the office and pay my salary would follow. Fortunately, the Joseph Rowntree Trust and the Cadbury Trust agreed to support the project financially, and thanks to these, the network has flourished and now employs three women.

The first six months' work consisted of building up a good network of reliable women parliamentarians in each of the NATO countries. Each one had to be identified, contacted and persuaded to take part. They also had to guarantee that, at short notice, any one of them would be available to take part in a meeting with a NATO ambassador or minister, in any of the 16 countries.

In 1987, a World Conference of Women was held in Moscow. Several women from our network were among the 3,000 from North, South, East and West – women whose countries were in conflict spent three days together in the period before the Cold War ended. During the event, Margarita Papandreou organised a reception. After a round of polite introductions, the proposal was made for a joint international women's delegation from both NATO and the Warsaw Treaty Organisation to meet together with our respective defence and foreign ministers. It was a daunting project for such a small group, with few human or financial resources at our disposition: but it was very urgent. Our male leaders were still pointing nuclear missiles at each other (and us), and preparing new ones.

Margarita Papandreou's office in Athens had built up a good relationship with many women's organisations in the Warsaw Treaty Organisation (WTO). Meanwhile, the NATO Alerts Network had an extensive data-base of women in the NATO countries; all that was left was to begin the letter-writing and political contact necessary to get near to the different foreign ministers whom we wanted to meet at NATO headquarters on the very next available occasion. For women in the WTO countries, the task at that time was easier, for most of the women's committees were sponsored by the state and the Party and therefore there were direct contacts. Women from NATO countries were not so fortunate: our democracies left little time or place for a meeting of ministers with uninfluential women.

Our intentions and objectives were the same as in our previous meetings with ambassadors and defence ministers; but this time we wanted to meet them accompanied by women from the military bloc called 'the enemy'. It must not be forgotten that at that time, no NATO ambassador had any contact, formal or informal, with WTO ambassadors. There was no direct governmental contact outside the USSR and US. We were suggesting women as a bridge. Our intentions were quite simple: to bring together at least 23 women from different parts of the world with political differences, Communists, Greens, Social Democrats and Christian Democrats, and then tell our male leaders the following:

> There are many principles that we can agree upon from the start. We do not believe that nuclear weapons protect us. We do not believe that increased defence spending guarantees our security. Nor do we believe that we are currently facing a threat from each other. As women, absent from all inter-

national political decision making, together we believe that vital national resources are necessary for the well being of ourselves and our children. They are not in terms of huge armies to protect us. But in terms of co-operation, exchange, education, health, well-being and full participation in a society.

The Warsaw Pact women's dialogue in Sofia, Bulgaria brought together in March 1988 a delegation of 13 women parliamentarians and peace activists from 10 NATO countries to meet the WTO foreign ministers. The dialogue was arranged by the Committee of the Movement of Bulgarian Women. The event, the first of its kind, took place in the Bulgarian Ministry of Foreign Affairs the evening before the WTO foreign ministers held their biannual meeting. Women members of parliament from Hungary, Czechoslovakia, the German Democratic Republic and Bulgaria were also present. This new phase in peace-making would not have been possible without the hard work of our friends in the Bulgarian Committee, and those women who expended the effort necessary to get the ministers of all countries involved to agree to meet us.

We were part of an international feminist movement. In one year, we organised two international meetings of women from 22 countries with ministers from the two military blocs facing each other with the largest armies in the world, unable to speak to each other. We have done this with very few resources. Our energy and our commitment to each other played a large role. By being part of the network, we became bound to each other.

The next NATO meeting was scheduled for Copenhagen in April 1988. NATO Defence Ministers were to meet for a biannual Defence Planning Committee meeting. A group of 12 women members of parliament had arranged to meet the defence ministers. Flights to Copenhagen and accommodation in private homes had been arranged. Mobilisation of women in several different countries took place. Child care organised, parliamentary meetings rescheduled, the press alerted: everything was ready. Then the Norwegian parliament collapsed. A serious argument erupted about whether foreign shipping coming into Norwegian ports should have to declare whether or not they were carrying nuclear weapons. NATO defence ministers, anxious that their planned meeting should not be sidetracked into discussing NATO nuclear weapons on shipping, decided to move their meeting to Brussels. In just seven days, we were able to reschedule everything, change flights – which was expensive – find accommodation, and a very beautiful meeting room at Quaker House. Channel 4 TV in the UK produced a *Dispatches* programme, in which the whole discussion about NATO's modernisation of nuclear weapons and the lies of ministers to Parliament were exposed. The programme followed our women's delegation both to NATO and to the WTO meeting in Sofia.

Warsaw Pact–NATO women's defence dialogue

To reciprocate the Sofia meeting, we aimed to bring eminent women representatives from the Warsaw Treaty nations to Brussels to meet with the foreign ministers of NATO nations on the occasion of the North Atlantic Council meeting of NATO. At first the organisers, NATO Alerts Network and the International Liaison Office of Women for a Meaningful Summit, found great resistance from NATO foreign ministers to this idea. Letters written six months in advance to individual ministers received either vague or negative replies. However, only a few days before the North Atlantic Council meeting, and as a result of substantial efforts in various NATO capitals, one by one the foreign ministers or their permanent representatives to NATO agreed to meet. Some agreed to meet the entire group, and some only to meet with women nationals of their own country, plus two representatives from the Warsaw Pact.

Women parliamentarians and representatives of 13 NATO nations were able to be present in Brussels, each one paying her own fare and expenses, in addition to representatives of the Soviet Union, Bulgaria, the German Democratic Republic, Hungary, Poland and Czechoslovakia. This was a historic moment, for a Soviet member of parliament, a woman, to go into NATO headquarters to address a NATO foreign minister and to express her anxieties. On arrival, the women met to discuss their priorities for the dialogue, and together decided on a list of questions to discuss with the foreign ministers. Individual meetings were scheduled throughout the three days, either at NATO or at individual embassies in Brussels, involving considerable logistical complexity for those trying to attend several meetings in succession. Careful notes of the discussions were compiled and have been set out briefly. The full version is in the archives of the NAN offices in Brussels.

East? West? 'NATO's best!'

'We do not want to talk about threat any more, we want to talk about risk.' These words of Henning Wegener, NATO's Deputy Secretary-General, were repeated faithfully by NATO defence ministers in their discussions with women MPs from East and West Europe, on 22 May 1990. The women, many of them recently elected to the new parliaments of former Warsaw Pact nations, were unimpressed. They had come to Brussels before, for individual meetings with NATO defence ministers and ambassadors at the time of the Defence Planning Committee. They were eager to find concrete signs of new thinking in line with the dramatic political changes taking place in Europe. 'Please give examples of what you mean by these nice words,' said Dr Evka

Razvigorva, member of the Bulgarian Parliament and director of a chemical engineering institute, addressing Denmark's permanent representative to NATO, Ambassador Ole Bierring. The ambassador's mouth opened and closed. A long silence followed. Then: 'You must wait for the July summit meeting in London.'

The six very specific questions put by women in all their interviews revealed confusion among member nations as to what actual changes in strategy NATO is prepared to make. According to the Belgian representative, 'the strategy of flexible response must be reviewed', while, according to Admiral Papadongonas, defence minister of Greece, 'NATO still believes in flexible response – it's the only way to avoid an attack.'

The tensest moment in all the meetings came when the women asked about NATO's proposed new tactical air-to-surface missile, the nuclear 'stand-off' missile, which the US will be ready to deploy in 1995. Britain, in collaboration with France and with the US, is also developing its own version of this missile at a cost of several billion pounds. At the mention of this weapon faces changed, polite smiles vanished. Precision and consensus returned. 'This is a missile we have to have.' The reasons given were many and varied, but the message was the same. 'I do not want to take this message home,' said Ludmila Enutina, representing the (then) Soviet Women's Committee. 'Gorbachev is not popular at home. If NATO ministers are genuine in saying they want to help Gorbachev survive, this is a very bad sign to send. It will undermine his position. It looks as though he is getting no return for all his concessions.'

The women also raised the issue of low flying, which was causing outrage among constituents in West Germany, where most low flying has now been banned and the lowest level permitted is 250 ft above ground. In Britain, levels of 100 ft above ground are still permitted, and in Canada, in areas inhabited by the Innu people, planes fly as low as 50 ft, causing deafness and nightmares among Innu children. The delegation, which included two West German and four East German MPs, wanted to know why, if the threat of a Soviet invasion was generally agreed to be negligible, it was still necessary to fly at these terrifying and dangerous levels, and why a new NATO flight training base is planned. Once again, the replies received were contradictory. Admiral Papadongonas assured the delegation that the NATO tactical weapons and flight-training centre would not now be built. The same opinion came from Per Ditlev Simonsen, Norwegian defence minister: 'This base is not going to be. Just forget about it.' At the same time the women were being told by the Canadian defence minister and by NATO's Assistant Secretary-General that no decision had been made about the base.

The most positive signs concerned the size of future defence budgets, which the women said their constituents wanted to see decreasing in favour of more money being available for environmental protection. In some cases they were able to obtain precise figures. The Netherlands ambassador proudly announced a decrease of 1 per cent for 1990, to be repeated in 1991. Belgium declared 'at least a freeze' for the 1991 budget. Greece saw a continuing reduction, perhaps as much as 25 per cent over five years. The East German MP reported that his government would have reduced its defence budget by 46 per cent in one year by the end of 1990. Against this background the women were very surprised indeed to hear the official NATO position from the Assistant Secretary-General for Political Affairs: 'If things develop well, we shall abandon the 3 per cent standard for growth in defence budgets of member nations.'

In most of their 12 meetings, with two notable exceptions, the women found they were treated to lengthy monologues on subjects on which they were themselves very knowledgeable. The notable exceptions were the Belgian representative, who responded concisely and factually to the women's questions, and the Netherlands ambassador, who listened carefully to the women, asked them questions, and invited them to visit NATO again. Other defence ministers and ambassadors seemed uninterested in hearing the views of members of the new Eastern European parliaments. West Germany's representative Hans Friedrich von Ploetz would not permit any interruption of his 25-minute lecture on the principles underlying NATO policy. 'Kindly assume we are familiar with these principles,' said German MEP Eva Quistorp, 'and give us an answer to our question concerning your reasons why nuclear weapons should remain in West Germany.' 'This is not the right way to approach the issue,' returned von Ploetz. In several instances the women were told to wait for answers to their specific questions for the results of NATO's strategy review. 'On past experience, this could take as much as seven years,' said Cecile Goldet, former member of the French Senate. 'I had hoped that NATO's approach had changed, but from these conversations I see it hasn't.'

Can we talk about international feminism today? I think more than ever it is urgent. The political changes in Europe have been so vast and so rapid that unless we find the ways to communicate and understand each other, we risk losing the opportunity that has been given to us all, for political change to barriers and political frontiers that have existed for two generations. Women must come together again, look at ways that we can guarantee our mutual security, develop trust and co-operation. The only forum in which I can see that possibility is via the process of the Conference for Co-operation and Security in Europe (CSCE). It is the only forum that provides a real vote for each European nation and includes the two military superpowers. Decisions taken within those nations will affect women in all countries of the world, because the forum of the CSCE covers all aspects of our society and aspirations: security, ecology, economy, human rights and people-to-people. Women must play an equal part in this process, must be informed, free to voice their opinions, disagree, say no, and be present when decisions need to be made for the future. Ultimately we have to be at the table.

Note

1. For description of WOE, see *Women's Studies International Forum, Summer* 1985, a special edition entitled 'An International Evaluation of the Decade for Women', guest editor Georgina Ashworth.

16

Piercing the Eye: Taking Feminism into Mainstream Political Processes

Georgina Ashworth

'If the purpose of research is to reveal, the purpose of advocacy is to see the revelation into wider consciousness and then into policy and remedial actions.'[1] This chapter is concerned not with an analysis of feminism or of mainstream policies, but of the process of making known the gender dimensions of, and feminist perspectives on, international policy and politics, as a commitment to feminism. Persistence, that rather indefinable motivation called empathy, and a range of self-evolved tactics have given me a great deal of experience and some success in this activity: there is awareness where it was not before, and there are processes under way which might not have been but for these efforts. The analogy of entering through the eye-slot to the brain, and particularly to the nervous and endocrine systems of the body politic, may conjure up painful images for the reader, but – realised in retrospect – this was the strategy adopted, being the most efficient use of the scarce resources of time, money and immediately available human support. It also transforms what the eye sees.

Excluded from many institutions, as women and then as feminists, particularly those who entered employment before the (however inadequate) equal opportunities legislation, women will find that the most direct route to the brain-centre is through the eye. From there the strategy is to persuade the 'brain' to change participation, priorities, procedures, processes, policies, and representation in the interests of the missing half of the society. While it may seem a long way from community or 'grassroots' action, this strategy requires interaction and co-operation with the widest spectrum of activists and academics, for it entails taking their knowledge and research into the 'brain' as the substance of the arguments for change. There are reciprocal gains to be made, too, for the activists and the academic, in the dispersal of ideas, and out of this many-sided process have emerged employment, courses, research contracts, book, films, articles and friendship.

The stimuli

The origins of this practice were probably those which obliged me to form CHANGE in 1979. The chief prompt was the wilful ignorance of the eminent board members and senior staff of my previous place of employment, involved in work on ethnic relations and human rights internationally, when I naively attempted to persuade them that there was a dimension missing from our work. It was even a potentially explosive dimension, for inter-ethnic conflict is not acted out by self-contained armies, but often through the victimisation of the 'enemies' women', or through natalist policies coercing women to produce more future men-at-arms. Nationalism is very much concerned with conformity and control of women, and religious minorities may repress the female sex even more than the state represses the overall group. Therefore intellectual and practical integrity were at stake, qualities that I still expect to find in others, though all too often with as much disappointment as then. For the suggestion that their life's work, the basis of their eminence, might have a substantial chunk of meaning and reality left out of it was too threatening to contemplate. Similar eminent and influential persons within various institutions, usually but not exclusively men, are still the chief targets of this advocacy on the gender dimension and the functioning of sexism in international issues. Smoothing of the paths of feminist women, perhaps as trapped, frustrated and angry as I was then, was also extremely important.

It should be mentioned that although I tried to take the ideas behind what was to become CHANGE to development agencies, human rights groups, women's organisations and to internationally minded academia, to share the opportunity with any of them, these advances were rejected. Women-as-a-category were not yet valid, 'gender' as yet unused, and feminism still a dirty word. To the international organisations it was 'why women?' For the women's organisations approached, the ideas were too international, while for academia they were too interdisciplinary and not 'rigorous' enough to support. So the effort spent trying *not* to form CHANGE as a separate entity was wasted. However, the distinctive character of CHANGE, in its principles and accessibility, and as one of the first international documentation collections on women, gave energy, strength and legitimacy to the subsequent 'mainstreaming'. There are many locations of our advocacy where other women's organisations are still not to be found.

There were probably many other stimuli; one was the dissatisfaction of attending purely academic events from which emerged no collective or personal commitment to action. The academic critique, so often merely the mauling of a rival, destructive rather than supportive of innovation, can be extremely unattractive, and CHANGE has freely contributed support, documentation and references to many students whose academic advisers opposed their research on women; however, we have also been concerned with synthesising academic work and making it accessible to policy-makers and others. Swasti Mitter, author of *Common Fate, Common Bond,* has spoken of being persuaded by our arguments, and of CHANGE's 'intellectual children' being widespread. Today I joke that the unexpected advantage of being middle-aged is that no amount of academic eminence, or political status, can succeed in trivialising me, and the issues I carry around. This enables me to support younger women who might be dismissed or humiliated for their age. Brought up and educated on an equal basis with people of all nationalities, races and religions, I make no distinctions about 'first' and 'third' worlds, and therefore CHANGE does not separate these spheres any more than it does the public from the private.

The early years

The first purpose of CHANGE was to produce brief, comprehensive profiles describing the social, legal, economic and political position of women in a given country, outlining the difference ethnicity made and linking the individual situation to the macro political economy. These were to be written by women from the country in question, and were to inform the general public, men as well as women, but in particular people in ministries of foreign affairs and development, and in United Nations agencies.[2] The outward simplicity of this approach, which seemed so much common sense, belied its novelty as well as the complexity of its execution.[3]

Shortly before starting this series, my attention had been drawn to the UN Decade for Women, which was being ignored in the UK. Over the subsequent years, campaigning on the Decade and its issues, and using the Decade as a campaigning tool itself, became an important part of CHANGE's presence. After attending the Copenhagen Mid-Decade Conference, I formed the Decade Network, which held innumerable informal meetings with visiting overseas women activists who shared their experiences, perspectives and visions with women from development agencies, academia, and 'private life' in the UK. It was an exhilarating way of learning from each other, and we were all hungry to learn, but without the sense of either alienation or superiority. The knowledge was transformed into the Thinkbook series, into packs

(Farmers, Food and Famine and *Women and Debt)* and information sheets so that it would not be lost and so that others would gain. These opened up discussion and analysis in directions rarely taken by feminists or by economists. It was a continuous exchange, but to broaden its outreach still further, in 1985 CHANGE organised a national conference on Women, Aid and Development, with a coalition of people from diverse organisations and occupations, intended to attract academia, NGOs and government. This caused a very visible change in many agencies – including the Overseas Development Administration, which had declined the invitation, for we paraded their shame to the press.[4]

Evidence (based on the CHANGE reports) was also given to enquiries on Bangladesh and famine in Africa, held by the Select Committee on Foreign Affairs,[5] and a range of tactics for 'educating the educator' (now called gender awareness) was undertaken. Almost every time the incumbent Minister for Overseas Development spoke at an accessible meeting, such as the Development Journalists Group, I would carefully compose and ask questions that could not be easily dismissed and that required an intelligent response. Supported by the friendly legitimacy of a friend in the British Council, we would penetrate fortress ODA to harass reluctant social development advisers into acknowledging the gender dimensions of their work, and the work of the ODA in general. Other agencies, sometimes honestly, sometimes cynically, invited us to talk and 'light fires of consciousness beneath them'.[6]

From the Decade Network emerged the Thinkbook series, sometimes published jointly with others. One such was *Shaming the World: the Needs of Women Refugees,*[7] in which, among many other issues, we clamoured for a redefinition of 'refugee'. Many women flee sexual persecution, which is not recognised as grounds for refugee status; many women engage in feminist activity (whether they call it that or not), and are persecuted for it, but are not recognised as undertaking political work; many women are sexually assaulted and violated during movement across borders and in camps. As copies of the book – originals and photocopies – spread, practice and work with women refugees began to change; policy – for example in Canada – began to change, but the 'status' issue did not change. But in 1992, as a result of a modest campaign based on the book and the energy of a volunteer, it became part of the agenda of a UNA think-tank on 'What is a Refugee?'

Related to this last area of work was the development, through papers and with other organisations, of the linkage between militarisation and the impoverishment and repression of women. In the early 1980s, most studies, theoretical or functional, demonstrating the social deprivation resulting from militarisation did so in general terms. Combining instinct with the understanding gained from my time working on minorities, along with some secondary research, my papers for the Star Campaign (see Paula Rose's chapter on NATO Alert Network), the FAO Human Rights Group and later for the Finnish Peace Centre, seemed both innovative and self-evident. It is sad that so much has to be relearned not only by each generation – the indicators from pre-Second World War fascism were always there to be read – but by groups simultaneously across the world. In publishing in 1992 *Unheard Voices*,[8] a study on the impact of war and sanctions on Iraqi women, we also repeated the cry that women should be involved in conflict resolution (see Judith Large's chapter in this volume) and in post-conflict research teams, prison visiting teams, and so on, to care for women's interests in medical, psychological and social rehabilitation, and in economic and constitutional reconstruction.

There was no neglect on the domestic front. Much of it is recorded in *The Invisible Decade: UK Women and the UN Decade*.[9] The lethargy, superiority and bouts of duplicity on the part of the British government towards the Plans and Programmes of Action (as well as towards the International Convention on the Elimination of Discrimination Against Women – CEDAW) provided more than adequate ammunition. In 1982 I persuaded the Women's National Commission to engage in a consultation process, which it did, although without the outreach and intensity of action proposed. So I formed a group to write the book mentioned above as an 'alternative report' to that of the British government, with policy and strategies – including a Ministry for Women. Speaking engagements all over the country roused other women to take action. Before the World Conference, CHANGE organised six meetings in Parliament and a campaign of parliamentary questions directed at every government department, including defence, on the non-implementation of the Decade. Male and female MPs from all parties co-operated over a period of six weeks, putting the questions we wrote for them based on the UK's answers to the UN questionnaire. Although governments never acknowledge their anxiety, and rarely the effectiveness of those who persuade them – in case the pressure continues – these activities clearly worried them into further action.

During and after the Nairobi World Conference in 1985, the pressure was maintained by a number of individual and collective actions, ensuring daily consultations between the official delegation and British NGO representatives. Later we persuaded the Home Secretary (Douglas Hurd) to initiate the Inter-Ministerial Working Group on Women's Issues, and to take up the issue of violence against women as its first area of activity. Our role was never acknowledged, however, and the Inter-Ministerial Group remains very inaccessible to women themselves. I was asked to organise a national conference on the implementation of the Forward-Looking Strategies within the United Kingdom. The convenor was the National Council for Voluntary Organisations, Women's Organisations

Interest Group,[10] which, from this national exposure, was able to evolve into the National Alliance of Women's Organisations. When the UK ratified CEDAW, the authorities did offer congratulations upon the success of the campaign, but it was a bitter victory, as there were so many reservations that its spirit and objectives were actually contradicted.

As international debt, structural adjustment agreements and inequitable terms of trade had come to dominate relations between governments of North and South, they naturally came to the fore in our advocacy. Our analysis had to be rapid and sometimes crude, but this was preferable to waiting twenty years to be able to research devastation. We found that 'the essential cultural limitations to women's rights or entitlements in their society predetermines their weak negotiating power, and enables the more powerful to dispose of their time, income and bodies through both micro and macro-economic policy.'[11]

In February 1986, again drawing in others, CHANGE organised a meeting on 'Development Issues After the Decade for Women' in Parliament, which was well attended by senior men from the Commonwealth and elsewhere, and at which one MP declared, 'Women in Development is the issue whose time has come.' Consequently it can be said that many of the pools of consciousness that exist today in the home departments of government, the Overseas Development Administration, amongst parliamentarians, and, especially, amongst NGOs are the outcome of these campaigns, even though the original source of advocacy and information may well not be known to a younger generation.

Human rights and democracy

Human rights concern the philosophy of the equal dignity and value of all human beings, expressed through standards drawn up in the immediate post-war period, encapsulated in the 1948 *Universal Declaration of Human Rights*, and subsequent international instruments including CEDAW. They bring with them active duties of the state towards every person, and their realisation applies everywhere; they concern economic conditions as much as political. In practice, however, they tend to be identified with male political prisoners, or with ethnic and religious minorities, and increasingly with children, but rarely with women: it would seem as though there is a fear and aversion to the self-determination of women. And there is a universal habit of distancing human rights abuse to somewhere else, anywhere that is not home, which is racist, patronising and convenient. These observations drove me into writing *Of Violence and Violation: Women and Human Rights* over a painful period up to 1985. There was an absence of human rights and self-determination within the very offices of human rights organisations, and, by any definition, conditions of slavery in many homes. There was also the documentation, the data and the details of man's inhumanity to woman that accumulated in the CHANGE office during its early years, and our *Report on Thailand* (1980) had made the link between culture and prostitution, and the economy and the abuse of women's human rights, which I had explored for conferences at the Council of Europe as elsewhere. Since human rights are intended to prevent the domination of one person over another, as well as persecution, torture, slavery and arbitrary imprisonment, and to guarantee freedom from fear and want, and freedom of belief and expression, they concern structural and personal violence, and are part of social and economic relations, not merely state-individual relations. Even within the latter, the individual woman is clearly at a disadvantage in her relationship with the state, and there is a marked indifference on the part of the state to protecting her from her chief aggressor, man. She is deemed not to have the full 'personality' that 'human rights' set out to honour and dignify, nor does she retain the traditional social protection (or at least limitations on men's capacity to control and abuse) of the community, which has been succeeded by the modern state.

> Women, because of their sex, have limited, indeed conditional access to the 'four freedoms' ... these conditions are not a divine oversight, but a continuation of the history of male supremacy ... No state should benefit from the violation, abuse or neglect by its agents or others, of the rights of its citizens – but it will be argued that all states do, because of their failure to create real and realisable equity and equality for the female sex. It is therefore incumbent upon the international and regional human rights systems to identify and rectify these violations.[12]

The object of the essay was to illustrate these points to the 'human rights industry', in which I had worked for five years and whose members have never put their backs into supporting women's rights. No particular campaign was involved, in the absence of resources, but a range of persons, including members of the UN Human Rights Subcommission, were sent copies. Quietly, *Of Violence and Violation* reached round the world inspiring women here and there to take up the issues, and it became a teaching text. A Fijian lawyer became a rape prosecutor. A French centre was sent a copy by a Turkish group. The American leader of the Amnesty International Women's Task Force said it had 'electrified' her. The Global Centre for Women's Leadership at Rutgers University used it as the basis of their teaching, which led to their campaign to take violence against women to the Human Rights Commission. The ideas and the approach appeared in other writings, and they in turn contributed to the new approach taken by OECD-DAC women's committee – which, coming full circle, I was asked to develop. Through this, indicators for participation and democracy will be proposed, to be added to the Human Development Index; they will include the right to decline sex and to prosecute a husband for marital rape, and possibly the right to strike over domestic work.

With the fall of the Berlin Wall and the revolutions in Eastern Europe, and with peoples in many countries tired of dictatorships, elected or otherwise, the word 'democracy' was much thrown about in the last few years. Invited to create a women's campaign for the UK Electoral Reform Society, I found myself reanalysing democracy from a feminist perspective, bringing in the question of 'participation' from much of the development literature, and the question of 'consent' on which democracy is supposed to be based, along with the questions concerning 'representation'. These are explored more in *When Will Democracy Include Women?*[13] which particularly examines the situation in the UK in 1992, where the constitutional debate had heated up, but in the knowledge that 'democracy', 'good governance' and human rights were rapidly becoming planks of overseas development policy. The Western model of democracy has consistently excluded women for many reasons and in many different ways, and the extension of these continuous exclusions within a neo-colonial model will be as disastrous as it was in the colonial model.

For example, consent to directions in policy is presumed although there is so little direct participation of women, and much policy is actually against women's interests and women's human rights. Britain's non-compliance with the European Directives is one instance; the US opposing equal pay is another. That these should be taken as examples of 'good governance' is hypocritical. Similarly women's consent to go to war is taken for granted, even when opinion polls show a majority against it; the absence of representation of that opinion, and of women's different life experiences and needs, in parliamentary assemblies all raise unanswered questions as to the sincerity of the 'democratic processes'. Political parties, often considered the cornerstone of democracy, are unwelcoming to women who want to make changes rather than sandwiches, and cannot be relied upon to defend or promote women's interests. The civil service and the courts have conspicuously discriminated against women, in lieu of serving or defending their human rights.

Alternative economics

Between the publication of these two 'Thinkbooks' was another, applying a human rights approach to economics, examining the way that gender inequalities are exploited by the state and by commerce, often in alliance with one another. This drew upon thoughts and ideas from many conferences, discussions and seminars in many parts of the world, and its tactic is to demonstrate the sources of these practices, or models, as well as their global application. Its title was *$£XONOMYC$: an Introduction to the Political Economy of Sex, Time and Gender,* whose time has yet to come. And yet, just as this was compiled from many sources, we are all moving forward with very similar thoughts and directions, but there is no specific co-ordination.

About the time of publishing *$£XONOMYC$,* CHANGE formed the Women's Alternative Budget Working Group. The absence of demands from women, of their voices in the media, and of consultation with them on the financing of the state, made me realise that, as no one else was doing it, I should take the initiative. The first proposal we made was that an annual 'Gender Impact Statement' of the distinct effects on women and men of the whole Budget should be published by the Treasury. There are precedents (always persuasive in Britain): the government of Australia now produces a Women's Budget Impact Statement regularly, while Canada's cabinet policy papers have to show the different effects on women and men. We aspired to show up the different patterns of expenditure and of poverty among women and men in all current social categories, with a view to correcting the inequalities.

The Group was brought together to present women's views and feminist perspectives on the Budget annually, and in the long run to draw up Alternative Budgets. As the chief form of national planning in Britain, which sets the priorities and directions for all government departments, the Budget should be reviewed in the light of all women's needs, interests and opinions – not only those with the time to advocate minor tax changes. As the programme for the distribution of national resources, it is the main instrument of social control in Britain – and the key means of improving women's economic and political self-determination and 'equality'. The government made much use of the expression 'creating a level playing field' for women and men, and for competition in the European internal market; at present it is severely pitched against women's economic independence and in favour of industry's demands, which are for control of a submissive, cheap and flexible labour force for which women's cultural subordination pre-determines them.

The Group welcomed separate taxation as a step towards the recognition of women as individuals, rather than adjuncts to their husbands, but recommended a thorough and public review of the taxation and social security systems to eliminate bias, discrimination and the hiding of unequal treatment. It is misleading of government, the Group also felt, to present such changes as a cost to the Exchequer when there were claw-backs elsewhere, and considering women's huge contribution to the economy. Unpaid family 'helpers', often full-time, are the backbone of farms and shops, ineligible for social benefits and pensions as individuals. Carers for the sick, disabled and elderly make an enormous, but unrecognised, contribution to the economy and need a range of supporting options and measures, enabling them to stay in employment longer before moving into what is often an isolated and exhausting life of sacrifice.

The Group also berated the government's record of implementation of the 1985 Forward-Looking Strategies, as a consciousness-raising tactic, and expressed its interest in the long-term conversion of armaments production, and of the armed services, into useful social services. Particular concern was also expressed that the biases and discrimination against women that exist in the British economy should not be carried into Eastern Europe with the new enthusiasm for investment and public administration training, as we have seen the disastrous effects of 'aid and development' on the Third World.

To begin with, the nucleus of the Group came from various national organisations (including non-feminist ones), with the Women's International League for Peace and Freedom, which has formed similar groups in other countries. Plans to draw in researchers, as well as other organisations have at last come to fruition, and the Budget Group is safely in the hands of others.

Into Europe

Many of the activities – failures and successes – undertaken in the period 1986–87, when I was invited to introduce the gender dimension into the work of several hundred development organisations, based in 20 countries, particularly related to debt and trade, are recounted in *An Elf Among the Gnomes: a Feminist in North–South Relations*.[14] My acceptance of the challenge was partly to broaden the analysis employed in the UK, and partly to accelerate the consciousness and transformation of those organisations from their central point of reference using all the strategies for advocacy already learned.

One site of activity was the 22-country European North–South Campaign on Interdependence and Solidarity, based within the Council of Europe, which was unique in having non-governmental participation at all the decision-making levels on an equal basis with parliamentarians[15] and diplomats. My presence as the only woman on the European Organising Committee and in the Bureau was an education in itself to those who thought women inferior beings, or who rarely met them in senior positions. We developed a cosmopolitan camaraderie which I relished and which enabled me often to convince my colleagues to make changes to their documents, priorities, plans, and behaviour with the 'novelty' of my presence. At my suggestion, the women from NGOs, governments, and other organisations met in irregular caucus during the EOC meetings, as well as the NGO representatives from the national delegations. This, of course, added to my work, but was useful in demystifying the Bureau and in sounding out NGO opinion to take into the Bureau. It was arranged that I should write a paper introducing women into each of the seven macro-economic areas of the Campaign. This contained the condition that each delegation should take it back to their national committee to apply at home; few, if any did, and sadly the women were reluctant to monitor progress sufficiently aggressively.

A number of other relatively democratic methods were introduced at my suggestion, for example, the seven Round Tables, intending to give equality to the participants. Some of the tables became very square, with key-note speakers, which was not the intention; but others tried. The effort was made at most (except the Germans) to include women, for which I had drawn up lists of relevant suggestions, but my influence was weakest in the nationally organised events. Earlier I had tried to make the Patrons into something very different from the usual list of ex-Prime Ministers who have created all the problems. I wanted them to be 100 grassroots activists and leaders, creators of new social and political movements around the world, which would make a difference to the overall ethos of the campaign. It was, after all, intended to change the relationship between Europe and the South, showing a capacity to listen, very different from the Americans. The point that they should be half from the North and half from the South (the chief opponent to this being the British ambassador) was won, as was the stipulation that some in each half should be women. But the Bureau refused to take a decision on the type of Patron until one Bureau meeting in Paris that I could not attend. At that they settled for the conventional, with the pop star Sting thrown in to appeal to the young. Perhaps it shows that I had more influence[16] than they would have liked to admit, but more non-governmental support and national lobbying, convinced that it could succeed, probably would have changed this archaic top-down formula. I failed also to bring about the abolition of masculine terminology – Chairman and so on – in the Council of Europe, where the meetings were held.[17]

Aware that 'something had to be done' about women, a conference was (dis)organised in Barcelona, for the 'Voice of Women' to be ex-pressed. As an exercise in futility this would have few competitors, for every effort was made to muffle women's voices – indeed to make women listen to the important men of Europe instead – especially at the final 'male' conference in Madrid. In response, an instant inter-national coalition was developed, leaving out the saboteurs, to co-ordinate our own last-minute strategies, and this body liaised with the report writer. It was a moderate success, but it should not have been such a struggle – even with other women.

Recognition

In 1990, CHANGE was contracted by the European Commission, through the Africa–Caribbean Pacific/EC Foundation for Cultural Co-operation, to manage research and produce 'country profiles' on the position of women. The countries covered were Botswana, Guyana, Madagascar, and Sierra Leone, with six more to follow. This project was formed under the third Lome Convention, after a Council of Ministers meeting held in November 1987 decided that the Directorate-General for Development required more information on which to base new initiatives in the country 'indicative programmes'. The two-and-a-half years of suspense after we were first approached made for difficult planning in the interim. It was CHANGE's unique character, in that the country profiles are written by women from the country concerned, which attracted the EC officials.

A sub-theme for the project was to encourage the local development of women's or gender studies, and to identify further research needs and participatory methods, as elements of 'institution-building', to which European funding might be directed. The authors were identified, usually by contact before my brief visit to the country in question, commissioned, and sent supporting documentation, where it was not evidently available. Circumstances were not easy: closed libraries for lack of librarians' pay in Sierra Leone, tension surrounding imminent elections in Guyana, and, as it turned out, revolution in Madagascar. Only Botswana with its diamonds, though with South Africa still dominating its economy, seemed to have the stability to give the more educated women the self-confidence to develop their own approach to national planning, to sue the government for its constitutional exclusion of nationality inherited through mothers, and to develop a gender studies unit in the university.

The support from the governments and the delegations both for my consultancy and for the authors varied considerably, depending substantially on the age and sex of the administrative officer. Each visit was made to explain the purpose of the study to a wide range of officials, particularly in the financial and planning ministries, both to gain the necessary support for the author, and to emphasise the centrality of women's contribution to the economy. The conditions already mentioned affected the efficacy of this considerably. Co-operation from other agencies visited, such as UNICEF and the World Bank, ranged from the magnificent to the dour.

In the mid-way report some of the most salient recommendations included:

• that the EC delegations should initiate inter-agency co-ordination meetings on women's programmes and maintain them on a regular basis;

- internal women's commissions should be fostered;
- documentation centres should be encouraged.

Further, the inter-agency meetings should have many products. One would be the recognition that all work concerning women is inter-sectoral, and all sectors have their gender dimensions. They would enable the agencies to monitor their own learning and build it into their own indicative programmes, especially into Structural Adjustment Programmes. They would save duplication, which would foster the applications of recommendations emerging from such meetings, and also reduce confusion amongst women's groups and organisations.[18]

The report commented on the ignorance amongst the agencies of the existing instruments – the Convention on the Elimination of Discrimination Against Women and the Forward-Looking Strategies, the Commonwealth Plan of Action and work on Structural Adjustment, which should be overcome by such meetings. However, the agencies could also share their successful experiences of 'integrating' women into programmes, supporting women's projects, using gender training and applying sex-segregated data, and develop 'good practice' as well as innovation. Women's groups and organisations are often forced to look outside their country for funds, at additional expense, so any rationalisation that simplifies and widens their access to resources is common sense.

It is noticeable that most women's 'national machineries' are marginal, based in the low-priority culture or social affairs ministries, with very little access in political – and psychological – terms to the financial decision-making processes. They are very often funded from outside, for example by UNICEF, rather than an integral part of government. This makes them vulnerable to the whims of donors, and never really integrates the gender dimensions of national life that they should, but makes women into an 'add-on' – while not giving the bureau the independence of an NGO. The consciousness that equality means that women should be able to mobilise national (as well as domestic and community) resources on an equal basis with men is hindered. With 'good governance' becoming the condition of development co-operation, this consciousness of the economic basis of equality needs raising amongst donors as much as amongst the countries of the ACP

The internal commissions would have several functions. They would inject new energy into national action on the Forward-Looking Strategies in preparation for the 1995 conference to review their implementation. They would bring together a range of women MPs, civil servants, lawyers and educators to assess what they know factually about women in their own country, and prepare strategies to integrate the gender dimension and women's specific short- and long-term needs into the planning, decision-making and administrative structures. This would entail drawing in the male administrators and politicians in the long run, but before that it would create a space for women to develop confidence in each other and make cross-ministry and organisational links, and networks outside. The women, it was envisaged, could make contacts with the sources of documentation and gender training, identify further areas of research – probably very participatory research would be the best – and develop outreach programmes: local consultation groups, to ensure that the remotest women's experience is sought and their needs recognised. A major area of confusion in most ex-colonies is the tension between customary law and the integration of the Convention into national law. A still little-recognised area of action research, damage limitation and policy, in these countries and others, is the issue of violence against women.

The importance of independent documentation centres, with a range of academic interdisciplinary and non-governmental materials, as well as the UN and other intergovernmental instruments which support and legitimise women's movements, cannot be overemphasised. Women's groups, hoping to lobby their own governments and to transform their bureaucracies, need information about what is taking place in the world at large, as well as about their own societies. They need data to be able to back up their arguments, and the networking of successful approaches and ideas on a regional basis, where cultures are shared, as well as on an international basis with common legal, political and administrative institutions.

These proposals were received with excitement by the Women's Desk Officer, and contributed to the stimulus of a practical gender education programme for the delegations. The first four profiles were finished in the almost impossible time frame of the contract. However, as no funds had been allocated to printing the profiles, and the Italian government failed to honour its commitment to second a replacement Women's Officer at the end of her term, causing personnel problems in the European Commission, time dragged on and the bureaucratic mud began to suck down the proposals, which still remained to be implemented in 1994.

Endpiece

To use the word 'conclusion' here would be a mistake, for such work can go on, alas, for ever. We are alert to the Beijing conference, and are a leading source of information. There have been many failures; there can be self-deluding optimism over chimerical modifications: the

Gulf war was fought, after all. Yet there are changes, noticeable, even tangible sometimes, and CHANGE, amongst others, is increasingly called upon for more than token – and it is possible to tell the difference – advice and contribution: the eye opens voluntarily to us. The gap between world events – political, economic and military – and feminist response is narrowing, so much so that perhaps we will, before long, contribute to diverting their outcome to real peace, security and development.

Notes

1. From the Introduction to my chapter, 'Politicising Women and Structural Adjustment' in Afshar and Dennis (eds), *Women and Adjustment in the Third World*, Macmillan, 1992.

2. A fuller description of the activities can be found in *CHANGE: A Decade of Achievement 1979–89*, written, it must be said, as a public relations exercise. The text of the CHANGE flyer outlines the objectives.

3. Particularly without funding, which in the UK is sparse for internationalism and non-existent for women. Paradoxically while external agencies such as the Ford Foundation will subsidise and contract men's research projects in Europe, they will not support women; while the more generous governments such as the Dutch and the Norwegian will subvent men's debt campaigns based in other European countries, they will not support women's debt campaigns on a similar basis.

4. See *Hard Cash: Man-made Development and its Consequences: A Feminist Perspective on Aid*, CHANGE and War on Want, 1986, for an account of the conference.

5. *Self-Twice Removed: Ugandan Woman*, Grace Akeilo, for CHANGE, 1983; *In Search of Ethiopian Women*, Tsehai Berhane Selassie, for CHANGE, 1984; *Minus Lives: Women of Bangladesh*, Naila Kabeer, for CHANGE, 1983.

6. An expression used by Richard Sandbrook, Director of the International Institute for Environment and Development, after my contribution to their seminar series.

7. By Lucy Bonnerjea, published with the World University Service, 1985.

8. By members of the International Task Force on the War, Bela Bhatia, Mary Sanwar.

9. See Georgina Ashworth and Lucy Bonnerjea, *The Invisible Decade: UK Women and the UN Decade*, Gower, 1985; also Georgina Ashworth, 'The International Women's Movement and the UN Women's Conference' in Peter Willetts (ed.), *Pressure Groups in the Global System*, Frances Pinter publishers and St Martin's Press, New York, 1981.

10. See UN, The Nairobi Forward-Looking Strategies, 1985; Report of the UK Conference on the Forward-Looking Strategies, NCVO, 1986.

11. From 'Politicising Gender and Structural Adjustment' in Afshar and Dennis, op. cit.

12. *Of Violence and Violation*, CHANGE, 1986.

13. Published by CHANGE and not the Electoral Reform Society.

14. *Millennium*, a journal of international relations, December 1988 (London School of Economics).

15. From the European Parliament and the Council of Europe Assembly, which is composed of selected national MPs.

16. At one stage I was asked by the Spanish diplomats to prepare notes for the King's Opening Speech in the Cortes/Senate. This I did (more or less on the back of an envelope, but carefully expressed, since the request was made in Geneva at an inconvenient time), and waited in anticipation at the ceremony. But they were not used, and the King gave a very boring, regular, non-feminist, state speech.

17. And in a ban on smoking.

18. Taken from an article written for *Femmes D'Abord*, the internal EC newsletter on women and development.

Index